THE INTERNATIONAL Children's DEVOTIONAL BIBLE

Robert J. Morgan, General Editor
Illustrations by Natalie Carabetta

INTERNATIONAL CHILDREN'S BIBLE

THOMAS NELSON PUBLISHERS
Nashville

About the Illustrator

Natalie Carabetta was born in Meriden, Connecticut, in 1963. She graduated from the Philadelphia College of Art in 1985 and has been illustrating books for children since 1990. Presently, Natalie lives in Perkasie, Pennsylvania, with her daughter, Grace.

About the General Editor

Robert John Morgan was born in Elizabethton, Tennessee, in 1952. He graduated from Columbia Bible College in Columbia, South Carolina, Wheaton Graduate School in Wheaton, Illinois, and Luther Rice Seminary in Atlanta, Georgia. He is the author of several books, including *On This Day* and *From This Verse,* and has published articles in numerous magazines. He is currently serving as pastor of The Donelson Fellowship in suburban Nashville, where he has pastored since 1980. He and his wife, Katrina, have three daughters.

Contents

The Devotionals
(Use the boxes to the left of the devotionals to check off the ones you've read.)

CONTENTS

CONTENTS

CONTENTS

Introduction

L ooking for a Best Friend?
We all need one. Someone we can share our secrets with. Someone who likes us. Someone who's fun to be around. We need somebody like that to talk to every day.

The International Children's Devotional Bible will help you become best friends with the *best* Best Friend of all—the wonderful God, creator of heaven and earth. He knows all about you, and he likes you very much. He loves you deeply. He's a joy to be with. You can tell him all your secrets. And you can spend time with him every day—for the rest of your life.

God becomes our Best Friend . . .

- when we ask Jesus Christ to forgive our sins and to give us everlasting life, and . . .
- when we begin reading our Bibles and praying every day.

Daily Bible reading and praying is like talking with God himself. He speaks to us when we read his book, the Bible. And we speak to him when we pray. These daily times of Bible reading and prayer make us more and more devoted to the Lord . . .

. . . which is why we call them—daily devotions.

Here are seven ways to get the most from *The International Children's Devotional Bible:*

1. Use it about the same time each day—maybe in the morning before school or at night just before going to bed.

2. Think of each day's passage as a special message from God just for you.

3. Study the pictures. Each has been drawn to accurately show something about the words you're reading.

4. Use the prayer starters to . . . well, to start your prayers. Then go on to tell the Lord whatever you'd like. Learn to talk to him naturally, just like talking to a friend.

5. Work hard on the memory verses. Collect all 52 in your mind.

6. Use weekends to look over Scriptures you've previously read and to review verses you've already learned.

7. If you *do* occasionally skip a day, make sure you don't miss the next one. Make your daily devotions a habit, and stick to them.

No matter how many—or how few—friends you have, you've got one Best Friend who will never leave you or let you down. And he's waiting for you to get to know him better . . .

. . . just as soon as you turn to page one.

A Word for Parents

My first Bible was given to me in the first grade as an award for memorizing Psalm 23. A year or two later, my parents gave me another Bible, a newer one with larger print. As I advanced through school, they kept updating my Bibles to match my age. I loved to burrow into the bedcovers and read, study, and memorize the Scripture. It's no wonder that at an early age, I gave my life to Christ, and I've been a lover of the Bible ever since.

Now that I'm a parent, my greatest longing is that my children grow up knowing, loving, and serving Jesus Christ. When they were younger, we gathered them around for family devotions. My wife or I would read a Bible story or a few verses then offer a brief prayer. But as they grew, we wanted them to cultivate their own daily devotions. We gave them Bibles appropriate for their ages, and encouraged them to have their "devos" each evening.

Our role shifted a little from instructing to modeling. Notice how Moses puts it in Deuteronomy 6:5-7:

> *Love the Lord your God with all your heart, soul and strength. Always remember these commands I give you today. Teach them to your children. Talk about them when you sit at home and walk along the road. Talk about them when you lie down and when you get up.*

The order is important. First, parents should love the Lord with all their hearts. Next we're to memorize his Word, his laws. Then we are to "talk about them . . ." to our children.

The International Children's Devotional Bible can help.

- For younger children, use this as a read-to-me picture book of daily devotions.

- For older children, gently monitor their use of this book and help them build the "daily devo" habit into their routine.

- Keep your own copy of *The International Children's Devotional Bible* (you can use it for your devotions, too) so you can talk more easily about the Scripture when you "sit at home and walk along the road . . . when you lie down and when you get up."

- Provide a full copy of the *International Children's Bible* so your children can look up surrounding passages for further study.

- Help your child learn the memory verses. John Ruskin, English social critic, said the verses his mother helped him memorize in childhood "set my soul for life." Use charts, stars, incentives, and rewards. Make it a family project.

- Involve your family in a good church with a strong youth ministry.

- Be a spiritual model for your children. The best way to entice your kids into the daily devotional habit is to let them see you enjoying yours.

Our spiritual vitality depends on two aspects of victorious Christian living: conversion and conversation. The first is a matter of heart; the second, of habit.

When we meet Christ at the cross, that's *conversion*. When we meet with him behind the closed door, that's *conversation*.

> *The teaching about **the cross** seems foolish to those who are lost. But to us who are being saved it is the power of God (1 Corinthians 1:18).*

> *When you pray, you should go into your room and **close the door**. Then pray to your Father who cannot be seen. Your Father can see what is done in secret, and he will reward you (Matthew 6:6).*

We're converted to Jesus Christ when we trust him as Savior, confessing our sins to him, asking him for eternal life, and committing ourselves to him as Lord and Master. Then the friendship starts. The God of the Universe wants to meet us each day over an old Book at the kitchen table. It's beyond comprehension. It's the *second* most astounding thing I know.

God is both infinite and intimate! He delights in being with his people, hearing us pray and talking to us through his Word. The Master, it seems, occupies two addresses: in a high and holy place and with the humblest hearts.

> *God lives forever and is holy.*
> *He is high and lifted up, and he says,*
> *"I live in a high and holy place.*
> *But I also live with people who are sad and humble.*
> *I give new life to those who are humble.*
> *I give new life to those whose hearts are broken" (Isaiah 57:15).*

The heavenly Father wants our earthly friendship. Could anything be more astonishing than that?

Only one: Many of us can't find time for him. And that's the *most* astounding thing I know. We're too busy for Bible study, and too pooped for prayer.

We rush into each day, bolting from bed like a thoroughbred from the gate. We gulp down our Colombian coffee, throw on designer labels, then veer onto the fast lane. We whirl through our daily tasks like a spinning top, then drive by the restaurant on the way home so they can throw food to us through the window. We drag ourselves to the couch for an hour of celluloid sex and video violence, then stagger to the bed for six hours of sleep.

Whatever happened to green pastures and still waters? We're too frazzled to find them!

It wasn't until my college years that I really understood the joy of spending a quiet half hour in regular conversation with God. Columbia Bible College's daily routine included a mandatory half hour for morning devotions. Now, over 20 years later, I wouldn't trade that habit for anything. It's my daily appointment with God, a personal conversation during which he speaks to me in the Bible and I speak to him in prayer. It enables me to start the day with confidence.

Suppose you go to bed at a reasonable hour and get up a half hour earlier to meet God the next morning—what do you do with those thirty minutes? I'd like to suggest a sequence called *JARS and Rs*.

J=Jot

J stands for "jot." You'll need a notebook for this, but any kind will do. At the top of the page, jot the date. You can then write anything you want about your feelings, your moods, or the circumstances of your life. Or, just use the margin of your Bible to jot down the date and any useful information.

I learned the notebook habit when a college buddy took me to visit Ruth Bell Graham one weekend. She talked with us at length, sharing lessons garnered through a lifetime of unusual ministry. I scribbled down much of what she said, including four words I've never forgotten, for they transformed my devotions: *"Cultivate the notebook habit."*

She explained that for many years she has kept a journal, recording the events of her life and the lessons she has learned from Scripture. When one notebook fills up, she slides it alongside its predecessors on the bookshelf, and starts a new one. Christians throughout history, she told us, have journaled to maintain their emotional equilibrium and to remember lessons they have learned from God.

I immediately went out and purchased a journal. In the two decades since, I've found that the notebook habit focuses my thoughts, especially when I'm troubled, forcing rip-roaring feelings into black ink on white paper so I can deal with them.

After you've jotted a sentence on a page, you're ready for the next step.

A=Ask

Take a moment to ask God to speak to you through his Word. Though some people read the Bible only as a textbook, it's primarily a love letter between the Lord and his people. It's designed to transform and invigorate our lives as the Holy Spirit applies it to our hearts. Repeat David's prayer in Psalm 119:18: *Open my eyes to see the wonderful things in your teachings.* Or Samuel's childlike prayer, *Speak, Lord. I am your servant, and I am listening (1 Samuel 3:10).*

R=Read

Then read your Bible. Begin each day where you left off the day before. Underline significant phrases. Study cross-references. Diagram sentences. Outline chapters. Check key words in a dictionary. Dig into the text, looking for contrasts and comparisons. Rewrite verses in your own words in your notebook. There are no rules for where or how much to read. The important thing is remembering as you read that God is talking to you as one talks to a friend.

S=Select

As you study the Bible, look for one verse to select as your *Verse-for-the-Day*—a verse that really hammers at your heart. When you find it, copy it in your journal and perhaps on a scrap of paper to carry with you all day. I know one man who writes his *VFTD* on the back of a business card that he props on his desk. Another friend jots hers on a sticky note to post on her dashboard. She memorizes it as she drives to work.

Find your *VFTD* in the morning, carry it in your heart all day, and at night meditate on it as you fall asleep. None sleep as well as those who have a promise for a pillow.

Then having listened to the Lord, it's time to speak to him. The last half of your quiet time centers around the three *Rs* of prayer.

R=Rejoice

Begin by rejoicing, praising, and thanking God for his grace and generosity. A good place to start is with your *VFTD*. Usually when engaged in conversation, I respond and react to the words of the one speaking to me. If he's talking about the Washington Redskins, I don't abruptly begin a discourse on the excavations of Crocodilopolis. I follow the flow of the conversation.

If your VFTD is Matthew 22:37—*Love the Lord your God with all your heart* . . .—tell God how much you love him and thank him for his love for you. Rejoice that you have a love-based relationship with the Almighty.

R=Repent

As you worship the Lord, you may begin to feel inadequate, like Peter in Luke 5:8, who, amazed at Christ's miracle of fish, fell at his knees saying, *"Go away from me, Lord. I am a sinful man!"*

So we move naturally from rejoicing to repenting. We admit to God faults and failures we've knowingly allowed to mar our lives since we last prayed.

R=Request

Then we're ready to obey Philippians 4:6: *Pray and ask God for everything you need.* The Lord promises to answer our prayers if we sincerely ask in the name of the Lord Jesus—with one condition inserted for our protection: He only promises to grant us those things that are good for us, that are according to his will (1 John 5:14-15).

So pray with confidence, using your journal to record your requests and to note God's answers. Pray aloud when you can, and talk to God naturally, as though speaking with a friend.

Because you are.

Don't grow discouraged if sometimes you don't feel like praying. Pray anyway.

Don't quit on mornings when you don't enjoy your Bible reading. Read anyway.

Don't despair if you miss a day. Start again the next.

Develop the habit, then the habit will develop you. Cultivate the friendship, and your Friend will stick closer than a brother. For . . .

> *God lives forever and is holy.*
> *He is high and lifted up, and he says,*
> *"I live in a high and holy place.*
> *But I also live with people who are sad and humble.*
> *I give new life to those who are humble.*
> *I give new life to those whose hearts are broken" (Isaiah 57:15).*

The effect on your children will be for keeps.

People You'll Meet in *The International Children's Devotional Bible*

Who in the world is Mephibosheth? Jehoshaphat? Nebuchadnezzar? Ever heard of Ananias and Sapphira?

These hard-to-say names belong to some very interesting people you'll meet in *The International Children's Devotional Bible*. The following list can help you get to know them. Beside every name is a helpful guide to pronouncing it correctly, and a description of the person's identity. At the end of each entry you'll find the page number first mentioning that character.

Adam *(ADD um)* **and Eve** *(eev)* - the first man and woman, created by God and placed in the Garden of Eden (p. 2)

Cain *(kane)* **and Abel** *(A buhl)* - Adam and Eve's first two sons (p. 6)

Noah *(NOE uh)* - the man who trusted and obeyed God by building a big boat (p. 8)

Abram/Abraham *(A bruhm/AY bruh ham)* - the man who received God's promise to make his descendants into a great nation (p. 15)

Sarai/Sarah *(SAR eye/SAR uh)* - Abraham's wife; she had her first son when she was 90 years old and Abraham was 100 years old (p. 15)

Lot *(laht)* - Abraham's nephew who traveled with him to the land of Canaan (p. 15)

Isaac *(EYE zik)* - the son of Abraham and Sarah through whom God fulfilled his promise to Abraham (p. 24)

Hagar *(HAY gahr)* - Sarah's Egyptian slave woman (p. 24)

Ishmael *(IHSH may ell)* - the son of Abraham and Hagar (p. 24)

Rebekah *(ruh BEK uh)* - Isaac's wife who was promised and chosen by God (p. 28)

Esau *(EE saw)* - Isaac and Rebekah's son who sold his birthright to his twin brother Jacob (p. 30)

Jacob *(JAY cub)* - Isaac and Rebekah's son who received his father's blessing in place of his twin brother Esau (p. 30)

Laban *(LAY bihn)* - Rebekah's wealthy brother for whom Jacob worked for over 14 years (p. 32)

Leah *(LEE uh)* - Laban's oldest daughter who became Jacob's wife through deceit (p. 32)

Rachel *(RAY chuhl)* - Leah's sister who became Jacob's wife after he had worked 14 years for her father Laban (p. 32)

Joseph *(JOE zeph)* - the second youngest of the twelve sons of Jacob; he became the ruler of all Egypt (p. 34)

Moses *(MOE zez)* - the man God used to deliver the children of Israel from Egyptian bondage (p. 42)

Aaron *(EHR un)* - the older brother of Moses who became his spokesman; he and his sons were the first priests of Israel (p. 46)

Balaam *(BAY lum)* - A magician in Mesopotamia whose donkey was enabled by God to talk (p. 63)

Joshua *(JAHSH oo uh)* - the man who became the leader of Israel following the death of Moses, and who led the nation into the Promised Land (p. 64)

Deborah *(DEB uh rah)* - a prophetess and leader of Israel who was used by God to defeat the enemies of Israel (p. 76)

Barak *(BAR ack)* - the leader of Israel's army who, along with Deborah, defeated the army of Sisera (p. 76)

Gideon *(GIDD ee un)* - the leader God used to rescue Israel from the Midianites with only 300 soldiers (p. 79)

Samson *(SAM suhn)* - a leader of Israel who had great strength when the Holy Spirit came upon him (p. 80)

Delilah *(dih LIE lah)* - the Philistine woman who tricked Samson, causing him to lose his great strength (p. 80)

Naomi *(nay OH mee)* - a woman whose family moved to Moab after a famine in their hometown of Bethlehem (p. 84)

Ruth *(rooth)* - the daughter-in-law of Naomi who returned with Naomi to Bethlehem after the death of both of their husbands (p. 84)

Boaz *(BOE az)* - a wealthy man from Bethlehem, a relative of Naomi's husband, who married Ruth and became an ancestor of David and Jesus (p. 86)

Hannah *(HAN nuh)* - the wife of Elkanah who prayed for a son and dedicated him to God before his birth (p. 89)

Eli *(EE lie)* - a priest and judge of Israel (p. 89)

Elkanah *(el KAY na)* - a Levite who was the husband of Hannah and the father of Samuel (p. 90)

Samuel *(SAM yoo uhl)* - a Hebrew prophet who, as a child, ministered to the Lord by helping Eli the priest (p. 90)

Saul *(sawl)* - the man who was anointed by Samuel as the first king of Israel (p. 93)

David *(DAY vid)* - a musician and warrior for Saul who eventually became king of Israel in Saul's place (p. 98)

Goliath *(goe LIE ahth)* - the gigantic Philistine whom David killed with a slingshot and stone (p. 100)

Jonathan *(JAHN uh thuhn)* - Saul's son and David's best friend (p. 104)

Mephibosheth *(meh FIB oh shehth)* - the son of Jonathan and grandson of Saul; David showed kindness to him for the sake of Jonathan (p. 114)

Solomon *(SAHL uh mun)* - David's son who became king of Israel; he was given special wisdom from God (p. 115)

Ahab *(A hab)* - a wicked king of Israel who built altars to Baal (p. 119)

Elijah *(ee LIE juh)* - a prophet of God during the reign of King Ahab (p. 119)

Elisha *(ee LIE shuh)* - the prophet of God who came after Elijah; he was given twice as much power as the other prophets (p. 124)

Naaman *(NAY a man)* - the commander of the Syrian army who was healed of a harmful skin disease (p. 126)

Jezebel *(JEZ uh bel)* - the evil wife of King Ahab and a worshiper of the false god Baal (p. 130)

Hezekiah *(hez uh KIGH uh)* - a king of Judah who trusted in the Lord for defeat of his enemies (p. 132)

Isaiah *(eye ZAY uh)* - a prophet of Judah during the reigns of four kings, including Hezekiah (p. 134)

Josiah *(joe SIGH uh)* - a godly king of Judah who took the throne when he was only eight years old (p. 136)

Jehoshaphat *(juh HAH shuh fat)* - a king of Judah who obeyed and worshiped the Lord; the Lord helped him keep control of his kingdom (p. 139)

Micaiah *(mie KAY yuh)* - a prophet of Judah who predicted to Ahab the defeat of Israel's army (p. 139)

Joash *(JOE ash)* - the king of Judah during the time when the temple was repaired (p. 142)

Uzziah *(you ZIE uh)* - the king of Judah who was struck with a harmful skin disease as a punishment from the Lord (p. 144)

Ahaz *(A haz)* - a wicked king of Judah who offered sacrifices to Baal (p. 145)

Nehemiah *(knee uh MY ah)* - a Jewish servant of the king of Persia who led in the rebuilding of the walls of Jerusalem (p. 146)

Esther *(ESS ter)* - the Jewish wife of King Xerxes and the queen of Persia who risked her life to save her people (p. 148)

Mordecai *(MAWR deh kie)* - the cousin of Esther and a palace official in Persia (p. 148)

Haman *(HAY mun)* - evil officer in Persia who wanted to destroy all the Jews in the world (p. 148)

Job *(jobe)* - a worshiper of God who trusted the Lord even when tested with the loss of all his possessions (p. 151)

Jeremiah *(jer uh MIGH uh)* - a priest and prophet of God who warned the people of their disobedience to God (p. 188)

Nebuchadnezzar *(neb you kad NEZ ur)* -

the king of Babylon who led his army in an attack on Jerusalem that captured the city (p. 194)

Ezekiel *(ih ZEEK e uhl)* - a priest and prophet of God before and after the fall of Jerusalem (p. 196)

Belshazzar *(bel SHAZ zur)* - the last king of Babylon whose evil ways caused the Lord to write a message of doom on the wall of his banquet room (p. 202)

Daniel *(DAN yuhl)* - a young Jew taken captive by the Babylonians who remained completely faithful to the Lord (p. 202)

Hosea *(hoe ZAY uh)* - a prophet in Israel for over 40 years (p. 208)

Joel *(JOE uhl)* - a prophet in Israel who used swarms of locusts to describe how God was going to destroy Israel (p. 209)

Amos *(AIM us)* - a man who left his hometown in Judah and went to the northern kingdom of Israel to deliver God's message to the people (p. 212)

Jonah *(JOE nuh)* - a prophet whose disobedience led to his being swallowed by a very big fish, but he repented and was sent to preach in Nineveh (p. 213)

Micah *(MIE kuh)* - a prophet who gave messages from the Lord especially to the cities of Samaria and Jerusalem (p. 217)

Nahum *(NAY hum)* - a prophet who told of justice and punishment to come upon Assyria (p. 220)

Habakkuk *(huh BAK uhk)* - a prophet of Judah who praised the Lord's power and glory (p. 221)

Zechariah *(zeck ah RIE a)* - a priest and prophet whose visions were used by God to help the people of Jerusalem with the rebuilding of the temple (p. 222)

Malachi *(MAL ah kie)* - a prophet who reminded the people of Israel to give to God what belonged to him (p. 227)

Jesus *(GEE zus)* - the Son of God, the Savior of the world, who was both God and man (p. 228)

Herod *(HEHR ud)* - the king of Israel when Jesus was born (p. 228)

Mary *(MAIR ee)* - the wife of Joseph and the woman chosen by the Lord as the mother of Jesus (p. 228)

Joseph *(JOE zeph)* - a carpenter from Nazareth; the husband of Mary, mother of Jesus (p. 229)

Simon Peter *(SIGH mun PEE ter)* - a fisherman who was brought to Jesus by his brother Andrew; he became one of Jesus' apostles (p. 235)

James *(jamez)* **and John** *(jahn)* - the sons of Zebedee; fishermen who became apostles of Jesus (p. 238)

Pilate *(PIE lat)* - the Roman governor of Judea during the time of Jesus (p. 243)

Jairus *(jay EYE ruhs)* - a ruler of the Jewish synagogue whose daughter needed healing from Jesus (p. 246)

Pharisees *(FARE uh sees)* - the religious teachers of Jesus' day (p. 249)

Elizabeth *(ee LIZ uh buth)* - the cousin of Mary and the mother of John (p. 256)

John *(jahn)* - the son of Zechariah and Elizabeth; the man God sent to prepare the people to receive Jesus (p. 264)

Zacchaeus *(za KEE us)* - a tax collector who climbed a tree to see Jesus (p. 277)

Judas *(JOO duhs)* - the apostle who betrayed Jesus (p. 278)

Nicodemus *(nick oh DEE mus)* - a Pharisee and Jewish leader who came to Jesus at night (p. 285)

Mary *(MAIR ee)* **and Martha** *(MAR thuh)* - sisters from the town of Bethany; Jesus was a close friend of their family (p. 291)

Lazarus *(LAZ ah russ)* - the brother of Mary and Martha who was raised from the dead by Jesus (p. 291)

Mary Magdalene *(MAIR ee MAG deh leen)* - a woman from Magdala of Galilee who was one of Jesus' most devoted followers (p. 299)

Thomas *(TAHM us)* - an apostle of Jesus who would not believe that Jesus had risen from the dead until he had seen the nail marks in Jesus' hands (p. 303)

Ananias *(an uh NYE us)* **and Sapphira** *(suh FIGH ruh)* - a husband and wife who were struck dead for lying to the Holy Spirit (p. 312)

Stephen *(STEE vun)* - a man of great faith and filled with God's Spirit who was chosen by the twelve apostles to serve God (p. 318)

Simon *(SIGH mun)* - a man of Samaria who

practiced magic, but came to believe in Jesus (p. 321)

Philip *(FILL ihp)* - one of seven men chosen by the apostles to serve God by going from place to place telling the good news (p. 321)

Saul *(sawl)* - a man from the city of Tarsus who hated Christians until he came to know Jesus as his Savior; he later became known as Paul, a great preacher of the gospel (p. 323)

Tabitha *(TAB ih thuh)* - a friend and helper of the poor; also known as Dorcas, she was raised from death by Peter (p. 327)

Paul *(pawl)* - a faithful follower of Jesus and an apostle to the Gentiles; he took the gospel throughout all the regions north of the Mediterranean Sea; he was originally known as Saul (p. 331)

Barnabas *(BAR nuh bus)* - a devoted follower of the Lord who sold all his goods to give to the work of Christ; he was known as the son of encouragement (p. 331)

Silas *(SIGH lus)* - a loyal companion and friend of Paul who went with him on one of his missionary trips (p. 338)

Timothy *(TIM uh thih)* - a faithful servant of the Lord who was like a son to Paul and served as his assistant (p. 339)

Aquila *(A kwil uh)* **and Priscilla** *(prih SIL uh)* - a Jewish couple who made tents for their living; followers of the Lord and friends of Paul (p. 346)

Philemon *(fie LEE mun)* - a wealthy man who used his large house for church meetings (p. 389)

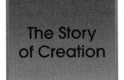

The Story of Creation

In the beginning God created the sky and the earth. ²The earth was empty and had no form. Darkness covered the ocean, and God's Spirit was moving over the water.

³Then God said, "Let there be light!" And there was light. ⁴God saw that the light was good. So he divided the light from the darkness. ⁵God named the light "day" and the darkness "night." Evening passed, and morning came. This was the first day.

⁶Then God said, "Let there be something to divide the water in two!" ⁷So God made the air to divide the water in two. Some of the water was above the air, and some of the water was below it. ⁸God named the air "sky." Evening passed, and morning came. This was the second day.

⁹Then God said, "Let the water under the sky be gathered together so the dry land will appear." And it happened. ¹⁰God named the dry land "earth." He named the water that was gathered together "seas." God saw that this was good.

¹¹Then God said, "Let the earth produce plants. Some plants will make grain for seeds. Others will make fruit with seeds in it. Every seed will produce more of its own kind of plant." And it happened. ¹²The earth produced plants. Some plants had grain for seeds. The trees made fruit with seeds in it. Each seed grew its own kind of plant. God saw that all this was good. ¹³Evening passed, and morning came. This was the third day.

¹⁴Then God said, "Let there be lights in the sky to separate day from night. These lights will be used for signs, seasons, days and years. ¹⁵They will be in the sky to give light to the earth." And it happened.

¹⁶So God made the two large lights. He made the brighter light to rule the day. He made the smaller light to rule the night. He also made the stars. ¹⁷God put all these in the sky to shine on the earth. ¹⁸They are to rule over the day and over the night. He put them there to separate the light from the darkness. God saw that all these things were good.

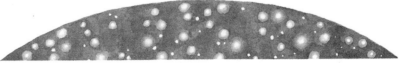

Prayer Starter: Thank you, Lord, for stars and sky, for trees and grass, and for making the world so beautiful.

Memory Verse: So God made the two large lights. . . . brighter one to rule the day.   *—Genesis 1:16*

Animals and Humans

Then God said, "Let the earth be filled with animals. And let each produce more of its own kind. Let there be tame animals and small crawling animals and wild animals. And let each produce more of its kind." And it happened.

²⁵So God made the wild animals, the tame animals and all the small crawling animals to produce more of their own kind. God saw that this was good.

²⁶Then God said, "Let us make human beings in our image and likeness. And let them rule over the fish in the sea and the birds in the sky. Let them rule over the tame animals, over all the earth and over all the small crawling animals on the earth."

²⁷So God created human beings in his image. In the image of God he created them. He created them male and female. ²⁸God blessed them and said, "Have many children and grow in number. Fill the earth and be its master. Rule over the fish in the sea and over the birds in the sky. Rule over every living thing that moves on the earth."

²⁹God said, "Look, I have given you all the plants that have grain for seeds. And I have given you all the trees whose fruits have seeds in them. They will be food for you. ³⁰I have given all the green plants to all the animals to eat. They will be food for every wild animal, every bird of the air and every small crawling animal." And it happened. ³¹God looked at everything he had made, and it was very good. Evening passed, and morning came. This was the sixth day.

2 So the sky, the earth and all that filled them were finished. ²By the seventh day God finished the work he had been doing. So on the seventh day he rested from all his work. ³God blessed the seventh day and made it a holy day. He made it holy because on that day he rested. He rested from all the work he had done in creating the world.

⁴This is the story of the creation of the sky and the earth.

Prayer Starter: Thank you, Lord, for dogs, cats, fish and birds. And thank you for men and women and boys and girls—and me.

Memory Verse: So God made the two large lights. He made the brighter light . . .   —*Genesis 1:16*

The First Sin

Now the snake was the most clever of all the wild animals the Lord God had made. One day the snake spoke to the woman. He said, "Did God really say that you must not eat fruit from any tree in the garden?"

[2]The woman answered the snake, "We may eat fruit from the trees in the garden. [3]But God told us, 'You must not eat fruit from the tree that is in the middle of the garden. You must not even touch it, or you will die.' "

[4]But the snake said to the woman, "You will not die. [5]God knows that if you eat the fruit from that tree, you will learn about good and evil. Then you will be like God!"

[6]The woman saw that the tree was beautiful. She saw that its fruit was good to eat and that it would make her wise. So she took some of its fruit and ate it. She also gave some of the fruit to her husband, and he ate it.

[7]Then, it was as if the man's and the woman's eyes were opened. They realized they were naked. So they sewed fig leaves together and made something to cover themselves.

[8]Then they heard the Lord God walking in the garden. This was during the cool part of the day. And the man and his wife hid from the Lord God among the trees in the garden. [9]But the Lord God called to the man. The Lord said, "Where are you?"

[10]The man answered, "I heard you walking in the garden. I was afraid because I was naked. So I hid."

[11]God said to the man, "Who told you that you were naked? Did you eat fruit from that tree? I commanded you not to eat from that tree."

[12]The man said, "You gave this woman to me. She gave me fruit from the tree. So I ate it."

[13]Then the Lord God said to the woman, "What have you done?"

She answered, "The snake tricked me. So I ate the fruit."

²⁰The man named his wife Eve.ⁿ This is because she is the mother of everyone who ever lived.

²¹The Lord God made clothes from animal skins for the man and his wife. And so the Lord dressed them. ²²Then the Lord God said, "Look, the man has become like one of us. He knows good and evil. And now we must keep him from eating some of the fruit from the tree of life. If he does, he will live forever." ²³So the Lord God forced the man out of the garden of Eden. He had to work the ground he was taken from. ²⁴God forced the man out of the garden. Then God put angels on the east side of the garden. He also put a sword of fire there. It flashed around in every direction. This kept people from getting to the tree of life.

ⁿ**Eve** This name sounds like the Hebrew word meaning "alive."

Prayer Starter: Father, forgive me for times when I disobey you and do things that make you sad. Help me to please you in all I do and say.

Memory Verse: So God made the two large lights. He made the brighter light to rule the day. . . .   —*Genesis 1:16*

Cain and Abel

Adam had sexual relations with his wife Eve. She became pregnant and gave birth to Cain.ⁿ Eve said, "With the Lord's help, I have given birth to a man." ²After that, Eve gave birth to Cain's brother Abel. Abel took care of sheep. Cain became a farmer.

³Later, Cain brought a gift to God. He brought some food from the ground. ⁴Abel brought the best parts of his best sheep. The Lord accepted Abel and his gift. ⁵But God did not accept Cain and his gift. Cain became very angry and looked unhappy.

⁶The Lord asked Cain, "Why are you angry? Why do you look so unhappy? ⁷If you do good, I will accept you. But if you do not do good, sin is ready to attack you. Sin wants you. But you must rule over it."

⁸Cain said to his brother Abel, "Let's go out into the field." So Cain and Abel went into the field. Then Cain attacked his brother Abel and killed him.

⁹Later, the Lord said to Cain, "Where is your brother Abel?"

Cain answered, "I don't know. Is it my job to take care of my brother?"

¹⁰Then the Lord said, "What have you done? Your brother's blood is on the ground. That blood is like a voice that tells me what happened. ¹¹And now you will be cursed in your work with the ground. It is the same ground where your brother's blood fell. Your hands killed

him. ¹²You will work the ground. But it will not grow good crops for you anymore. You will wander around on the earth."

¹³Then Cain said to the Lord, "This punishment is more than I can stand! ¹⁴Look! You have forced me to stop working the ground. And now I must hide from you. I will wander around on the earth. And anyone who meets me can kill me."

¹⁵Then the Lord said to Cain, "No! If anyone kills you, I will punish that person seven times more." Then the Lord put a mark on Cain. It was a warning to anyone who met him not to kill him.

ⁿ**Cain** This name sounds like the Hebrew word for "I have given birth."

Prayer Starter: Lord, help us love each other as you love us. Help me be concerned about others and treat them as I want to be treated.

Memory Verse: So God made the two large lights. He made the brighter light to rule the day. He made the smaller light to rule the night. . . .
—*Genesis 1:16*

Noah

The Lord saw that the human beings on the earth were very wicked. He also saw that their thoughts were only about evil all the time. ⁶The Lord was sorry he had made human beings on the earth. His heart was filled with pain. ⁷So the Lord said, "I will destroy all human beings that I made on the earth. And I will destroy every animal and everything that crawls on the earth. I will also destroy the birds of the air. This is because I am sorry that I have made them." ⁸But Noah pleased the Lord.

⁹This is the family history of Noah. Noah was a good man. He was the most innocent man of his time. He walked with God. ¹⁰Noah had three sons: Shem, Ham and Japheth.

¹¹People on earth did what God said was evil. Violence was everywhere. ¹²And God saw this evil. All people on the earth did only evil. ¹³So God said to Noah, "People have made the earth full of violence. So I will destroy all people from the earth. ¹⁴Build a boat of cypress wood for yourself. Make rooms in it and cover it inside and outside with tar. ¹⁵This is how big I want you to build the boat: 450 feet long, 75 feet wide and 45 feet high. ¹⁶Make an opening around the top of the boat. Make it 18 inches high from the edge of the roof down. Put a door in the side of the boat. Make an upper, middle and lower deck in it. ¹⁷I will bring a flood of water on the earth. I will destroy all living things that live under the sky. This includes everything

that has the breath of life. Everything on the earth will die. ¹⁸But I will make an agreement with you. You, your sons, your wife and your sons' wives will all go into the boat. ¹⁹Also, you must bring into the boat two of every living thing, male and female. Keep them alive with you. ²⁰There will be two of every kind of bird, animal and crawling thing. They will come to you to be kept alive. ²¹Also gather some of every kind of food. Store it on the boat as food for you and the animals."

²²Noah did everything that God commanded him.

Prayer Starter: Dear Lord, give me good friends who will help me to be a better person. Keep me from the wrong kind of friends.

Memory Verse: So God made the two large lights. He made the brighter light to rule the day. He made the smaller light to rule the night. He also made the stars. —*Genesis 1:16*

The Great Flood

Then the Lord said to Noah, "I have seen that you are the best man among the people of this time. So you and your family go into the boat. ²Take with you seven pairs, each male with its female, of every kind of clean animal. And take one pair, each male with its female, of every kind of unclean animal. ³Take seven pairs of all the birds of the sky, each male with its female. This will allow all these animals to continue living on the earth after the flood. ⁴Seven days from now I will send rain on the earth. It will rain 40 days and 40 nights. I will destroy from the earth every living thing that I made."

⁵Noah did everything that the Lord commanded him.

⁶Noah was 600 years old when the flood came. ⁷He and his wife and his sons and their wives went into the boat. They went in to escape the waters of the flood. ⁸The clean animals, the unclean animals, the birds and everything that crawls on the ground ⁹came to Noah. They went into the boat in groups of two, male and female. This was just as God had commanded Noah. ¹⁰Seven days later the flood started.

¹¹Noah was now 600 years old. The flood started on the seventeenth day of the second month of that year. That day the underground springs split open. And the clouds in the sky poured out rain. ¹²The rain fell on the earth for 40 days and 40 nights.

¹⁷Water flooded the earth for 40 days. As the water rose, it lifted the boat off the ground. ¹⁸The water continued to rise, and the boat floated on the water above the earth. ¹⁹The water rose so much that even the highest mountains under the sky were covered by it. ²⁰The water continued to rise until it was more than 20 feet above the mountains.

²¹All living things that moved on the earth died. This included all the birds, tame animals, wild animals and creatures that swarm on the earth. And all human beings died. ²²So everything on dry land died. This means everything that had the breath of life in its nose. ²³So God destroyed from the earth every living thing that was on the land. This was every man, animal, crawling thing and bird of the sky. All that was left was Noah and what was with him in the boat. ²⁴And the waters continued to cover the earth for 150 days.

Prayer Starter: I know you are a holy God, dear Father. Make me pure and holy like you are. Keep me from sin.

Memory Verse: It was by faith Noah heard . . . —*Hebrews 11:7*

A New Beginning

But God remembered Noah and all the wild animals and tame animals with him in the boat. God made a wind blow over the earth. And the water went down. ²The underground springs stopped flowing. And the clouds in the sky stopped pouring down rain. ³⁻⁴The water that covered the earth began to go down. After 150 days the water had gone down so much that the boat touched land again. It came to rest on one of the mountains of Ararat.ⁿ This was on the seventeenth day of the seventh month. ⁵The water continued to go down. By the first day of the tenth month the tops of the mountains could be seen.

⁶Forty days later Noah opened the window he had made in the boat. ⁷He sent out a raven. It flew here and there until the water had dried up from the earth. ⁸Then Noah sent out a dove. This was to find out if the water had dried up from the ground. ⁹The dove could not find a place to land because water still covered the earth. So it came back to the boat. Noah reached out his hand and took the bird. And he brought it back into the boat. ¹⁰After seven days Noah again sent out the dove from the boat. ¹¹And that evening it came back to him with a fresh olive leaf in its mouth. Then Noah knew that the ground was almost dry. ¹²Seven days later he sent the dove out again. But this time it did not come back.

¹³Noah was now 601 years old. It was the first day of the first month of that year. The water was dried up from the land. Noah removed the covering of the boat and saw that the land was dry. ¹⁴By the twenty-seventh day of the second month the land was completely dry.

¹⁵Then God said to Noah, ¹⁶"You and your wife, your sons and their wives should go out of the boat. ¹⁷Bring every animal out of the boat with you—the birds, animals and everything that crawls on the earth. Let them have many young ones and let them grow in number."

ⁿ**Ararat** The ancient land of Urartu, an area in Eastern Turkey.

Prayer Starter: Thank you for taking care of all the animals and people you have created. You give us food to eat, water to drink, air to breath. We love you, Father.

Memory Verse: It was by faith Noah heard God's warnings about things . . .
—Hebrews 11:7

The Rainbow

Then God blessed Noah and his sons. He said to them, "Have many children. Grow in number and fill the earth. ²Every animal on earth and every bird in the sky will respect and fear you. So will every animal that crawls on the ground and every fish in the sea respect and fear you. I have given them to you."

⁸Then God said to Noah and his sons, ⁹"Now I am making my agreement with you and your people who will live after you. ¹⁰And I also make it with every living thing that is with you. It is with the birds, the tame animals and the wild animals. It is with all that came out of the boat with you. I make my agreement with every living thing on earth. ¹¹I make this agreement with you: I will never again destroy all living things by floodwaters. A flood will never again destroy the earth."

¹²And God said, "I am making an agreement between me and you and every living creature that is with you. It will continue from now on. This is the sign: ¹³I am putting my rainbow in the clouds. It is the sign of the agreement between me and the earth. ¹⁴When I bring clouds over the earth, a rainbow appears in the clouds. ¹⁵Then I will remember my agreement. It is between me and you and every living thing. Floodwaters will never again destroy all life on the earth. ¹⁶When the rainbow appears in the clouds, I will see it. Then I will remember the agreement that continues forever. It is between me and every living thing on the earth."

¹⁷So God said to Noah, "That rainbow is a sign. It is the sign of the agreement that I made with all living things on earth."

¹⁸The sons of Noah came out of the boat with him. They were Shem, Ham and Japheth. (Ham was the father of Canaan.) ¹⁹These three men were Noah's sons. And all the people on earth came from these three sons.

Prayer Starter: You made all the colors in the rainbow, dear Lord—green and blue and yellow and red.

Memory Verse: It was by faith Noah heard God's warnings about things that he could not yet see. . . .   —*Hebrews 11:7*

Abram

After Terah [a descendant of Shem] was 70 years old, his sons Abram, Nahor and Haran were born.

²⁷This is the family history of Terah. Terah was the father of Abram, Nahor and Haran. Haran was the father of Lot. ²⁸Haran died while his father, Terah, was still alive. This happened in Ur in Babylonia, where he was born. ²⁹Abram and Nahor both married. Abram's wife was named Sarai. Nahor's wife was named Milcah. She was the daughter of Haran. Haran was the father of Milcah and Iscah. ³⁰Sarai was not able to have children.

³¹Terah took his son Abram, his grandson Lot (Haran's son) and his daughter-in-law Sarai (Abram's wife). They moved out of Ur of Babylonia. They had planned to go to the land of Canaan. But when they reached the city of Haran, they settled there.

³²Terah lived to be 205 years old. Then he died in Haran.

12Then the Lord said to Abram, "Leave your country, your relatives and your father's family. Go to the land I will show you.

²I will make you a great nation,
and I will bless you.
I will make you famous.
And you will be a blessing to others.
³I will bless those who bless you.
I will place a curse on those who harm you.
And all the people on earth
will be blessed through you."

⁴So Abram left Haran as the Lord had told him. And Lot went with him. At this time Abram was 75 years old. ⁵Abram took his wife Sarai, his nephew Lot and everything they owned. They took all the servants they had gotten in Haran. They set out from Haran, planning to go to the land of Canaan. In time they arrived there.

⁶Abram traveled through that land. He went as far as the great tree of Moreh at Shechem. The Canaanites were living in the land at that time. ⁷The Lord appeared to Abram. The Lord said, "I will give this land to your descendants." So Abram built an altar there to the Lord, who had appeared to him. ⁸Then Abram traveled from Shechem to the mountain east of Bethel. And he set up his tent there. Bethel was to the west, and Ai was to the east. There Abram built another altar to the Lord and worshiped him. ⁹After this, he traveled on toward southern Canaan.

Prayer Starter: Dear Lord, I know that you are wise and wonderful, more than anyone else in the universe. Lead me each day in doing what you wish.

Memory Verse: It was by faith Noah heard God's warnings about things that he could not yet see. He obeyed God and built a large boat . . .
                                                  —*Hebrews 11:7*

Abram and Lot

So Abram, his wife and Lot left Egypt. They took everything they owned and traveled to southern Canaan. ²Abram was very rich in cattle, silver and gold.

³He left southern Canaan and went back to Bethel. He went where he had camped before, between Bethel and Ai. ⁴It was the place where Abram had built an altar before. So he worshiped the Lord there.

⁵During this time Lot was traveling with Abram. Lot also had many sheep, cattle and tents. ⁶Abram and Lot had so many animals that the land could not support both of them together. ⁷Abram's herders and Lot's herders began to argue. The Canaanites and the Perizzites were living in the land at this time.

⁸So Abram said to Lot, "There should be no arguing between you and me. Your herders and mine should not argue either. We are brothers. ⁹We should separate. The whole land is there in front of you. If you go to the left, I will go to the right. If you go to the right, I will go to the left."

¹⁰Lot looked all around and saw the whole Jordan Valley. He saw that there was much water there. It was like the Lord's garden, like the land of Egypt in the direction of Zoar. (This was before the Lord destroyed Sodom and Gomorrah.) ¹¹So Lot chose to move east and live in the Jordan Valley. In this way Abram and Lot separated. ¹²Abram lived in the land of Canaan. But Lot lived among the cities in the Jordan Valley. He moved very near to Sodom. ¹³Now the people of Sodom were very evil. They were always sinning against the Lord.

¹⁴After Lot left, the Lord said to Abram, "Look all around you. Look north and south and east and west. ¹⁵All this land that you see I will give to you and your descendants forever. ¹⁶I will make your descendants as many as the dust of the earth. If anyone could count the dust on the earth, he could count your people. ¹⁷Get up! Walk through all this land. I am now giving it to you."

¹⁸So Abram moved his tents. He went to live near the great trees of Mamre. This was at the city of Hebron. There he built an altar to the Lord.

Prayer Starter: Father, I want to be unselfish. Keep me from complaining and bickering and being jealous. May I love others like you do.

Memory Verse: It was by faith Noah heard God's warnings about things that he could not yet see. He obeyed God and built a large boat to save his family.
                                                                    —*Hebrews 11:7*

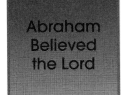

Abraham Believed the Lord

After these things happened, the Lord spoke his word to Abram in a vision. God said, "Abram, don't be afraid. I will defend you. And I will give you a great reward."

²But Abram said, "Lord God, what can you give me? I have no son. So my slave Eliezer from Damascus will get everything I own after I die." ³Abram said, "Look, you have given me no son. So a slave born in my house will inherit everything I have."

⁴Then the Lord spoke his word to Abram. He said, "That slave will not be the one to inherit what you have. You will have a son of your own. And your son will inherit what you have."

⁵Then God led Abram outside. God said, "Look at the sky. There are so many stars you cannot count them. And your descendants will be too many to count."

⁶Abram believed the Lord. And the Lord accepted Abram's faith, and that faith made him right with God.

17 When Abram was 99 years old, the Lord appeared to him. The Lord said, "I am God All-Powerful. Obey me and do what is right. ²I will make an agreement between us. I will make you the ancestor of many people."

³Then Abram bowed facedown on the ground. God said to him, ⁴"I am making my agreement with you: I will make you the father of many nations. ⁵I am changing your name from Abram[n] to Abraham.[n] This is because I am making you a father of many nations. ⁶I will give you many descendants. New nations will be born from you. Kings will come from you. ⁷And I will make an agreement between me and you and all your descendants from now on: I will be your God and the God of all your descendants. ⁸You live in the land of Canaan now as a stranger. But I will give you and your descendants all this land forever. And I will be the God of your descendants."

¹⁵God said to Abraham, "I will change the name of Sarai,[n] your wife. Her new name will be Sarah.[n] ¹⁶I will bless her. I will give her a son, and you will be the father. She will be the mother of many nations. Kings of nations will come from her."

[n]**Abram** This name means "honored father."
[n]**Abraham** The end of the Hebrew word for "Abraham" sounds like the beginning of the Hebrew word for "many."
[n]**Sarai** An Aramaic name meaning "princess."
[n]**Sarah** A Hebrew name meaning "princess."

Prayer Starter: Father, thank you for Jesus Christ, and for your promise of eternal life. Give me faith in Christ, and may I serve him each day.

Memory Verse: He never doubted . . . —*Romans 4:20*

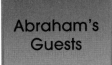

Abraham's Guests

Later, the Lord again appeared to Abraham near the great trees of Mamre. At that time Abraham was sitting at the door of his tent. It was during the hottest part of the day. ²He looked up and saw three men standing near him. When Abraham saw them, he ran from his tent to meet them. He bowed facedown on the ground before them. ³Abraham said, "Sir, if you think well of me, please stay awhile with me, your servant. ⁴I will bring some water so all of you can wash your feet. You may rest under the tree. ⁵I will get some bread for you, so you can regain your strength. Then you may continue your journey."

The three men said, "That is fine. Do as you said."

⁶Abraham hurried to the tent where Sarah was. He said to her, "Hurry, prepare 20 quarts of fine flour. Make it into loaves of bread." ⁷Then Abraham ran to his cattle. He took one of his best calves and gave it to a servant. The servant hurried to kill the calf and to prepare it for food. ⁸Abraham gave the three men the calf that had been cooked. He also gave them milk curds and milk. While the three men ate, he stood under the tree near them.

⁹The men asked Abraham, "Where is your wife Sarah?"

"There, in the tent," said Abraham.

¹⁰Then the Lord said, "I will certainly return to you about this time a year from now. At that time your wife Sarah will have a son."

Sarah was listening at the entrance of the tent which was behind him. ¹¹Abraham and Sarah were very old. Sarah was past the age when women normally have children. ¹²So she laughed to herself, "My husband and I are too old to have a baby."

¹³Then the Lord said to Abraham, "Why did Sarah laugh? Why did she say, 'I am too old to have a baby'? ¹⁴Is anything too hard for the Lord? No! I will return to you at the right time a year from now. And Sarah will have a son."

Prayer Starter: Heavenly father, you are very great. You know the past, the present, and the future. Thank you for having a plan for my life.

Memory Verse: He never doubted that God would keep his promise. . . .
—Romans 4:20

Sodom
and
Gomorrah

T he two angels came to Sodom in the evening.
Lot was sitting near the city gate and saw
them. He got up and went to them and bowed facedown
on the ground. ²Lot said, "Sirs, please come to my house
and spend the night. There you can wash your feet.
Then tomorrow you may continue your journey."

The angels answered, "No, we will spend the night
in the city's public square."

¹²The two men said to Lot, "Do you have any other relatives in this
city? Do you have any sons-in-law, sons, daughters or any other relatives?
If you do, tell them to leave now. ¹³We are about to destroy this city. The
Lord has heard of all the evil that is here. So he has sent us to destroy it."

¹⁴So Lot went out and spoke to his future sons-in-law. They were
pledged to marry his daughters. Lot said, "Hurry and leave this city! The
Lord is about to destroy it!" But they thought Lot was joking.

¹⁵At dawn the next morning, the angels begged Lot to hurry. They
said, "Go! Take your wife and your two daughters with
you. Then you will not be destroyed when the city is
punished."

¹⁶But Lot delayed. So the two men took the
hands of Lot, his wife and his two daughters. The
men led them safely out of the city. So the Lord
was merciful to Lot and his family.

²³The sun had already come up when Lot
entered Zoar. ²⁴The Lord sent a rain of burning
sulfur down from the sky on Sodom and Gomorrah. ²⁵So the Lord destroyed those cities. He
also destroyed the whole Jordan Valley, everyone living in the cities and even all the plants.

²⁶At that point Lot's wife looked back. When
she did, she became a pillar of salt.

Prayer Starter: Father, help me to never doubt or question your promises. I
know you are faithful. May I trust you more and more.

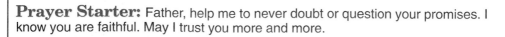

Memory Verse: He never doubted that God would keep his
promise. Abraham never stopped believing. . . .   —*Romans 4:20*

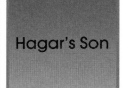

Hagar's Son

The Lord cared for Sarah as he had said. He did for her what he had promised. ²Sarah became pregnant. And she gave birth to a son for Abraham in his old age. Everything happened at the time God had said it would. ³Abraham named his son Isaac. Sarah gave birth to this son of Abraham.

⁸Isaac grew and became old enough to eat food. At that time Abraham gave a great feast. ⁹But Sarah saw Ishmael making fun of Isaac. (Ishmael was the son of Abraham by Hagar, Sarah's Egyptian slave.) ¹⁰So Sarah said to Abraham, "Throw out this slave woman and her son. When we die, our son Isaac will inherit everything we have. I don't want her son to inherit any of our things."

¹¹This troubled Abraham very much because Ishmael was also his son. ¹²But God said to Abraham, "Don't be troubled about the boy and the slave woman. Do whatever Sarah tells you. The descendants I promised you will be from Isaac. ¹³I will also make the descendants of Ishmael into a great nation. I will do this because he is your son, too."

¹⁴Early the next morning Abraham took some food and a leather bag full of water. He gave them to Hagar and sent her away. Hagar carried these things and her son. She went and wandered in the desert of Beersheba.

¹⁵Later, all the water was gone from the bag. So Hagar put her son under a bush. ¹⁶Then she went away a short distance and sat down. Hagar thought, "My son will die. I cannot watch this happen." She sat there and began to cry.

¹⁷God heard the boy crying. And God's angel called to Hagar from heaven. He said, "What is wrong, Hagar? Don't be afraid! God has heard the boy crying there. ¹⁸Help the boy up. Take him by the hand. I will make his descendants into a great nation."

¹⁹Then God showed Hagar a well of water. So she went to the well and filled her bag with water. Then she gave the boy a drink.

²⁰God was with the boy as he grew up. Ishmael lived in the desert. He learned to shoot with a bow very well. ²¹He lived in the Desert of Paran. His mother found a wife for him in Egypt.

Prayer Starter: Lord, many people around the world are hungry and thirsty. Please provide for their needs, and give me what I need each day, too.

Memory Verse: He never doubted that God would keep his promise. Abraham never stopped believing. He grew stronger in his faith . . .
—*Romans 4:20*

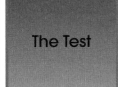

The Test

After these things God tested Abraham's faith. God said to him, "Abraham!"

And he answered, "Here I am."

²Then God said, "Take your only son, Isaac, the son you love. Go to the land of Moriah. There kill him and offer him as a whole burnt offering. Do this on one of the mountains there. I will tell you which one."

³Early in the morning Abraham got up and saddled his donkey. He took Isaac and two servants with him. He cut the wood for the sacrifice. Then they went to the place God had told them to go. ⁴On the third day Abraham looked up and saw the place in the distance. ⁵He said to his servants, "Stay here with the donkey. My son and I will go over there and worship. Then we will come back to you."

⁶Abraham took the wood for the sacrifice and gave it to his son to carry. Abraham took the knife and the fire. So Abraham and his son went on together.

⁷Isaac said to his father Abraham, "Father!"

Abraham answered, "Yes, my son."

Isaac said, "We have the fire and the wood. But where is the lamb we will burn as a sacrifice?"

⁸Abraham answered, "God will give us the lamb for the sacrifice, my son."

So Abraham and his son went on together. ⁹They came to the place God had told him about. There, Abraham built an altar. He laid the wood on it. Then he tied up his son Isaac. And he laid Isaac on the wood on the altar. ¹⁰Then Abraham took his knife and was about to kill his son.

¹¹But the angel of the Lord called to him from heaven. The angel said, "Abraham! Abraham!"

Abraham answered, "Yes."

¹²The angel said, "Don't kill your son or hurt him in any way. Now I can see that you respect God. I see that you have not kept your son, your only son, from me."

¹³Then Abraham looked up and saw a male sheep. Its horns were caught in a bush. So Abraham went and took the sheep and killed it. He offered it as a whole burnt offering to God. Abraham's son was saved. ¹⁴So Abraham named that place The Lord Gives. Even today people say, "On the mountain of the Lord it will be given."

Prayer Starter: Thank you, Lord, for helping me to love you more than anything else in the world. I love you because you first loved me.

Memory Verse: He never doubted that God would keep his promise. Abraham never stopped believing. He grew stronger in his faith and gave praise to God. —*Romans 4:20*

A Wife for Isaac

Abraham was now very old. The Lord had blessed him in every way. [2]Abraham's oldest servant was in charge of everything Abraham owned. Abraham called that servant to him and said, "Put your hand under my leg." [3]Make a promise to me before the Lord, the God of heaven and earth. Don't get a wife for my son from the Canaanite girls who live around here. [4]Instead, go back to my country, to the land of my relatives. Get a wife for my son Isaac from there."

[9]So the servant put his hand under his master's leg. He made a promise to Abraham about this. [10]The servant took ten of Abraham's camels and left. He carried with him many different kinds of beautiful gifts. He went to Northwest Mesopotamia to Nahor's city. [11]He made the camels kneel down at the well outside the city. It was in the evening when the women come out to get water.

[12]The servant said, "Lord, you are the God of my master Abraham. Allow me to find a wife for his son today. Please show this kindness to my master Abraham. [13]Here I am, standing by the spring of water. The girls from the city are coming out to get water. [14]I will say to one of the girls, 'Please put your jar down so I can drink.' Then let her say, 'Drink, and I will also give water to your camels.' If that happens, I will know she is the right one for your servant Isaac. And I will know that you have shown kindness to my master."

[15]Before the servant had finished praying, Rebekah came out of the city. She was the daughter of Bethuel. (Bethuel was the son of Milcah and Nahor, Abraham's brother.) Rebekah was carrying her water jar on her shoulder. [16]She was very pretty. She was a virgin; she had never had sexual relations with a man. She went down to the spring and filled her jar. Then she came back up. [17]The servant ran to her and said, "Please give me a little water from your jar."

[18]Rebekah said, "Drink, sir." She quickly lowered the jar from her shoulder and gave him a drink. [19]After he finished drinking, Rebekah said, "I will also pour some water for your camels." [20]So she quickly poured all the water from her jar into the drinking trough for the camels. Then she kept running to the well until she had given all the camels enough to drink.

Put . . . leg This showed that a person would keep the promise.

Prayer Starter: You lead those who trust you, Lord. Please be my guide and show me what to do and how to live all my life.

Memory Verse: We know that in everything . . .　　　*—Romans 8:28*

Jacob and Esau

This is the family history of Isaac. Abraham had a son named Isaac. [20]When Isaac was 40 years old, he married Rebekah. Rebekah was from Northwest Mesopotamia. She was Bethuel's daughter and the sister of Laban the Aramean. [21]Isaac's wife could not have children. So Isaac prayed to the Lord for her. The Lord heard Isaac's prayer, and Rebekah became pregnant.

[22]While she was pregnant, the babies struggled inside her. She asked, "Why is this happening to me?" Then she went to get an answer from the Lord.

[23]The Lord said to her,

"Two nations are in your body.
    Two groups of people will be taken from you.
One group will be stronger than the other.
    The older will serve the younger."

[24]And when the time came, Rebekah gave birth to twins. [25]The first baby was born red. His skin was like a hairy robe. So he was named Esau.[n] [26]When the second baby was born, he was holding on to Esau's heel. So that baby was named Jacob.[n] Isaac was 60 years old when they were born.

[27]When the boys grew up, Esau became a skilled hunter. He loved to be out in the fields. But Jacob was a quiet man. He stayed among the tents. [28]Isaac loved Esau. Esau hunted the wild animals that Isaac enjoyed eating. But Rebekah loved Jacob.

[29]One day Jacob was boiling a pot of vegetable soup. Esau came in

from hunting in the fields. He was weak from hunger. [30]So Esau said to Jacob, "Let me eat some of that red soup. I am weak with hunger." (That is why people call him Edom.[n])

[31]But Jacob said, "You must sell me your rights as the firstborn son."[n]

[32]Esau said, "I am almost dead from hunger. If I die, all of my father's wealth will not help me."

[33]But Jacob said, "First, promise me that you will give it to me." So Esau made a promise to Jacob. In this way he sold his part of their father's wealth to Jacob. [34]Then Jacob gave Esau bread and vegetable soup. Esau ate and drank and then left. So Esau showed how little he cared about his rights as the firstborn son.

[n]**Esau** This name may mean "hairy."
[n]**Jacob** This name sounds like the Hebrew word for "heel." "Grabbing someone's heel" is a Hebrew saying for tricking someone.
[n]**Edom** This name sounds like the Hebrew word for "red."
[n]**rights . . . son** Usually the firstborn son had a high rank in the family. The firstborn son usually became the new head of the family.

Prayer Starter: If I have friends who tempt me to do what is wrong, Lord, help me to say no. May I always do what pleases you.

Memory Verse: We know that in everything God works for the good . . .
—*Romans 8:28*

Jacob and Rachel

Then Jacob continued his journey. He came to the land of the people of the East. ²He looked and saw a well in the field. Three flocks of sheep were lying nearby, because they drank water from this well. A large stone covered the mouth of the well. ³All the flocks would gather there. The shepherds would roll the stone away from the well and water the sheep. Then they would put the stone back in its place.

⁴Jacob said to the shepherds there, "My brothers, where are you from?"

They answered, "We are from Haran."

⁵Then Jacob asked, "Do you know Laban grandson of Nahor?"

They answered, "We know him."

⁶Then Jacob asked, "How is he?"

They answered, "He is well. Look, his daughter Rachel is coming now with his sheep."

⁷Jacob said, "But look, it is still the middle part of the day. It is not time for the sheep to be gathered for the night. So give them water and let them go back into the pasture."

[8]But they said, "We cannot do that until all the flocks are gathered. Then we will roll away the stone from the mouth of the well and water the sheep."

[9]While Jacob was talking with the shepherds, Rachel came with her father's sheep. It was her job to take care of the sheep. [10]Then Jacob saw Laban's daughter Rachel and Laban's sheep. So he went to the well and rolled the stone from its mouth. Then he watered Laban's sheep. Now Laban was the brother of Rebekah, Jacob's mother. [11]Then Jacob kissed Rachel and cried. [12]He told her that he was from her father's family. He said that he was the son of Rebekah. So Rachel ran home and told her father.

[13]When Laban heard the news about his sister's son Jacob, Laban ran to meet him. Laban hugged him and kissed him and brought him to his house. Jacob told Laban everything that had happened.

[14]Then Laban said, "You are my own flesh and blood."

So Jacob stayed there a month. [15]Then Laban said to Jacob, "You are my relative. But it is not right for you to keep on working for me without pay. What would you like me to pay you?"

[16]Now Laban had two daughters. The older was Leah, and the younger was Rachel. [17]Leah had weak eyes, but Rachel was very beautiful. [18]Jacob loved Rachel. So he said to Laban, "Let me marry your younger daughter Rachel. If you will, I will work seven years for you."

[19]Laban said, "It would be better for her to marry you than someone else. So stay here with me." [20]So Jacob worked for Laban seven years so he could marry Rachel. But they seemed to him like just a few days. This was because he loved Rachel very much.

[21]After seven years Jacob said to Laban, "Give me Rachel so that I may marry her. The time I promised to work for you is over."

[22]So Laban gave a feast for all the people there. [23]That evening Laban brought his daughter Leah to Jacob. Jacob and Leah had sexual relations together. [24](Laban gave his slave girl Zilpah to his daughter to be her servant.) [25]In the morning Jacob saw that he had had sexual relations with Leah! He said to Laban, "What have you done to me? I worked hard for you so that I could marry Rachel! Why did you trick me?"

[26]Laban said, "In our country we do not allow the younger daughter to marry before the older daughter. [27]But complete the full week of the marriage ceremony with Leah. I will give you Rachel to marry also. But you must serve me another seven years."

[28]So Jacob did this and completed the week with Leah. Then Laban gave him his daughter Rachel as a wife.

Prayer Starter: Thank you for my family, dear Lord. Help us to always take care of each other.

Memory Verse: We know that in everything God works for the good of those who love him. . . .   —*Romans 8:28*

Jacob's Name Is Changed

When Jacob also went his way, the angels of God met him. [2]When Jacob saw them, he said, "This is the camp of God!" So Jacob named that place Mahanaim.[n]

[3]Jacob's brother Esau was living in the area called Seir in the country of Edom. Jacob sent messengers to Esau. [4]Jacob told the messengers, "Give this message to my master Esau: 'This is what Jacob, your servant, says: I have lived with Laban and have remained there until now. [5]I have cattle, donkeys, flocks, and male and female servants. I send this message to you and ask you to accept us.' "

[6]The messengers returned to Jacob and said, "We went to your brother Esau. He is coming to meet you. And he has 400 men with him."

[7]Then Jacob was very afraid and worried. He divided the people who were with him into two camps. He also divided all the flocks, herds and camels into two camps. [8]Jacob thought, "Esau might come and destroy one camp. But the other camp can run away and be saved."

[16]Jacob gave each separate flock of animals to one of his servants. Then he said to them, "Go ahead of me and keep some space between each herd." [17]Jacob gave them their orders. To the servant with the first group of animals he said, "My brother Esau will come to you. He will ask you, 'Whose servant are you? Where are you going? Whose animals are these?' [18]Then you will answer, 'These animals belong to your servant Jacob. He sent them as a gift to you my master, Esau. And Jacob also is coming behind us.' "

[19]Jacob ordered the second servant, the third servant and all the other servants to do the same thing. He said, "Say the same thing to Esau when you meet him. [20]Say, 'Your servant Jacob is coming behind us.' " Jacob thought, "If I send this gift ahead of me, maybe Esau will forgive me. Then when I see him, perhaps he will accept me." [21]So Jacob sent the gift to Esau. But Jacob stayed that night in the camp.

[22]During the night Jacob rose and crossed the Jabbok River at the crossing. He took his 2 wives, his 2 slave girls and his 11 sons with him. [23]He sent his family and everything he had across the river. [24]But Jacob stayed behind alone. And a man came and wrestled with him until the sun came up. [25]The man saw that he could not defeat Jacob. So he struck Jacob's hip and put it out of joint. [26]Then the man said to Jacob, "Let me go. The sun is coming up."

But Jacob said, "I will let you go if you will bless me."

[27]The man said to him, "What is your name?"

And he answered, "Jacob."

[28]Then the man said, "Your name will no longer be Jacob. Your name will now be Israel,[n] because you have wrestled with God and with men. And you have won."

[29]Then Jacob asked him, "Please tell me your name."

But the man said, "Why do you ask my name?" Then he blessed Jacob there.

³⁰So Jacob named that place Peniel.ⁿ He said, "I have seen God face to face. But my life was saved." ³¹Then the sun rose as he was leaving that place. Jacob was limping because of his leg. ³²So even today the people of Israel do not eat the muscle that is on the hip joint of animals. This is because Jacob was touched there.

ⁿ**Mahanaim** This name means "two camps."
ⁿ**Israel** This name means "he wrestles with God."
ⁿ**Peniel** This name means "the face of God."

Prayer Starter: Dear Lord, may I be strong and cheerful, for I know you give me victory.

Memory Verse: We know that in everything God works for the good of those who love him. They are the people God called . . .

—*Romans 8:28*

Eight Ounces of Silver

Ozne day Joseph's brothers went to Shechem to herd their father's sheep. ¹³Jacob said to Joseph, "Go to Shechem. Your brothers are there herding the sheep."

Joseph answered, "I will go."

¹⁷So Joseph went to look for his brothers and found them in Dothan.

¹⁸Joseph's brothers saw him coming from far away. Before he reached them, they made a plan to kill him. ¹⁹They said to each other, "Here comes that dreamer. ²⁰Let's kill him and throw his body into one of the wells. We can tell our father that a wild animal killed him. Then we will see what will become of his dreams."

²³So when Joseph came to his brothers, they pulled off his robe with long sleeves. ²⁴Then they threw him into the well. It was empty. There was no water in it.

²⁵While Joseph was in the well, the brothers sat down to eat. When they looked up, they saw a group of Ishmaelites. They were traveling from Gilead to Egypt. Their camels were carrying spices, balm and myrrh.

²⁶Then Judah said to his brothers, "What will we gain if we kill our brother and hide his death? ²⁷Let's sell him to these Ishmaelites. Then we will not be guilty of killing our own brother. After all, he is our brother, our own flesh and blood." And the other brothers agreed. ²⁸So when the Midianite traders came by, the brothers took Joseph out of the well. They sold him to the Ishmaelites for eight ounces of silver. And the Ishmaelites took him to Egypt.

39Now Joseph had been taken down to Egypt. An Egyptian named Potiphar was an officer to the king of Egypt. He was the captain of the palace guard. He bought Joseph from the Ishmaelites who had brought him down there. ²The Lord was with Joseph, and he became a successful man. He lived in the house of his master, Potiphar the Egyptian.

Prayer Starter: Protect me from bad people, Lord. Keep me safe from those who could harm me. And keep me from ever harming another person.

Memory Verse: We know that in everything God works for the good of those who love him. They are the people God called, because that was his plan.   —*Romans 8:28*

The King's Dreams

Two years later the king had a dream. He dreamed he was standing on the bank of the Nile River. ²He saw seven fat and beautiful cows come up out of the river. They stood there, eating the grass. ³Then seven more cows came up out of the river. But they were thin and ugly. They stood beside the seven beautiful cows on the bank of the Nile. ⁴The seven thin and ugly cows ate the seven beautiful fat cows. Then the king woke up. ⁵The king slept again and dreamed a second time. In his dream he saw seven full and good heads of grain growing on one stalk. ⁶After that, seven more heads of grain sprang up. But they were thin and burned by the hot east wind. ⁷The thin heads of grain ate the seven full and good heads. Then the king woke up again. And he realized it was only a dream. ⁸The next morning the king was troubled about these dreams. So he sent for all the magicians and wise men of Egypt. The king told them his dreams. But no one could explain their meaning to him.

¹⁴So the king called for Joseph. The guards quickly brought him out of the prison. He shaved, put on clean clothes and went before the king.

¹⁵The king said to Joseph, "I have had a dream. But no one can explain its meaning to me. I have heard that you can explain a dream when someone tells it to you."

¹⁶Joseph answered the king, "I am not able to explain the meaning of dreams. God will do this for the king."

²⁹"You will have seven years of good crops and plenty to eat in all the land of Egypt. ³⁰But after those seven years, there will come seven years of hunger. All the food that grew in the land of Egypt will be forgotten. The time of hunger will eat up the land. ³¹People will forget what it was like to have plenty of food. This is because the hunger that follows will be so great. ³²You had two dreams which mean the same thing. This shows that God has firmly decided that this will happen. And he will make it happen soon."

Prayer Starter: Thank you, Lord, for always being at work for Joseph's good—and for mine. May I love you and be chosen for your purpose.

Memory Verse: If someone does wrong to you . . .—*Romans 12:17–18*

Joseph Becomes Ruler

So the king said to Joseph, "God has shown you all this. There is no one as wise and understanding as you are. ⁴⁰I will put you in charge of my palace. All the people will obey your orders. Only I will be greater than you."

⁴¹Then the king said to Joseph, "Look! I have put you in charge of all the land of Egypt." ⁴²Then the king took off from his own finger his ring with the royal seal on it. And he put it on Joseph's finger. He gave Joseph fine linen clothes to wear. And he put a gold chain around Joseph's neck. ⁴³The king had Joseph ride in the second royal chariot. Men walked ahead of his chariot calling, "Bow down!" By doing these things, the king put Joseph in charge of all of Egypt.

⁴⁴The king said to him, "I am the king. And I say that no one in all the land of Egypt may lift a hand or a foot unless you say he may." ⁴⁵The king gave Joseph the name Zaphenath-Paneah. He also gave Joseph a wife named Asenath. She was the daughter of Potiphera, priest of On. So Joseph traveled through all the land of Egypt.

⁴⁶Joseph was 30 years old when he began serving the king of Egypt. And he left the king's court and traveled through all the land of Egypt. ⁴⁷During the seven good years, the crops in the land grew well. ⁴⁸And Joseph gathered all the food which was produced in Egypt during those seven years of good crops. He stored the food in the cities. In every city he stored grain that had been grown in the fields around that city. ⁴⁹Joseph stored much grain, as much as the sand of the seashore. He stored so much grain that he could not measure it.

Prayer Starter: Make me wise, O Lord, that I might help other people like Joseph did.

Memory Verse: If someone does wrong to you, do not pay him back . . .
　　　　　　　　　　　　　　　　—*Romans 12:17–18*

God Sent Me Here

Jacob learned that there was grain in Egypt. So he said to his sons, "Why are you just sitting here looking at one another. ²I have heard that there is grain in Egypt. Go down there and buy grain for us to eat. Then we will live and not die."

⁶Now Joseph was governor over Egypt. He was the one who sold the grain to people who came to buy it. So Joseph's brothers came to him. They bowed facedown on the ground before him. ⁷When Joseph saw his brothers, he knew who they were. But he acted as if he didn't know them. He asked unkindly, "Where do you come from?"

They answered, "We have come from the land of Canaan to buy food."

⁸Joseph knew they were his brothers. But they did not know who he was.

45 He said to his brothers, "I am Joseph. Is my father still alive?" But the brothers could not answer him, because they were very afraid of him.

⁴So Joseph said to them, "Come close to me." So the brothers came close to him. And he said to them, "I am your brother Joseph. You sold me as a slave to go to Egypt. ⁵Now don't be worried. Don't be angry with yourselves because you sold me here. God sent me here ahead of you to save people's lives."

Prayer Starter: Dear Lord, don't let me mistreat those who mistreat me. Help me do my best to live at peace with others.

Memory Verse: If someone does wrong to you, do not pay him back by doing wrong to him. . . .   —*Romans 12:17–18*

My Son Is Alive!

So the king said to Joseph, "Tell your brothers to load their animals and go back to the land of Canaan. [18]Tell them to bring their father and their families back here to me. I will give them the best land in Egypt. And they will eat the best food we have here. [19]Tell them to take some wagons from Egypt for their children and their wives. And tell them to bring their father back also. [20]Tell them not to worry about bringing any of their things with them. We will give them the best of what we have in Egypt."

[21]So the sons of Israel did this. Joseph gave them wagons as the king had ordered. And he gave them food for their trip. [22]He gave each brother a change of clothes. But he gave Benjamin five changes of clothes. And Joseph gave him about seven and one-half pounds of silver. [23]Joseph also sent his father ten donkeys loaded with the best things from Egypt. And he sent ten female donkeys. They were loaded with grain, bread and other food for his father on his trip back. [24]Then Joseph told his brothers to go. As they were leaving, he said to them, "Don't quarrel on the way home."

[25]So the brothers left Egypt and went to their father Jacob in the land of Canaan. [26]They told him, "Joseph is still alive. He is the ruler over all the land of Egypt." Their father was shocked and did not believe them. [27]But the brothers told him everything Joseph had said. Then Jacob saw the wagons that Joseph had sent to carry him back to Egypt. Now Jacob felt better. [28]Jacob, also called Israel, said, "Now I believe you. My son Joseph is still alive. I will go and see him before I die."

46 So Jacob, also called Israel, took all he had and started his trip. He went to Beersheba. There he offered sacrifices to the God of his father Isaac. [2]During the night God spoke to Israel in a vision. He said, "Jacob, Jacob."

And Jacob answered, "Here I am."

[3]Then God said, "I am God, the God of your father. Don't be afraid to go to Egypt. I will make your descendants a great nation there. [4]I will go to Egypt with you. And I will bring you out of Egypt again. Joseph's own hands will close your eyes when you die."

[5]Then Jacob left Beersheba. The sons of Israel loaded their father, their children and their wives. They put them in the wagons the king of Egypt had sent. [6]They also took their farm animals and everything they had gotten in Canaan. So Jacob went to Egypt with all his descendants. [7]He took his sons and grandsons, his daughters and granddaughters. He took all his family to Egypt with him.

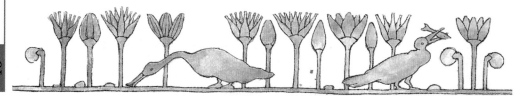

Prayer Starter: Bless my family, Lord, those I love. May we praise you together.

Memory Verse: If someone does wrong to you, do not pay him back by doing wrong to him. Try to do what everyone thinks is right. . . .

—*Romans 12:17–18*

Baby on the Nile

Then a new king began to rule Egypt. He did not know who Joseph was. ⁹This king said to his people, "Look! The people of Israel are too many! And they are too strong for us to handle! ¹⁰We must make plans against them. If we don't, the number of their people will grow even more. Then if there is a war, they might join our enemies. Then they could fight us and escape from the country!"

¹¹So the Egyptians made life hard for the people of Israel. They put slave masters over the Israelites. The slave masters forced the Israelites to build the cities Pithom and Rameses for the king. These cities were supply centers in which the Egyptians stored things. ¹²The Egyptians forced the Israelites to work even harder. But this made the Israelites grow in number and spread more. So the Egyptians became more afraid of them. ¹³They forced the Israelites to work even harder. ¹⁴The Egyptians made life hard for the Israelites. They forced the Israelites to work very hard making bricks and mortar. They also forced them to do all kinds of hard work in the fields. The Egyptians were not merciful to them in all their hard work.

¹⁵There were two Hebrew nurses named Shiphrah and Puah. These nurses helped the Israelite women give birth to their babies. The king of Egypt said to the nurses, ¹⁶"When you are helping the Hebrew women give birth to their babies, watch! If the baby is a girl, let the baby live. But if it is a boy, kill it!" ¹⁷But the nurses feared God. So they did not do as the king told them. They let all the boy babies live. ¹⁸Then the king of Egypt sent for the nurses. He said, "Why did you do this? Why did you let the boys live?"

¹⁹The nurses said to him, "The Hebrew women are much stronger than the Egyptian women. They give birth to their babies before we can get there." ²⁰God was good to the nurses. And the Hebrew people continued to grow in number. So they became even stronger. ²¹Because the nurses feared God, he gave them families of their own.

²²So the king commanded all his people: "Every time a boy is born to the Hebrews, you must throw him into the Nile River. But let all the girl babies live."

Prayer Starter: Lord, watch over me each night as I'm asleep and keep me from all harm. May your angels keep me safe.

Memory Verse: If someone does wrong to you, do not pay him back by doing wrong to him. Try to do what everyone thinks is right. Do your best to live in peace with everyone.   —*Romans 12:17–18*

2 There was a man from the family of Levi. He married a woman who was also from the family of Levi. ²She became pregnant and gave birth to a son. She saw how wonderful the baby was, and she hid him for three months. ³But after three months, she was not able to hide the baby any longer. So she got a basket and covered it with tar so that it would float. She put the baby in the basket. Then she put the basket among the tall grass at the edge of the Nile River. ⁴The baby's sister stood a short distance away. She wanted to see what would happen to him.

⁵Then the daughter of the king of Egypt came to the river. She was going to take a bath. Her servant girls were walking beside the river. She saw the basket in the tall grass. So she sent her slave girl to get it. ⁶The king's daughter opened the basket and saw the baby boy. He was crying, and she felt sorry for him. She said, "This is one of the Hebrew babies."

⁷Then the baby's sister asked the king's daughter, "Would you like me to find a Hebrew woman to nurse the baby for you?"

⁸The king's daughter said, "Yes, please." So the girl went and got the baby's own mother.

⁹The king's daughter said to the woman, "Take this baby and nurse him for me. I will pay you." So the woman took her baby and nursed him. ¹⁰After the child had grown older, the woman took him to the king's daughter. She adopted the baby as her own son. The king's daughter named him Moses,ⁿ because she had pulled him out of the water.

ⁿ**Moses** The name Moses sounds like the Hebrew word for "to pull out."

The Burning Bush

One day Moses was taking care of Jethro's sheep. Jethro was the priest of Midian and also Moses' father-in-law. Moses led the sheep to the west side of the desert. He came to Sinai, the mountain of God. ²There the angel of the Lord appeared to Moses in flames of fire coming out of a bush. Moses saw that the bush was on fire, but it was not burning up. ³So Moses said, "I will go closer to this strange thing. How can a bush continue burning without burning up?"

⁴The Lord saw Moses was coming to look at the bush. So God called to him from the bush, "Moses, Moses!"

And Moses said, "Here I am."

⁵Then God said, "Do not come any closer. Take off your sandals. You are standing on holy ground. ⁶I am the God of your ancestors. I am the God of Abraham, the God of Isaac and the God of Jacob." Moses covered his face because he was afraid to look at God.

⁷The Lord said, "I have seen the troubles my people have suffered in Egypt. And I have heard their cries when the Egyptian slave masters hurt them. I am concerned about their pain. ⁸I have come down to save them from the Egyptians. I will bring them out of that land. I will lead them to a good land with lots of room. This is a land where much food grows. This is the land of these people: the Canaanites, Hittites, Amorites, Perizzites, Hivites and Jebusites. ⁹I have heard the cries of the people of Israel. I have seen the way the Egyptians have made life hard for them. ¹⁰So now I am sending you to the king of Egypt. Go! Bring my people, the Israelites, out of Egypt!"

Prayer Starter: Dear Lord, you are the God worshiped by Abraham, Joseph, and Moses. Help us to honor and worship and praise you, too.

Memory Verse: Are there any gods like you, Lord? . . . —*Exodus 15:11*

What Is That in Your Hand?

Then Moses answered, "What if the people of Israel do not believe me or listen to me? What if they say, 'The Lord did not appear to you'?"

²The Lord said to him, "What is that in your hand?"

Moses answered, "It is my walking stick."

³The Lord said, "Throw it on the ground."

So Moses threw it on the ground. And it became a snake. Moses ran from the snake. ⁴But the Lord said to him, "Reach out and grab the snake by its tail." So Moses reached out and took hold of the snake. When he did this, it again became a stick in his hand. ⁵The Lord said, "When this happens, the Israelites will believe that the Lord appeared to you. I am the God of their ancestors. I am the God of Abraham, the God of Isaac and the God of Jacob."

⁶Then the Lord said to Moses, "Put your hand inside your coat." So Moses put his hand inside his coat. When he took his hand out, it was white with a harmful skin disease.

⁷Then the Lord said, "Now put your hand inside your coat again." So Moses put his hand inside his coat again. When he took it out, his hand was healthy again. It was like the rest of his skin.

⁸Then the Lord said, "The people may not believe you or be convinced by the first miracle. They may believe you when you show them this second miracle. ⁹After these two miracles they still may not believe or listen to you. Then take some water form the Nile River. Pour it on the dry ground. The water will become blood when it touches the ground."

¹⁰But Moses said to the Lord, "But Lord, I am not a skilled speaker. I have never been able to speak well. And now, even after talking to you, I am not a good speaker. I speak slowly and can't find the best words."

¹¹Then the Lord said to him, "Who made man's mouth? And who makes him deaf or not able to speak? Or who gives a man sight or makes him blind? It is I, the Lord. ¹²Now go! I will help you speak. I will tell you what to say."

Prayer Starter: Lord, help me to speak up for you whenever I need to. Give me great courage and wise words. May I be your witness.

Memory Verse: Are there any gods like you, Lord? No! There are no gods like you. . . .
                                                                    —*Exodus 15:11*

¹³But Moses said, "Please, Lord, send someone else."

¹⁴The Lord became angry with Moses. He said, "Your brother Aaron, from the family of Levi, is a skilled speaker. He is already coming to meet you. And he will be happy when he sees you. ¹⁵I will tell you what to say. Then you will tell Aaron. I will help both of you know what to say and do. ¹⁶And Aaron will speak to the people for you. You will tell him what God says. And he will speak for you. ¹⁷Take your walking stick with you. Use it to do miracles."

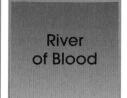

River of Blood

Then the Lord said to Moses, "The king is being stubborn. He refuses to let the people go. [15]In the morning the king will go out to the Nile River. Go meet him by the edge of the river. Take with you the walking stick that became a snake. [16]Tell him this: The Lord, the God of the Hebrews, sent me to you. He said, 'Let my people go worship me in the desert.' Until now you have not listened. [17]This is what the Lord says: 'This is how you will know that I am the Lord. I will strike the water of the Nile River with this stick in my hand. And the water will change into blood. [18]Then the fish in the Nile will die, and the river will begin to stink. And the Egyptians will not be able to drink the water from the Nile.' "

[19]The Lord said to Moses, "Tell Aaron to stretch the walking stick in his hand over the rivers, canals, ponds and pools in Egypt. The water will become blood everywhere in Egypt. There even will be blood in the wooden buckets and stone jars."

[20]So Moses and Aaron did just as the Lord had commanded. Aaron raised his walking stick and struck the water in the Nile River. He did this in front of the king and his officers. So all the water in the Nile changed into blood. [21]The fish in the Nile died, and the river began to stink. So the Egyptians could not drink water from it. Blood was everywhere in the land of Egypt.

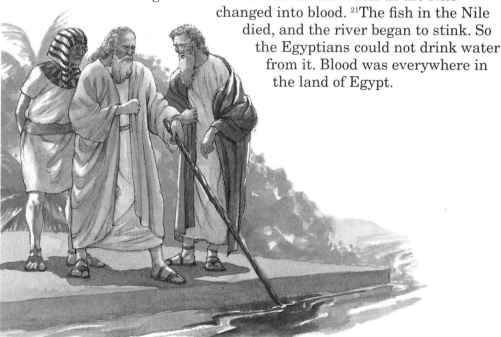

Prayer Starter: Thank you for being more powerful than anything or anyone else in all the universe, Lord. And thank you for your powerful love to me.

Memory Verse: Are there any gods like you, Lord? No! There are no gods like you. You are wonderfully holy. . . .   —*Exodus 15:11*

Leave My People

Then Moses called all the older leaders of Israel together. He told them, "Get the animals for your families. Kill the animals for the Passover. ²²Take a branch of the hyssop plant and dip it into the bowl filled with blood. Wipe the blood on the sides and tops of the doorframes. No one may leave his house until morning. ²³The Lord will go through Egypt to kill the Egyptians. He will see the blood on the sides and tops of the doorframes. Then the Lord will pass over that house. He will not let the one who brings death come into your houses and kill you.

²⁴"You must keep this command. This law is for you and your descendants from now on. ²⁵Do this when you go to the land the Lord has promised to give to you. ²⁶When your children ask you, 'Why are we doing these things?' ²⁷you will say, 'This is the Passover sacrifice to honor the Lord. When we were in Egypt, the Lord passed over the houses of Israel. The Lord killed the Egyptians, but he saved our homes.' " So now the people bowed down and worshiped the Lord. ²⁸They did just as the Lord commanded Moses and Aaron.

²⁹At midnight the Lord killed all the firstborn sons in the land of Egypt. The firstborn of the king, who sat on the throne, died. Even the firstborn of the prisoner in jail died. Also all the firstborn farm animals died. ³⁰The king, his officers and all the Egyptians got up during the night. Someone had died in every house. So there was loud crying everywhere in Egypt.

³¹During the night the king called for Moses and Aaron. He said to them, "Get up and leave my people. You and your people may do as you have asked. Go and worship the Lord. ³²Take all of your sheep and cattle as you have asked. Go. And also bless me." ³³The Egyptians also asked the Israelites to hurry and leave. They said, "If you don't leave, we will all die!"

Prayer Starter: O Lord, no other gods compare with you. You are majestic and holy. I love you.

Memory Verse: Are there any gods like you, Lord? No! There are no gods like you. You are wonderfully holy. You are amazingly powerful. . . .
—*Exodus 15:11*

49

Walls of Water

The king of Egypt was told that the people of Israel had already left. Then he and his officers changed their minds about them. They said, "What have we done? We have let the people of Israel leave. We have lost our slaves!" ⁶So the king prepared his war chariot and took his army with him. ⁷He took 600 of his best chariots. He also took all the other chariots of Egypt. Each chariot had an officer in it. ⁸The Lord made the king of Egypt stubborn. So he chased the Israelites, who were leaving victoriously. ⁹The king of Egypt came with his horses, chariot drivers and army. And they chased the Israelites. They caught up with the Israelites while they were camped by the Red Sea. This was near Pi Hahiroth and Baal Zephon.

¹⁰The Israelites saw the king and his army coming after them. They were very frightened and cried to the Lord for help. ¹¹They said to Moses, "What have you done to us? Why did you bring us out of Egypt to die in the desert? There were plenty of graves for us in Egypt. ¹²We told you in Egypt, 'Let us alone! Let us stay and serve the Egyptians.' Now we will die in the desert."

¹³But Moses answered, "Don't be afraid! Stand still and see the Lord save you today. You will never see these Egyptians again after today. ¹⁴You will only need to remain calm. The Lord will fight for you."

¹⁵Then the Lord said to Moses, "Why are you crying out to me? Command the people of Israel to start moving. ¹⁶Raise your walking stick and hold it over the sea. The sea will split. Then the people can cross the sea on dry land. ¹⁷I have made the Egyptians stubborn so they will chase the Israelites. But I will be honored when I defeat the king and all of his chariot drivers and chariots. ¹⁸I will defeat the king, his chariot drivers and chariots. Then Egypt will know that I am the Lord."

²¹Moses held his hand over the sea. All that night the Lord drove back the sea with a strong east wind. And so he made the sea become dry ground. The water was split. ²²And the Israelites went through the sea on dry land. A wall of water was on both sides.

Prayer Starter: Thank you, Lord, for the story of Moses and the children of Israel. Help me to trust you just as Moses did.

Memory Verse: Are there any gods like you, Lord? No! There are no gods like you. You are wonderfully holy. You are amazingly powerful. You do great miracles.   —*Exodus 15:11*

What Is It?

Then the whole Israelite community left Elim. They came to the Desert of Sin. This place was between Elim and Sinai. They came to this place on the fifteenth day of the second month after they had left Egypt. [2]Then the whole Israelite community grumbled to Moses and Aaron in the desert. [3]The Israelites said to them, "It would have been better if the Lord had killed us in the land of Egypt. There we had meat to eat. We had all the food we wanted. But you have brought us into this desert. You will starve us to death here."

[4]Then the Lord said to Moses, "I will cause food to fall like rain from the sky. This food will be for all of you. Every day the people must go out and gather what they need for that day. I will do this to see if the people will do what I teach them. [5]On the sixth day of each week, they are to gather twice as much as they gather on other days. Then they are to prepare it."

[6]So Moses and Aaron said to all the Israelites: "This evening you will know that the Lord is the one who brought you out of Egypt. [7]Tomorrow morning you will see the greatness of the Lord. He has heard you grumble against him. We are nothing. You are not grumbling against us, but against the Lord."

[11]The Lord said to Moses, [12]"I have heard the grumblings of the people of Israel. So tell them, 'At twilight you will eat meat. And every morning you will eat all the bread you want. Then you will know I am the Lord, your God.'"

[13]That evening, quail came and covered the camp. And in the morning dew lay around the camp. [14]When the dew was gone, thin flakes like frost were on the desert ground. [15]When the Israelites saw it, they asked each other, "What is that?" They asked this question because they did not know what it was.

So Moses told them, "This is the bread the Lord has given you to eat. [16]The Lord has commanded, 'Each one of you must gather what he needs. Gather about two quarts for every person in your family.'"

[17]So the people of Israel did this. Some people gathered much, and some gathered little.

Prayer Starter: Give us each day the food we need, Lord. Give me clothes and shelter and friends and family. Please provide for all my needs.

Memory Verse: Honor your father and your mother. . . .

—*Exodus 20:12*

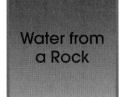

Water from a Rock

The whole Israelite community left the Desert of Sin. They traveled from place to place as the Lord commanded. They camped at Rephidim. But there was no water there for the people to drink. ²So they quarreled with Moses. They said, "Give us water to drink."

But Moses said to them, "Why do you quarrel with me? Why are you testing the Lord?"

³But the people were very thirsty for water. So they grumbled against Moses. They said, "Why did you bring us out of Egypt? Was it to kill us, our children and our farm animals with thirst?"

⁴So Moses cried to the Lord, "What can I do with these people? They are almost ready to kill me with stones."

⁵The Lord said to Moses, "Go ahead of the people of Israel. And take some of the older leaders of Israel with you. Carry with you the walking stick that you used to strike the Nile River. Now go! ⁶I will stand in front of you on a rock at Mount Sinai. Hit that rock with the stick, and water will come out of it. Then the people can drink." Moses did these things as the older leaders of Israel watched. ⁷Moses named that place Massah[n] because the Israelites tested the Lord. They asked, "Is the Lord with us or not?" He also named it Meribah[n] because they quarreled.

[n]**Massah** This name sounds like the Hebrew word for "testing."
[n]**Meribah** This name sounds like the Hebrew word for "quarreled."

Prayer Starter: Thank you, Lord, for making water. Thanks for giving us water for drinking, bathing, and swimming.

Memory Verse: Honor your father and your mother. Then you will live a long time . . .   —*Exodus 20:12*

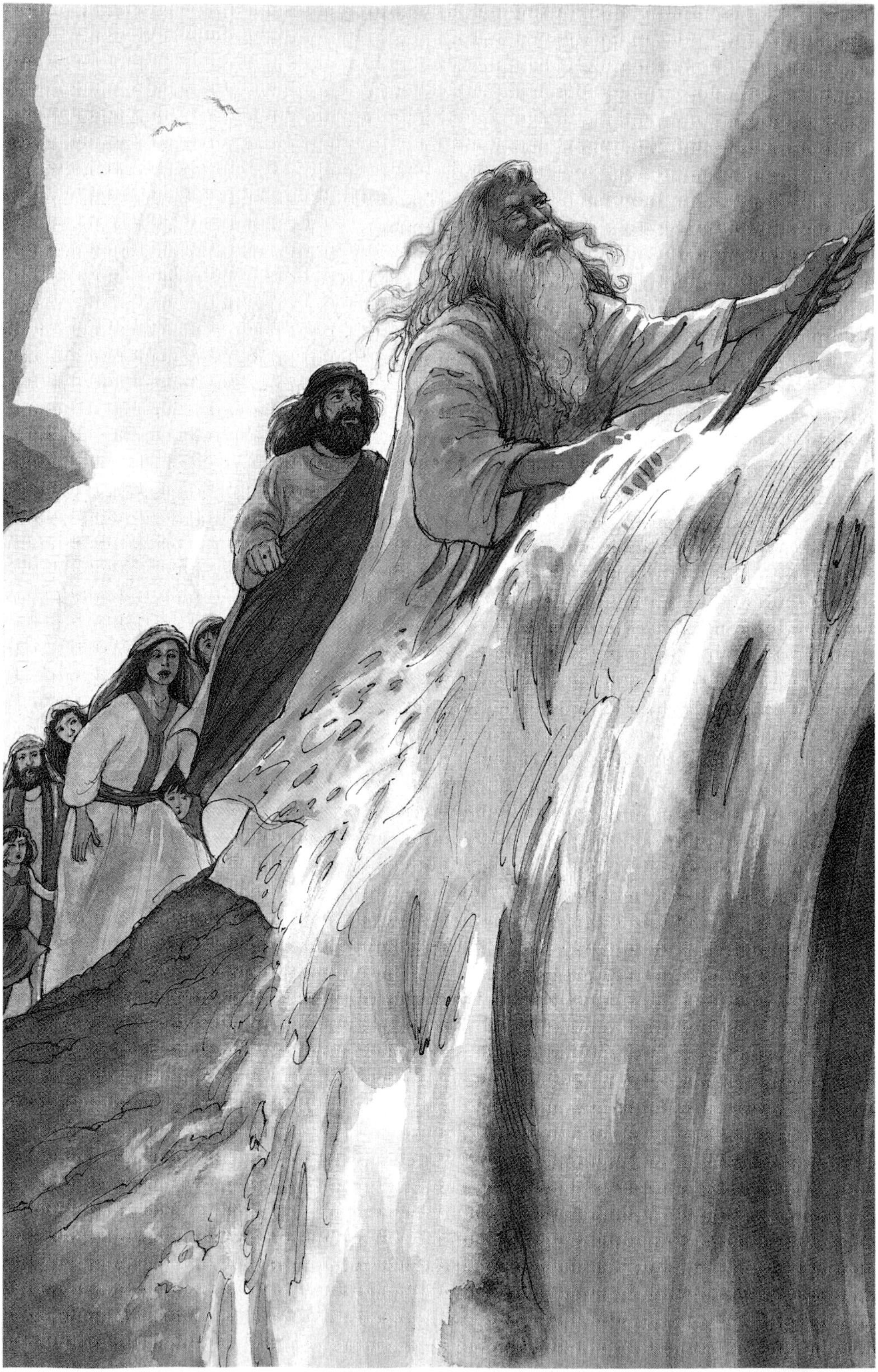

God's Commands

Exactly three months after the Israelites had left Egypt, they reached the Desert of Sinai. ²They had left Rephidim and had come to the Desert of Sinai. The Israelites camped in the desert in front of Mount Sinai.

¹⁶It was the morning of the third day. There was thunder and lightning with a thick cloud on the mountain. And there was a very loud blast from a trumpet. All the people in the camp were frightened. ¹⁷Then Moses led the people out of the camp to meet God. They stood at the foot of the mountain. ¹⁸Mount Sinai was covered with smoke. This happened because the Lord came down on it in fire. The smoke rose from the mountain like smoke from a furnace. And the whole mountain shook wildly. ¹⁹The sound from the trumpet became louder. Then Moses spoke, and the voice of God answered him.

20 Then God spoke all these words:
²"I am the Lord your God. I brought you out of the land of Egypt where you were slaves.

³"You must not have any other gods except me.

⁴"You must not make for yourselves any idols. Don't make something that looks like anything in the sky above or on the earth below or in the water below the land. ⁵You must not worship or serve any idol. This is because I, the Lord your God, am a jealous God.

⁷"You must not use the name of the Lord your God thoughtlessly. The Lord will punish anyone who is guilty and misuses his name.

⁸"Remember to keep the Sabbath as a holy day.

¹²"Honor your father and your mother. Then you will live a long time in the land. The Lord your God is going to give you this land.

¹³"You must not murder anyone.

¹⁴"You must not be guilty of adultery.

¹⁵"You must not steal.

¹⁶"You must not tell lies about your neighbor in court.

¹⁷"You must not want to take your neighbor's house. You must not want his wife or his men or women slaves. You must not want his ox or his donkey. You must not want to take anything that belongs to your neighbor."

Prayer Starter: O Lord, you are the Lord my God. May I never worship anyone except you.

Memory Verse: Honor your father and your mother. Then you will live a long time in the land. . . .
        —Exodus 20:12

The Broken Agreement

So the Lord finished speaking to Moses on Mount Sinai. Then the Lord gave him the two stone tablets with the agreement written on them. The finger of God wrote the commands on the stones.

32 The people saw that a long time had passed. And Moses had not come down from the mountain. So they gathered around Aaron. They said to him, "Moses led us out of Egypt. But we don't know what has happened to him. So make us gods who will lead us."

²Aaron said to the people, "Take off the gold earrings that your wives, sons and daughters are wearing. Bring them to me." ³So all the people took their gold earrings and brought them to Aaron. ⁴Aaron took the gold from the people. Then he melted it and made a statue of a calf. He finished it with a tool. Then the people said, "Israel! These are your gods who brought you out of the land of Egypt!"

⁵Aaron saw all this, and he built an altar before the calf. Then he made an announcement. He said, "Tomorrow there will be a special feast to honor the Lord." ⁶The people got up early the next morning. They offered whole burnt offerings and fellowship offerings. First the people sat down to eat and drink. Then they got up and sinned sexually.

⁷And the Lord said to Moses, "Go down from this mountain. Your people, the people you brought out of the land of Egypt, have done a terrible sin."

¹⁵Then Moses went down the mountain. In his hands he had the two stone tablets with the agreement on them. The commands were written on both sides of each stone, front and back. ¹⁶God himself had made the stones. And God himself had written the commands on the stones.

¹⁹When Moses came close to the camp, he saw the gold calf and the dancing. He became very angry. He threw down the stone tablets which he was carrying. He broke them at the bottom of the mountain.

Prayer Starter: Dear Lord, I know that many people act badly in this world. Keep me from following their example.

Memory Verse: Honor your father and your mother. Then you will live a long time in the land. The Lord your God . . .   —Exodus 20:12

His Face Was Shining

The Lord said to Moses, "Cut two more stone tablets like the first two. I will write the same words on them that were on the first two stones which you broke. ²Be ready tomorrow morning. Then come up on Mount Sinai. Stand before me there on the top of the mountain. ³No one may come with you. No one should even be seen any place on the mountain. Not even the sheep or cattle may eat grass near that mountain."

⁴So Moses cut two stone tablets like the first ones. Then early the next morning he went up Mount Sinai. He did this just as the Lord had commanded him. Moses carried the two stone tablets with him. ⁵Then the Lord came down in the cloud and stood there with Moses. And the Lord called out his name, the Lord.

²⁸Moses stayed there with the Lord 40 days and 40 nights. During that time he did not eat food or drink water. And Moses wrote the words of the agreement—the Ten Commandments—on the stone tablets.

²⁹Then Moses came down from Mount Sinai. In his hands he was carrying the two stone tablets of the agreement. But Moses did not know that his face was shining because he had talked with the Lord. ³⁰Aaron and all the people of Israel saw that Moses' face was shining. So they were afraid to go near him. ³¹But Moses called to them. So Aaron and all the leaders of the people returned to Moses. Moses talked with them. ³²After that, all the people of Israel came near him. And he gave them all the commands that the Lord had given him on Mount Sinai.

³³When Moses finished speaking to the people, he put a covering over his face. ³⁴Anytime Moses went before the Lord to speak with him, Moses took off the covering until he came out. Then Moses would come out and tell the people of Israel the things the Lord had commanded. ³⁵The Israelites would see that Moses' face was shining. So he would cover his face again. He did this until the next time he went in to speak with the Lord.

Prayer Starter: Give me a cheerful face, dear Lord. Help me to smile easily. Give me eyes that express your love.

Memory Verse: Honor your father and your mother. Then you will live a long time in the land. The Lord your God is going to give you this land.
                                                    —*Exodus 20:12*

Two Goats

Now two of Aaron's sons had died while offering incense to the Lord. At that time the Lord spoke to Moses. ²He said, "Talk to your brother Aaron. Tell him there are times when he cannot go behind the curtain into the Most Holy Place where the Holy Box is. If he goes in when I appear in a cloud over the lid on the Holy Box, he will die.

³"Aaron may enter the Most Holy Place only on the Day of Cleansing. Before he enters, he must offer a bull for a sin offering. And he must offer a male sheep for a whole burnt offering. ⁴He must put on these clothes. He will put on the holy linen inner robe. The linen underclothes will be next to his body. His belt will be the cloth belt. And he will wear the linen turban. These are holy clothes. So he must wash his whole body with water before he puts them on.

⁵"Aaron must take from the people of Israel two male goats for a sin offering. And he must take one male sheep for a burnt offering. ⁶Then he will offer the bull for the sin offering. This sin offering is for himself. Then he will perform the acts to remove sins from him and his family so they will belong to the Lord.

⁷"Next Aaron will take the two goats. He will bring them before the Lord at the entrance to the Meeting Tent. ⁸Aaron will throw lots for the two goats. One lot will be for the Lord. The other lot will be for the goat that removes sin. ⁹Then Aaron will take the goat that was chosen for the Lord by throwing the lot. He must offer this goat as a sin offering. ¹⁰The other goat was chosen by lot to remove the sin. It must be brought alive before the Lord. The priest will use it to perform the acts to remove Israel's sin so they will belong to the Lord. Then this goat will be sent out into the desert."

Prayer Starter: O Lord, help me to understand more and more about what Christ has done for me.

Memory Verse: Moses lifted up the snake in the desert. . . .

—*John 3:14*

59

Twelve Spies

The Lord said to Moses, [2]"Send men to explore the land of Canaan. I will give that land to the Israelites. Send one leader from each tribe."

[3]So Moses obeyed the Lord's command. He sent the Israelite leaders out from the Desert of Paran.

[17]Moses sent them to explore Canaan. He said, "Go through southern Canaan and then into the mountains. [18]See what the land looks like. Are the people who live there strong or weak? Are there a few or many? [19]What kind of land do they live in? Is it good or bad? What about the towns they live in—do they have walls, or are they open like camps? [20]What about the soil? Is it fertile or poor? Are there trees there? Try to bring back some of the fruit from that land." (It was the season for the first grapes.)

[21]So they went up and explored the land. They went from the Desert of Zin all the way to Rehob by Lebo Hamath. [22]They went through the southern area to Hebron. That is where Ahiman, Sheshai and Talmai lived. They were the descendants of Anak. (The city of Hebron had been built seven years before Zoan in Egypt.) [23]In the Valley of Eshcol, they cut off a branch of a grapevine. It had one bunch of grapes on it. They carried that branch on a pole between two of them. They also got some pomegranates and figs. [24]They call that place the Valley of Eshcol.[n] That is because the Israelites cut off the bunch of grapes there. [25]After 40 days of exploring the land, the man returned to the camp.

[26]They came back to Moses and Aaron and all the Israelites at Kadesh. This was in the Desert of Paran. The men reported to them and showed everybody the fruit from the land. [27]They told Moses, "We went to the land where you sent us. It is a land where much food grows! Here is some of its fruit. [28]But the people who live there are strong. Their cities are walled and large."

[30]Then Caleb told the people near Moses to be quiet. Caleb said, "We should go up and take the land for ourselves. We can do it."

[n]**Eschol** This name in Hebrew means "bunch."

Prayer Starter: Give me more and more faith in you, O Lord. Help me to trust your word.

Memory Verse: Moses lifted up the snake in the desert. It is the same . . .
—*John 3:14*

The Bronze Snake

The Israelites left Mount Hor and went on the road toward the Gulf of Aqaba. They did this to go around the country of Edom. But the people became impatient on the way. ⁵They grumbled at God and Moses. They said, "Why did you bring us out of Egypt? We will die in this desert! There is no bread! There is no water! And we hate this terrible food!"

⁶So the Lord sent them poisonous snakes. They bit the people, and many of the Israelites died. ⁷The people came to Moses and said, "We sinned when we grumbled at you and the Lord. Pray that the Lord will take away these snakes." So Moses prayed for the people.

⁸The Lord said to Moses, "Make a bronze snake. And put it on a pole. If anyone is bitten, he should look at it. Then he will live." ⁹So Moses made a bronze snake. And he put it on a pole. Then when a snake bit anyone, he looked at the bronze snake and lived.

¹⁰The Israelites went and camped at Oboth. ¹¹They went from Oboth to Iye Abarim. This was in the desert east of Moab. ¹²From there they went and camped in the Zered Valley. ¹³From there they went and camped across the Arnon. This was in the desert just inside the Amorite country. The Arnon is the border between the Moabites and the Amorites. ¹⁴That is why the Book of the Wars of the Lord says:

". . . and Waheb in Suphah, and the ravines,
　　the Arnon, [15]and the slopes of the ravines
that lead to the settlement of Ar.
　　These places are at the border of Moab."

[16]The Israelites went from there to Beer. A well is there where the Lord said to Moses, "Gather the people. I will give them water."

[17]Then the Israelites sang this song:
"Pour out water, well!
　　Sing about it.
[18]Princes dug this well.
　　Important men made this hole.
　　With their scepters and poles, they dug it."

The people went from the desert to Mattanah. [19]From Mattanah they went to Nahaliel and on to Bamoth. [20]From Bamoth they went to the valley of Moab. There the top of Mount Pisgah looks over the desert.

Prayer Starter: Forgive me, Lord, when I complain and grumble and make others unhappy. Give me a happy spirit.

Memory Verse: Moses lifted up the snake in the desert. It is the same with the Son of Man. . . .　　　　　　　　　　　*—John 3:14*

Balaam's Donkey

Balaam got up the next morning. He put a saddle on his donkey. Then he went with the Moabite leaders. ²²But God became angry because Balaam went. So the angel of the Lord stood in the road to stop Balaam. Balaam was riding his donkey. And he had two servants with him. ²³The donkey saw the angel of the Lord standing in the road. The angel had a sword in his hand. So the donkey left the road and went into the field. Balaam hit the donkey to force her back on the road.

²⁴Later, the angel of the Lord stood on a narrow path between two vineyards. There were walls on both sides. ²⁵Again the donkey saw the angel of the Lord. So the donkey walked close to one wall. This crushed Balaam's foot against the wall. So he hit her again.

²⁶The angel of the Lord went ahead again. The angel stood at a narrow place. It was too narrow to turn left or right. ²⁷The donkey saw the angel of the Lord. So she lay down under Balaam. Balaam was very angry and hit her with his stick. ²⁸Then the Lord made the donkey talk. She said to Balaam, "What have I done to make you hit me three times?"

²⁹Balaam answered the donkey, "You have made me look foolish! I wish I had a sword in my hand! I would kill you right now!"

³⁰But the donkey said to Balaam, "I am your very own donkey. You have ridden me for years. Have I ever done this to you before?"

"No," Balaam said.

³¹Then the Lord let Balaam see the angel. The angel of the Lord was standing in the road with his sword drawn. Then Balaam bowed facedown on the ground.

³²The angel of the Lord asked Balaam, "Why have you hit your donkey three times? I have stood here to stop you. What you are doing is wrong. ³³The donkey saw me. She turned away from me three times. If she had not turned away, I would have killed you by now. But I would let her live."

³⁴Then Balaam said to the angel of the Lord, "I have sinned. I did not know you were standing in the road to stop me. If I am wrong, I will go back."

Prayer Starter: How wonderful you are, dear Lord. How wise and powerful!

Memory Verse: Moses lifted up the snake in the desert. It is the same with the Son of Man. The Son of Man . . .   *—John 3:14*

The Death of Moses

Then Moses climbed up Mount Nebo. He went from the plains of Moab to the top of Mount Pisgah. It is across from Jericho. From there the Lord showed him all the land. He could see from Gilead to Dan. ²He could see all of Naphtali and the lands of Ephraim and Manasseh. He would see all the land of Judah as far as the Mediterranean Sea. ³He could see the southern desert and the whole Valley of Jericho up to Zoar. Jericho is called the city of palm trees. ⁴Then the Lord said to Moses, "This is the land I promised to Abraham, Isaac and Jacob. I said to them, 'I will give this land to your descendants.' I have let you look at it, Moses. But you will not cross over there."

⁵Then Moses, the servant of the Lord, died there in Moab. It was as the Lord had said. ⁶The Lord buried Moses in Moab in the valley opposite Beth Peor. But even today no one knows where his grave is. ⁷Moses was 120 years old when he died. His eyes were not weak. And he was still strong. ⁸The Israelites cried for Moses for 30 days. They stayed in the plains of Moab until the time of sadness was over.

⁹Joshua son of Nun was then filled with wisdom. Moses had put his hands on Joshua. So the Israelites listened to Joshua. And they did what the Lord had commanded Moses.

Prayer Starter: I love your promises in the Bible, dear Lord. Thank you for each one.

Memory Verse: Moses lifted up the snake in the desert. It is the same with the Son of Man. The Son of Man must be lifted up too.

—John 3:14

Rahab

Joshua son of Nun secretly sent out two spies from Acacia. Joshua said to them, "Go and look at the land. Look closely at the city of Jericho."

So the men went to Jericho. They went to the house of a prostitute and stayed there. This woman's name was Rahab.

²Someone told the king of Jericho, "Some men from Israel have come here tonight. They are spying out the land."

³So the king of Jericho sent this message to Rahab: "Bring out the men who came to you and entered your house. They have come to spy out our whole land."

⁴Now the woman had hidden the two men. She said, "They did come here. But I didn't know where they came from. ⁵In the evening, when it was time to close the city gate, they left. I don't know where they went. Go quickly. Maybe you can catch them." ⁶(But the woman had taken the men up to the roof.ⁿ She had hidden them there under stalks of flax. She had spread the flax out there to dry.) ⁷So the king's men went out looking for the spies from Israel. They went to the places where people cross the Jordan River. The city gate was closed just after the king's men left the city.

⁸The spies were ready to sleep for the night. So Rahab went to the roof and talked to them. ⁹She said, "I know the Lord has given this land to your people. You frighten us very much. Everyone living in this land is terribly afraid of you. ¹⁰We are afraid because we have heard how the Lord helped you. We heard how he dried up the Red Sea when you came out of Egypt. We heard how you destroyed Sihon and Og. They were the two Amorite kings who lived east of the Jordan. ¹¹When we heard this, we became very frightened. Now our men are afraid to fight you. This is because the Lord your God rules the heavens above and the earth below! ¹²So now, make me a promise before the Lord. Promise that you will show kindness to my family just as I showed you kindness. Give me some proof that you will do this. ¹³Promise me you will allow my family to live. Save my father, mother, brothers, sisters and all of their families from death."

¹⁴The men agreed. They said, "We will trade our lives for your lives. Don't tell anyone what we are doing. When the Lord gives us our land, we will be kind to you. You may trust us."

ⁿ**roof** In Bible times houses were built with flat roofs. The roof was used for drying things such as flax and fruit. And it was used as an extra room, as a place for worship and as a place to sleep in the summer.

Prayer Starter: Keep me safe each day, O Lord, and protect me throughout every night.

Memory Verse: Remember that I commanded you . . . —*Joshua 1:9*

Amazing Things

Then Joshua told the people, "Make yourselves holy for the Lord. Tomorrow the Lord will do amazing things among you."

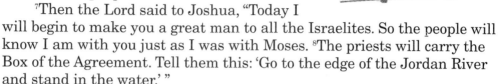

⁶Joshua said to the priests, "Take the Box of the Agreement. Cross over the river ahead of the people." So the priests lifted the Holy Box and carried it ahead of the people.

⁷Then the Lord said to Joshua, "Today I will begin to make you a great man to all the Israelites. So the people will know I am with you just as I was with Moses. ⁸The priests will carry the Box of the Agreement. Tell them this: 'Go to the edge of the Jordan River and stand in the water.'"

⁹Then Joshua said to the people of Israel, "Come here. Listen to the words of the Lord your God. ¹⁰Here is proof that the living God is with you. Here is proof that he will drive out the Canaanites, Hittites, Hivites, Perizzites, Girgashites, Amorites and the Jebusites. ¹¹This is the proof: The Box of the Agreement will go ahead of you into the Jordan River. It is the Agreement with the Lord of the whole world. ¹²Now choose 12 men from among you. Choose 1 from each of the 12 tribes of Israel. ¹³The priests will carry the Holy Box of the Lord, the Master of the whole world. They will carry it into the Jordan ahead of you. When they enter the water, the river will stop flowing. The water will be stopped. It will stand up in a heap as if a dam were there."

¹⁴So the priests carried the Box of the Agreement. And the people left the place where they had camped. Then they started across the Jordan River. ¹⁵During harvest the Jordan is flooded. So the river was at its fullest. The priests who were carrying the Holy Box came to the edge of the river. And they stepped into the water. ¹⁶Just at that moment, the water stopped flowing. It stood up in a heap a great distance away at Adam. This is a town near Zarethan. The water flowing down to the Sea of Arabah (the Dead Sea) was completely cut off. So the people crossed the river near Jericho. ¹⁷The ground there became dry. The priests carried the Box of the Agreement with the Lord to the middle of the river and stopped. They waited there while all the people of Israel walked across. They crossed the Jordan River on dry land.

Prayer Starter: Lord, help me to worship you as I should, because you are going to do amazing things for me.

Memory Verse: Remember that I commanded you to be strong and brave. . . .
—Joshua 1:9

The Walls of Jericho

Now the people of Jericho were afraid because the Israelites were near. So they closed the city gates and guarded them. No one went into the city. And no one came out.

²Then the Lord spoke to Joshua. He said, "Look, I have given you Jericho, its king and all its fighting men. ³March around the city with your army one time every day. Do this for six days. ⁴Have seven priests carry trumpets made from horns of male sheep. Tell them to march in front of the Holy Box. On the seventh day march around the city seven times. On that day tell the priests to blow the trumpets as they march. ⁵They will make one long blast on the trumpets. When you hear that sound, have all the people give a loud shout. Then the walls of the city will fall. And the people will go straight into the city."

⁶So Joshua son of Nun called the priests together. He said to them, "Carry the Box of the Agreement with the Lord. Tell seven priests to carry trumpets and march in front of it." ⁷Then Joshua ordered the people, "Now go! March around the city. The soldiers with weapons should march in front of the Box of the Agreement with the Lord."

⁸So Joshua finished speaking to the people. Then the seven priests began marching before the Lord. They carried the seven trumpets and blew them as they marched. The priests carrying the Box of the Agreement with the Lord followed them. ⁹The soldiers with weapons marched in front of the priests. And armed men walked behind the Holy Box. They were blowing their trumpets. ¹⁰But Joshua had told the people not to give a war cry. He said, "Don't shout. Don't say a word until the day I tell you. Then shout!" ¹¹So Joshua had the Holy Box of the Lord carried around the city one time. Then they went back to camp for the night.

¹²Early the next morning Joshua got up. And the priests carried the Holy Box of the Lord again. ¹³The seven priests carried the seven trumpets. They marched in front of the Holy Box of the Lord, blowing their trumpets. The soldiers with weapons marched in front of them. Other soldiers walked behind the Holy Box of the Lord. All this time the priests were blowing their trumpets. ¹⁴So on the second day they marched around the city one time. Then they went back to camp. They did this every day for six days.

¹⁵On the seventh day they got up at dawn. They marched around the city seven times. They marched just as they had on the days before. But on that day they marched around the city seven times. ¹⁶The seventh time around the priests blew their trumpets. Then Joshua gave the command: "Now, shout! The Lord has given you this city! ¹⁷The city and everything in it are to be destroyed as an offering to the Lord. Only Rahab the prostitute and everyone in her house should remain alive. They must not be killed. This is because Rahab hid the two spies we sent out. ¹⁸Don't take any of the things that are to be destroyed as an offering to the Lord. If you take them and bring them into our camp, then you yourselves will be destroyed. You will also bring trouble to all of Israel. ¹⁹All the silver and gold and things made from bronze and iron belong to the Lord. They must be saved for him."

²⁰When the priests blew the trumpets, the people shouted. At the sound of the trumpets and the people's shout, the walls fell. And everyone ran straight into the city. So the Israelites defeated that city.

Prayer Starter: You are a God who does miracles, Lord. I praise and worship you.

Memory Verse: Remember that I commanded you to be strong and brave. So don't be afraid. . . .   *—Joshua 1:9*

The Longest Day

Then these five Amorite kings joined their armies. They were the kings of Jerusalem, Hebron, Jarmuth, Lachish and Eglon. These armies went to Gibeon, surrounded it and attacked it.

⁶The Gibeonites sent a message to Joshua in his camp at Gilgal. The message said: "We are your servants. Don't let us be destroyed. Come quickly and help us! Save us! All the Amorite kings from the mountains have joined their armies. They are fighting against us."

⁷So Joshua marched out of Gilgal with his whole army. His best fighting men were with him. ⁸The Lord said to Joshua, "Don't be afraid of those armies. I will allow you to defeat them. None of them will be able to defeat you."

⁹Joshua and his army marched all night to Gibeon. So Joshua surprised them when he attacked. ¹⁰The Lord confused those armies when Israel attacked. So Israel defeated them in a great victory. They chased them from Gibeon on the road going to Beth Horon. The army of Israel killed men all the way to Azekah and Makkedah. ¹¹They chased the enemy down the road from Beth Horon to Azekah. While they were chasing them, the Lord threw large hailstones on them from the sky. Many of the enemy were killed by the hailstones. More men were killed by the hailstones than the Israelites killed with their swords.

¹²That day the Lord allowed the Israelites to defeat the Amorites. And that day Joshua stood before all the people of Israel and said to the Lord:

"Sun, stand still over Gibeon.
Moon, stand still over the Valley of Aijalon."
¹³So the sun stood still.
And the moon stopped
until the people defeated their enemies.
These words are written in the Book of Jashar.

The sun stopped in the middle of the sky. It waited to go down for a full day. ¹⁴That has never happened at any time before that day or since. That was the day the Lord listened to a man. Truly the Lord was fighting for Israel!

Prayer Starter: Thank you, Father, for the sun and moon. And thank you for the day they stood still.

Memory Verse: Remember that I commanded you to be strong and brave. So don't be afraid. The Lord your God will be with you . . . —*Joshua 1:9*

Choose for Yourselves

Then all the tribes of Israel met together at Shechem. Joshua called them all together there. Then he called the older leaders, heads of families, judges and officers of Israel. These men stood before God.

²Then Joshua spoke to all the people. He said, "Here's what the Lord, the God of Israel, says to you: 'A long time ago your ancestors lived on the other side of the Euphrates River. I am talking about men like Terah, the father of Abraham and Nahor. They worshiped other gods. ³But I, the Lord, took your ancestor Abraham out of the land on the other side of the river. I led him through the land of Canaan. And I gave him many children. I gave him his son Isaac. ⁴And I gave Isaac two sons named Jacob and Esau. I gave the land around the mountains of Edom to Esau. But Jacob and his sons went down to Egypt. ⁵Then I sent Moses and Aaron to Egypt. I caused many terrible things to happen to the Egyptians. Then I brought you people out. ⁶When I brought your fathers out of Egypt, they came to the Red Sea. And the Egyptians chased them. There were chariots and men on horses. ⁷So the people asked me, the Lord, for help. And I caused great trouble to come to the Egyptians. I caused the sea to cover them. You yourselves saw what I did to the army of Egypt. After that, you lived in the desert for a long time.

⁸" 'Then I brought you to the land of the Amorites. This was east of

the Jordan River. They fought against you, but I gave you the power to defeat them. I destroyed them before you. Then you took control of that land. ⁹But the king of Moab, Balak son of Zippor, prepared to fight against the Israelites. The king sent for Balaam son of Beor to curse you. ¹⁰But I, the Lord, refused to listen to Balaam. So he asked for good things to happen to you! He blessed you many times. I saved you and brought you out of his power.

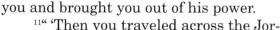

¹¹" 'Then you traveled across the Jordan River and came to Jericho. The people in the city of Jericho fought against you. Also, the Amorites, Perizzites, Canaanites, Hittites, Girgashites, Hivites and Jebusites fought against you. But I allowed you to defeat them all. ¹²While your army traveled forward, I sent hornets ahead of them. These hornets made the people leave before you came. So you took the land without using your swords and bows. ¹³It was I, the Lord, who gave you that land. I gave you land where you did not have to work. I gave you cities that you did not have to build. And now you live in that land and in those cities. You eat from vineyards and olive trees. But you did not have to plant them.' "

¹⁴Then Joshua spoke to the people. He said, "Now you have heard the Lord's words. So you must respect the Lord and serve him fully and sincerely. Throw away the false gods that your people worshiped. That happened on the other side of the Euphrates River and in Egypt. Now you must serve the Lord. ¹⁵But maybe you don't want to serve the Lord. You must choose for yourselves today. You must decide whom you will serve. You may serve the gods that your people worshiped when they lived on the other side of the Euphrates River. Or you may serve the gods of the Amorites who lived in this land. As for me and my family, we will serve the Lord."

Prayer Starter: Father, may my family and I worship and obey the Lord!

Memory Verse: Remember that I commanded you to be strong and brave. So don't be afraid. The Lord your God will be with you everywhere you go.
—Joshua 1:9

Deborah and Barak

There was a prophetess named Deborah. She was the wife of Lappidoth. She was judge of Israel at that time. ⁵Deborah would sit under the Palm Tree of Deborah. This was between the cities of Ramah and Bethel, in the mountains of Ephraim. And the people of Israel would come to her to settle their arguments.

⁶Deborah sent a message to a man named Barak. He was the son of Abinoam. Barak lived in the city of Kedesh, which is in the area of Naphtali. Deborah said to Barak, "The Lord, the God of Israel, commands you: 'Go and gather 10,000 men of Naphtali and Zebulun. Lead them to Mount Tabor. ⁷I will make Sisera, the commander of Jabin's army, come to you. Sisera, his chariots and his army will meet you at the Kishon River. I will help you to defeat Sisera there.'"

⁸Then Barak said to Deborah, "I will go if you will go with me. But if you will not go with me, I won't go."

⁹"Of course I will go with you," Deborah answered. "But you will not get credit for the victory. The Lord will let a woman defeat Sisera." So Deborah went with Barak to Kedesh. ¹⁰At Kedesh, Barak called the people of Zebulun and Naphtali together. From them, he gathered 10,000 men to follow him. Deborah went with Barak also.

¹¹Now Heber the Kenite had left the other Kenite people. (The Kenites were descendants of Hobab, Moses' brother-in-law.) Heber had put up his tent by the great tree in Zaanannim. This is near Kedesh.

¹²Then Sisera was told that Barak son of Abinoam had gone up to Mount Tabor. ¹³So Sisera gathered his 900 iron chariots and all the men with him. They went from Harosheth Haggoyim to the Kishon River.

¹⁴Then Deborah said to Barak, "Get up! Today is the day the Lord will help you defeat Sisera. You know the Lord has already cleared the way for you." So Barak led 10,000 men down from Mount Tabor. ¹⁵He and his men attacked Sisera and his men. During the battle the Lord confused Sisera and his army and chariots. So Barak and his men used their swords to defeat Sisera's army. But Sisera left his chariot and ran away on foot.

Prayer Starter: Father, help my friends to live for you as they should. May they love and serve Jesus.

Memory Verse: Since God has shown us great mercy . . .

—Romans 12:1

Praise the Lord!

O n that day Deborah and Barak son of Abinoam sang this song:

2 "The leaders led Israel.
> The people volunteered to go to battle.
> Praise the Lord!
3 Listen, kings.
Pay attention, rulers!
I myself will sing to the Lord.
> I will make music to the Lord, the God of Israel.

4 "Lord, in the past you came from Edom.
> You marched from the land of Edom,
and the earth shook.
> The skies rained,
> and the clouds dropped water.
5 The mountains shook before the Lord,
> > the God of Mount Sinai.
They shook before the Lord, the God of Israel!

6 "In the days of Shamgar son of Anath,
> in the days of Jael, the main roads were empty.
> Travelers went on the back roads.
7 There were no warriors in Israel
> until I, Deborah, arose.
> I arose to be a mother to Israel.
8 At that time they chose to follow new gods.
> Because of this, enemies fought us at our city gates.
No one could find a shield or a spear
> among the 40,000 men of Israel.
9 My heart is with the commanders of Israel.
> They volunteered freely from among the people.
Praise the Lord!

Prayer Starter: We praise you, O Lord, for giving us what we need each day. Thank you for loving me so much.

Memory Verse: Since God has shown us great mercy, I beg you to offer your lives . . .   *—Romans 12:1*

Gideon

The angel of the Lord came and sat down under an oak tree at Ophrah. The oak tree belonged to Joash, who was one of the Abiezrite people. Joash was the father of Gideon. Gideon was separating some wheat from the chaff in a winepress. Gideon did this to keep wheat from the Midianites. [12]The angel of the Lord appeared to Gideon and said, "The Lord is with you, mighty warrior!"

[13]Then Gideon said, "Pardon me, sir. If the Lord is with us, why are we having so many troubles? Our ancestors told us he did miracles. They told us the Lord brought them out of Egypt. But now he has left us. He has allowed the Midianites to defeat us."

[14]The Lord turned to Gideon and said, "You have the strength to save the people of Israel. Go and save them from the Midianites. I am the one who is sending you."

[15]But Gideon answered, "Pardon me, Lord. How can I save Israel? My family group is the weakest in Manasseh. And I am the least important member of my family."

[16]The Lord answered him, "I will be with you. It will seem as if you are fighting only one man."

[36]Then Gideon said to God, "You said you would help me save Israel. [37]I will put some wool on the threshing floor. Let there be dew only on the wool. But let all of the ground be dry. Then I will know what you said is true. I will know that you will use me to save Israel." [38]And that is just what happened. Gideon got up early the next morning and squeezed the wool. He got a full bowl of water from the wool.

[39]Then Gideon said to God, "Don't be angry with me. Let me ask just one more thing. Please let me make one more test. Let the wool be dry while the ground around it gets wet with dew." [40]That night God did that very thing. Just the wool was dry, but the ground around it was wet with dew.

Prayer Starter: When I'm tempted to doubt your promises, Lord, strengthen my faith. Help me trust you as I should.

Memory Verse: Since God has shown us great mercy, I beg you to offer your lives as a living sacrifice to him. . . . —*Romans 12:1*

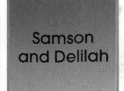

Samson and Delilah

After this, Samson fell in love with a woman named Delilah. She lived in the Valley of Sorek. [5]The kings of the Philistines went to Delilah. They said, "Try to find out what makes Samson so strong. Try to trick him into telling you. Find out how we could capture him and tie him up. Then we will be able to control him. If you do this, each one of us will give you 28 pounds of silver."

[6]So Delilah said to Samson, "Tell me why you are so strong. How could someone tie you up and take control of you?"

[7]Samson answered, "Someone would have to tie me up. He would have to use seven new bowstrings that have not been dried. If he did that, I would be as weak as any other man."

[8]Then the kings of the Philistines brought seven new bowstrings to Delilah. They had not been dried. She tied Samson with them. [9]Some men were hiding in another room. Delilah said to Samson, "Samson, the Philistines are about to capture you!" But Samson easily broke the bowstrings. They broke like pieces of string burned in a fire. So the Philistines did not find out the secret of Samson's strength.

[15]Then Delilah said to him, "How can you say, 'I love you,' when you don't even trust me? This is the third time you have made me look foolish. You haven't told me the secret of your great strength." [16]She kept bothering Samson about his secret day after day. He became so tired of it he felt he was going to die!

[17]So he told her everything. He said, "I have never had my hair cut. I have been set apart to God as a Nazirite since I was born. If someone shaved my head, then I would lose my strength. I would become as weak as any other man."

[18]Delilah saw that he had told her everything sincerely. So she sent a message to the kings of the Philistines. She said, "Come back one more time. He has told me everything." So the kings of the Philistines came

Prayer Starter: Keep me from sin, Lord, and keep me from making foolish mistakes.

Memory Verse: Since God has shown us great mercy, I beg you to offer your lives as a living sacrifice to him. Your offering must be only for God . . .
—*Romans 12:1*

back to Delilah. They brought the silver they had promised to give her. ¹⁹Delilah got Samson to go to sleep. He was lying in her lap. Then she called in a man to shave off the seven braids of Samson's hair. In this way she began to make him weak. And Samson's strength left him.

²⁰Then she called out to him, "Samson, the Philistines are about to capture you!"

He woke up and thought, "I'll get loose as I did before and shake myself free." But he did not know that the Lord had left him.

²¹Then the Philistines captured Samson. They tore out his eyes. And they took him down to Gaza. They put bronze chains on him. They put him in prison and made him grind grain. ²²But his hair began to grow again.

One Last Time

The kings of the Philistines gathered to celebrate. They were going to offer a great sacrifice to their god Dagon. They said, "Our god has given us Samson our enemy." [24]When they saw him, they praised their god. They said,

"This man destroyed our country.
He killed many of us!

But our god helped us
capture our enemy."

[25]The people were having a good time at the celebration. They said, "Bring Samson out to perform for us." So they brought Samson from the prison. He performed for them. They made him stand between the pillars of the temple of Dagon. [26]A servant was holding his hand. Samson said to him, "Let me feel the pillars that hold up the temple. I want to lean against them." [27]Now the temple was full of men and women. All the kings of the Philistines were there. There were about 3,000 men and women on the roof.[n] They watched Samson perform. [28]Then Samson prayed to the Lord. He said, "Lord God, remember me. God, please give me strength one more time. Let me pay these Philistines back for putting out my two eyes!" [29]Then Samson held the two center pillars of the temple. These two pillars supported the whole temple. He braced himself between the two pillars. His right hand was on one, and his left hand was on the other. [30]Samson said, "Let me die with these Philistines!" Then he pushed as hard as he could. And the temple fell on the kings and all the people in it. So Samson killed more of the Philistines when he died than when he was alive.

[n]**roof** In Bible times houses were built with flat roofs. The roof was used for drying things such as flax and fruit. And it was used as an extra room, as a place for worship and as a place to sleep in the summer.

Prayer Starter: Help those in prison, dear Lord. May they learn to love and serve you.

Memory Verse: Since God has shown us great mercy, I beg you to offer your lives as a living sacrifice to him. Your offering must be only for God and pleasing to him.   —*Romans 12:1*

Ruth and Naomi

Long ago the judges[n] ruled Israel. During their rule, there was a time in the land when there was not enough food to eat. A man named Elimelech left Bethlehem in Judah and moved to the country of Moab. He took his wife and his two sons with him. His wife was named Naomi, and his two sons were named Mahlon and Kilion. These people were from the Ephrathah district around Bethlehem in Judah. The family traveled to Moab and lived there.

³Later, Naomi's husband, Elimelech, died. So only Naomi and her two sons were left. ⁴These sons married women from Moab. The name of one wife was Orpah. The name of the other wife was Ruth. Naomi and her sons lived in Moab about ten years. ⁵Then Mahlon and Kilion also died. So Naomi was left alone without her husband or her two sons.

⁶While Naomi was in Moab, she heard that the Lord had taken care of his people. He had given food to them in Judah. So Naomi got ready to leave Moab and go back home. The wives of Naomi's sons also got ready to go with her. ⁷So they left the place where they had lived. And they started back on the way to the land of Judah. ⁸But Naomi said to her two daughters-in-law, "Go back home. Each of you go to your own mother's house. You have been very kind to me and to my sons who are now dead. I hope the Lord will also be kind to you in the same way. ⁹I hope the Lord will give you another home and a new husband."

Then Naomi kissed the women. And they began to cry out loud. ¹⁰Her daughters-in-law said to her, "No. We will go with you to your people."

¹¹But Naomi said, "My daughters, go back to your own homes. Why do you want to go with me? I cannot give birth to more sons to give you new husbands. ¹²So go back to your own homes. I am too old to have another husband. But even if I had another husband tonight and if I had more sons, it wouldn't help! ¹³Would you wait until the babies were grown into men? Would you live for so many years without husbands? Don't do this thing. My life is much too sad for you to share. This is because the Lord is against me!"

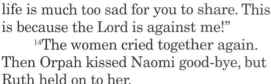

¹⁴The women cried together again. Then Orpah kissed Naomi good-bye, but Ruth held on to her.

¹⁵Naomi said, "Look, your sister-in-law is going back to her own people and her own gods. Go back with her."

¹⁶But Ruth said, "Don't ask me to leave you! Don't beg me not to follow you! Every place you go, I will go. Every place you live, I will live. Your people will be my people. Your God will be my God. ¹⁷And where you die, I will die. And there I will be buried. I ask the Lord to punish me terribly if I do not keep this promise: Only death will separate us."

¹⁸Naomi saw that Ruth had made up her mind to go with her. So Naomi stopped arguing with her. ¹⁹Naomi and Ruth went on until they came to the town of Bethlehem. When the two women entered Bethlehem, all the people became very excited. The women of the town said, "Is this Naomi?"

²⁰But Naomi told the people, "Don't call me Naomi.ⁿ Call me Mara,ⁿ because God All-Powerful has made my life very sad. ²¹When I left, I had all I wanted. But now, the Lord has brought me home with nothing. So why should you call me Naomi when the Lord has spoken against me? God All-Powerful has given me much trouble."

²²So Naomi and her daughter-in-law Ruth, the woman from Moab, came back from Moab. They came to Bethlehem at the beginning of the barley harvest.

ⁿ**judges** They were not judges in courts of law, but leaders of the people in times of emergency.
ⁿ**Naomi** This name means "happy" or "pleasant."
ⁿ**Mara** This name means "bitter" or "sad."

Prayer Starter: Thanks for giving us families, Lord. Bless my family today.

Memory Verse: When you pray, you should go into your room . . .
—*Matthew 6:6*

Boaz
and
Ruth

Now there was a rich man living in Bethlehem whose name was Boaz. Boaz was one of Naomi's close relatives from Elimelech's family.

²One day Ruth, the woman from Moab, said to Naomi, "Let me go to the fields. Maybe someone will be kind and let me gather the grain he leaves in his field."

Naomi said, "Go, my daughter."

³So Ruth went to the fields. She followed the workers who were cutting the grain. And she gathered the grain that they had left. It just so happened that the field belonged to Boaz. He was a close relative from Elimelech's family.

⁴When Boaz came from Bethlehem, he spoke to his workers: "The Lord be with you!"

And the workers answered, "May the Lord bless you!"

⁵Then Boaz spoke to his servant who was in charge of the workers. He asked, "Whose girl is that?"

⁶The servant answered, "She is the Moabite woman who came with Naomi from the country of Moab. ⁷She said, 'Please let me follow the workers and gather the grain that they leave on the ground.' She came and has remained here. From morning until just now, she has stopped only a few moments to rest in the shelter."

⁸Then Boaz said to Ruth, "Listen, my daughter. Stay here in my field to gather grain for yourself. Do not go to any other person's field. Continue following behind my women workers. ⁹Watch to see which fields they go to and follow them. I have warned the young men not to bother you. When you are thirsty, you may go and drink. Take water from the water jugs that the servants have filled."

¹⁰Then Ruth bowed low with her face to the ground. She said to Boaz, "I am a stranger. Why have you been so kind to notice me?"

¹¹Boaz answered her, "I know about all the help you have given to Naomi, your mother-in-law. You helped her even after your husband died. You left your father and mother and your own country. You came to this nation where you did not know anyone. ¹²The Lord will reward you for all you have done. You will be paid in full by the Lord, the God of Israel. You have come to him as a little bird finds shelter under the wings of its mother."

Prayer Starter: Lead me each day, dear Father. Guide me to the people you want me to meet, and to the work you want me to do.

Memory Verse: When you pray, you should go into your room and close the door. . . .
—Matthew 6:6

Better Than Seven Sons

Then Boaz spoke to the older leaders and to all the people. He said, "You are witnesses today of what I am buying from Naomi. I am buying everything that belonged to Elimelech and Kilion and Mahlon. [10]I am also taking Ruth as my wife. She is the Moabite who was the wife of Mahlon. I am doing this so her dead husband's property will stay with his family. This way, his name will not be separated from his family and his land. You are witnesses this day."

[11]So all the people and older leaders who were at the city gate said, "We are witnesses. This woman will be coming into your home. We hope the Lord will make her like Rachel and Leah. They had many children. So the people of Israel grew in number. May you become powerful in the district of Ephrathah. May you become famous in Bethlehem! [12]Tamar gave birth to Judah's son Perez.[n] In the same way, may the Lord give you many children through Ruth. And may your family be great like his."

[13]So Boaz took Ruth and married her. The Lord let her become pregnant, and she gave birth to a son. [14]The women told Naomi, "Praise the Lord who gave you this grandson. And may he become famous in Israel. [15]He will give you new life. And he will take care of you in your old age. This happened because of your daughter-in-law. She loves you. And she is better for you than seven sons. She has given birth to your grandson."

[16]Naomi took the boy, held him in her arms and cared for him. [17]The neighbors gave the boy his name. These women said, "This boy was born for Naomi." The neighbors named him Obed. Obed was Jesse's father. And Jesse was the father of David.

[n]**Perez** One of Boaz's ancestors.

Prayer Starter: Thank you for my parents, Lord. And for my grandparents, too.

Memory Verse: When you pray, you should go into your room and close the door. Then pray to your Father who cannot be seen. . . .
—*Matthew 6:6*

Hannah Prayed in Her Heart

Once, after they had eaten their meal in Shiloh, Hannah got up. Now Eli the priest was sitting on a chair near the entrance to the Lord's Holy Tent. [10]Hannah was very sad. She cried much and prayed to the Lord. [11]She made a promise. She said, "Lord of heaven's armies, see how bad I feel. Remember me! Don't forget me. If you will give me a son, I will give him back to you all his life. And no one will ever use a razor to cut his hair."[n]

[12]While Hannah kept praying, Eli watched her mouth. [13]She was praying in her heart. Her lips moved, but her voice was not heard. So Eli thought she was drunk. [14]He said to her, "Stop getting drunk! Throw away your wine!"

[15]Hannah answered, "No, master, I have not drunk any wine or beer. I am a woman who is deeply troubled. I was telling the Lord about all my problems. [16]Don't think of me as an evil woman. I have been praying because of my many troubles and much sadness."

[17]Eli answered, "Go in peace. May the God of Israel give you what you asked of him."

[18]Hannah said, "I want to be pleasing to you always." Then she left and ate something. She was not sad anymore.

[n]**And . . . hair** People who made special promises not to cut their hair or to drink wine or beer were called Nazirites. These people gave their lives to the Lord.

Prayer Starter: Lord, I am sure you answer prayer. Please help me pray to you each day.

Memory Verse: When you pray, you should go into your room and close the door. Then pray to your Father who cannot be seen. Your Father can see what is done in secret . . . —*Matthew 6:6*

Samuel

Early the next morning Elkanah's family got up and worshiped the Lord. Then they went back home to Ramah. Elkanah had sexual relations with his wife Hannah. And the Lord remembered her. [20]So Hannah became pregnant, and in time she gave birth to a son. She named him Samuel.[n] She said, "His name is Samuel because I asked the Lord for him."

[21]Every year Elkanah went to Shiloh to offer sacrifices. He went to keep the promise he had made to God. He brought his whole family with him. So once again he went up to Shiloh. [22]But Hannah did not go with him. She told him, "When the boy is old enough to eat solid food, I will take him to Shiloh. Then I will give him to the Lord. He will become a Nazirite. He will always live there at Shiloh."

[23]Elkanah, Hannah's husband, said to her, "Do what you think is best. You may stay home until the boy is old enough to eat. May the Lord do what you have said." So Hannah stayed at home to nurse her son until he was old enough to eat.

[24]When Samuel was old enough to eat, Hannah took him to the Tent of the Lord at Shiloh. She also took a three-year-old bull, one-half bushel of flour and a leather bag filled with wine. [25]They killed the bull for the sacrifice. Then Hannah brought Samuel to Eli. [26]She said to Eli, "As surely as you live, my master, I am the same woman who stood near you praying to the Lord. [27]I prayed for this child. The Lord answered my prayer and gave him to me. [28]Now I give him back to the Lord. He will belong to the Lord all his life." And he worshiped the Lord there.

[n]**Samuel** This name sounds like the Hebrew word for "God heard."

Prayer Starter: I want to be your servant as long as I live, dear Lord.

Memory Verse: When you pray, you should go into your room and close the door. Then pray to your Father who cannot be seen. Your Father can see what is done in secret, and he will reward you.   *—Matthew 6:6*

I Am Listening

The boy Samuel served the Lord under Eli. In those days the Lord did not speak directly to people very often. There were very few visions. ²Eli's eyes were so weak he was almost blind. One night he was lying in bed. ³Samuel was also in bed in the Lord's Holy Tent. The Box of the Agreement was in the Holy Tent. God's lamp was still burning.

⁴Then the Lord called Samuel. Samuel answered, "I am here!" ⁵He ran to Eli and said, "I am here. You called me."

But Eli said, "I didn't call you. Go back to bed." So Samuel went back to bed.

⁶The Lord called again, "Samuel!"

Samuel again went to Eli and said, "I am here. You called me."

Again Eli said, "I didn't call you. Go back to bed."

⁷Samuel did not yet know the Lord. The Lord had not spoken directly to him yet.

⁸The Lord called Samuel for the third time. Samuel got up and went to Eli. He said, "I am here. You called me."

Then Eli realized the Lord was calling the boy. ⁹So he told Samuel, "Go to bed. If he calls you again, say, 'Speak, Lord. I am your servant, and I am listening.'" So Samuel went and lay down in bed.

¹⁰The Lord came and stood there. He called as he had before. He said, "Samuel, Samuel!"

Samuel said, "Speak, Lord. I am your servant, and I am listening."

¹¹The Lord said to Samuel, "See, I am going to do something in Israel. It will shock those who hear about it. ¹²At that time I will do to Eli and his family everything I promised. I will not stop until I have finished. ¹³I told Eli I would punish his family forever. I will do it because Eli knew his sons were evil. They spoke against me, but he did not control them."

¹⁷Eli asked, "What did the Lord say to you? Don't hide it from me. May God punish you terribly if you hide from me anything he said to you." ¹⁸So Samuel told Eli everything. He did not hide anything from him. Then Eli said, "He is the Lord. Let him do what he thinks is best."

¹⁹The Lord was with Samuel as he grew up. He did not let any of Samuel's messages fail to come true.

Prayer Starter: I'm listening to your word each day, dear Lord. Help me to do what you want me to do.

Memory Verse: Samuel answered, "What pleases the Lord more: . . ."
— *1 Samuel 15:22*

Saul Is Anointed King

Samuel took a jar of olive oil. He poured the oil on Saul's head. He kissed Saul and said, "The Lord has appointed you to be leader of his people Israel. You will rule over the people of the Lord. You will save them from their enemies all around. This will be the sign that the Lord has appointed you as leader of his people. ²After you leave me today, you will meet two men. They will be near Rachel's tomb on the border of Benjamin at Zelzah. They will say to you, 'The donkeys you were looking for have been found. But now your father has stopped thinking about his donkeys. He is worrying about you. He is asking, "What will I do about my son?" '

³"Then you will go on until you reach the great tree at Tabor. There three men will meet you. They will be on their way to worship God at Bethel. One man will be carrying three young goats. The second man will be carrying three loaves of bread. And the third one will have a leather bag full of wine. ⁴They will greet you and

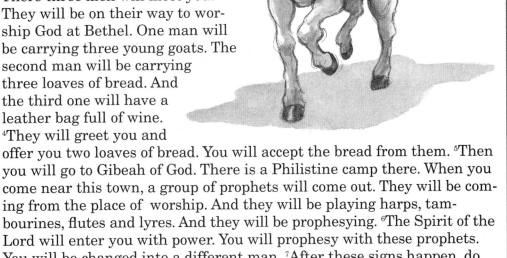

offer you two loaves of bread. You will accept the bread from them. ⁵Then you will go to Gibeah of God. There is a Philistine camp there. When you come near this town, a group of prophets will come out. They will be coming from the place of worship. And they will be playing harps, tambourines, flutes and lyres. And they will be prophesying. ⁶The Spirit of the Lord will enter you with power. You will prophesy with these prophets. You will be changed into a different man. ⁷After these signs happen, do whatever you find to do. God will help you.

⁸"Go ahead of me to Gilgal. I will come down to you. Then I will offer whole burnt offerings and fellowship offerings. But you must wait seven days. Then I will come and tell you what to do."

⁹When Saul turned to leave Samuel, God changed Saul's heart. All these signs came true that day.

Prayer Starter: Father, I know you have a plan for my life. Thanks for loving me so much.

Memory Verse: Samuel answered, "What pleases the Lord more: burnt offerings and sacrifices or obedience? . . ."   *—1 Samuel 15:22*

Saul was 30 years old when he became king. He was king over Israel 42 years.ⁿ ²Saul chose 3,000 men from Israel. There were 2,000 men who stayed with him at Micmash in the mountains of Bethel. And 1,000 men stayed with Jonathan at Gibeah in Benjamin. Saul sent the other men in the army back home.

³Jonathan attacked the Philistine camp in Geba. And the other Philistines heard about it. Saul said, "Let the Hebrew people hear what happened." So he told the men to blow trumpets through all the land of Israel. ⁴All the Israelites heard the news. The men said, "Saul has defeated the Philistine camp. Now the Philistines really hate us!" Then the Israelites were called to join Saul at Gilgal.

⁵The Philistines gathered to fight Israel. They had 3,000ⁿ chariots and 6,000 men to ride in the chariots. Their soldiers were many in number, like the grains of sand on the seashore. The Philistines went and camped at Micmash which is east of Beth Aven. ⁶The Israelites saw that they were in trouble. So they went to hide in caves and bushes. They also hid among the rocks and in pits and wells. ⁷Some Hebrews even went across the Jordan River to the land of Gad and Gilead.

But Saul stayed at Gilgal. All the men in his army were shaking with fear. ⁸Saul waited seven days, because Samuel had said he would meet him then. But Samuel did not come to Gilgal. And the soldiers began to leave.

⁹So Saul said, "Bring me the whole burnt offering and the fellowship

offerings." Then Saul offered the whole burnt offering. [10]Just as he finished, Samuel arrived. Saul went to meet him.

[11]Samuel asked, "What have you done?"

Saul answered, "I saw the soldiers leaving me, and you were not here. The Philistines were gathering at Micmash. [12]Then I thought, 'The Philistines will come against me at Gilgal. And I haven't asked for the Lord's approval.' So I forced myself to offer the whole burnt offering."

[13]Samuel said, "You acted foolishly! You haven't obeyed God's command. If you had obeyed him, God would make your kingdom continue in Israel forever. [14]But now your kingdom will not continue. The Lord has looked for the kind of man he wants. The Lord has appointed him to become ruler of his people. He is doing this because you haven't obeyed his command."

[15]Then Samuel left Gilgal and went to Gibeah in Benjamin. The rest of the army followed Saul into battle. Saul counted the men still with him, and there were about 600.

[16]Saul and his son Jonathan stayed in Geba in the land of Benjamin. The soldiers with them also stayed there. The Philistines made their camp at Micmash.

[n]**Saul . . . years** This is how the verse is worded in some early Greek copies. The Hebrew is not clear here.
[n]**3,000** Some Greek copies say 3,000. The Hebrew copies say 30,000.

Prayer Starter: Forgive us, Lord, when we aren't as patient as you want us to be.

Memory Verse: Samuel answered, "What pleases the Lord more: burnt offerings and sacrifices or obedience? It is better to obey God than to offer a sacrifice. . . ."
—1 Samuel 15:22

It Is Better to Obey

Then the Lord spoke his word to Samuel: [11]"Saul has stopped following me. And I am sorry I made him king. He has not obeyed my commands." Samuel was upset, and he cried out to the Lord all night long.

[12]Early the next morning Samuel got up and went to meet Saul. But the people told Samuel, "Saul has gone to Carmel. He has put up a monument in his own honor. Now he has gone down to Gilgal."

[13]Then Samuel came to Saul. And Saul said, "May the Lord bless you! I have obeyed the Lord's commands."

[14]But Samuel said, "Then why do I hear cattle mooing and sheep bleating?"

[15]Saul answered, "The soldiers took them from the Amalekites. They saved the best sheep and cattle to offer as sacrifices to the Lord your God. But we destroyed all the other animals."

[16]Samuel said to Saul, "Stop! Let me tell you what the Lord said to me last night."

Saul answered, "Tell me."

[17]Samuel said, "Once you didn't think much of yourself. But now you have become the leader of the tribes of Israel. The Lord appointed you to be king over Israel. [18]And he told you to do something. He said, 'Go and destroy those evil people, the Amalekites. Make war on them until all of them are dead.' [19]Why didn't you obey the Lord? Why did you take the best things? Why did you do what the Lord said was wrong?"

[20]Saul said, "But I did obey the Lord. I did what the Lord told me to do. I destroyed all the Amalekites. And I brought back Agag their king. [21]The soldiers took the best sheep and cattle to sacrifice to the Lord your God at Gilgal."

[22]But Samuel answered,

"What pleases the Lord more:
burnt offerings and sacrifices or obedience?
It is better to obey God than to offer a sacrifice.
It is better to listen to God than to offer the fat of male sheep."

Prayer Starter: I know you want me to obey you, Lord. Give me an obedient heart.

Memory Verse: Samuel answered, "What pleases the Lord more: burnt offerings and sacrifices or obedience? It is better to obey God than to offer a sacrifice. It is better to listen to God . . ." —1 Samuel 15:22

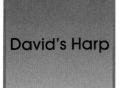

David's Harp

But the Lord's spirit had gone out of Saul. And an evil spirit from the Lord troubled him. ¹⁵Saul's servants said to him, "See, an evil spirit from God is troubling you. ¹⁶Give us the command. We will look for someone who can play the harp. When the evil spirit from the Lord enters you, he will play. Then the evil spirit will leave you alone. And you will feel better."

¹⁷So Saul said to his servants, "Find someone. If he plays well, bring him to me."

¹⁸One of the servants said, "Jesse of Bethlehem has a son who plays the harp. I have seen him play it. He is a brave man and fights well. He is a good speaker and handsome. And the Lord is with him."

¹⁹Then Saul sent messengers to Jesse. The message said, "Send me your son David, who is with the sheep." ²⁰So Jesse loaded a donkey with bread and a leather bag full of wine. He also took a young goat. He sent them all with his son David to Saul.

²¹When David came to Saul, he began to serve him. Saul loved David very much. And David became the officer who carried Saul's armor. ²²Saul sent a message to Jesse. He said, "Let David stay and serve me. I like him."

²³When the evil spirit from God entered Saul, David would take his harp and play. Then the evil spirit would go out of him. And Saul would feel relief. He would feel better again.

Prayer Starter: So many people are sad, dear Lord. Give me a message to cheer them up.

Memory Verse: Samuel answered, "What pleases the Lord more: burnt offerings and sacrifices or obedience? It is better to obey God than to offer a sacrifice. It is better to listen to God than to offer the fat of male sheep."
—1 Samuel 15:22

David's Sling

The Philistines had a champion fighter named Goliath. He was from Gath. He was about nine feet four inches tall. He came out of the Philistine camp.

⁸Goliath stood and shouted to the Israelite soldiers, "Why have you taken positions for battle? I am a Philistine, and you are Saul's servants! Choose a man and send him to fight me."

²⁶David asked the men who stood near him, "What will be done to reward the man who kills this Philistine? What will be done for whoever takes away the shame from Israel? Goliath is a Philistine. He is not circumcised. Why does he think he can speak against the armies of the living God?"

³¹Some men heard what David said and told Saul. Then Saul ordered David to be sent to him.

³²David said to Saul, "Don't let anyone be discouraged. I, your servant, will go and fight this Philistine!

³⁷"The Lord saved me from a lion and a bear. He will also save me from this Philistine."

Saul said to David, "Go, and may the Lord be with you." ³⁸Saul put his own clothes on David. He put a bronze helmet on David's head and armor on his body. ³⁹David put on Saul's sword and tried to walk around. But he was not used to all the armor Saul had put on him.

He said to Saul, "I can't go in this. I'm not used to it." Then David took it all off. ⁴⁰He took his stick in his hand. And he chose five smooth stones from a stream. He put them in his pouch and held his sling in his hand. Then he went to meet Goliath.

⁴¹At the same time, the Philistine was coming closer to David. The man who held his shield walked in front of him. ⁴²Goliath looked at David. He saw that David was only a boy, tanned and handsome. He looked down at David with disgust. ⁴³He said, "Do you think I am a dog, that you come at me with a stick?" He used his gods' names to curse David. ⁴⁴He said to David, "Come here. I'll feed your body to the birds of the air and the wild animals!"

⁴⁵But David said to him, "You come to me using a sword, a large spear and a small spear. But I come to you in the name of the Lord of heaven's armies. He's the God of the armies of Israel! You have spoken out against him. ⁴⁶Today the Lord will give you to me. I'll kill you, and I'll cut off your head. Today I'll feed the bodies of the Philistine soldiers to the birds of the air and the wild animals. Then all the world will know there is a God in Israel! ⁴⁷Everyone gathered here will know the Lord does not need swords or spears to save people. The battle belongs to him! And he will help us defeat all of you."

⁴⁸As Goliath came near to attack him, David ran quickly to meet him. ⁴⁹He took a stone from his pouch. He put it into his sling and slung it. The stone hit the Philistine on his forehead and sank into it. Goliath fell face-down on the ground.

⁵⁰So David defeated the Philistine with only a sling and a stone! He hit him and killed him. He did not even have a sword in his hand.

Prayer Starter: Keep me strong and safe against bullies, dear Lord, and against everyone who might harm me.

Memory Verse: I go to bed . . .   —*Psalm 4:8*

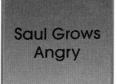

Saul Grows Angry

Saul sent David to fight in different battles. And David was very successful. Then Saul put David over the soldiers. When he did this, Saul's officers and all the other people were pleased.

⁶After David had killed the Philistine, he and the men returned home. Women came out from all the towns of Israel to meet King Saul. They sang songs of joy, danced and played tambourines and stringed instruments. ⁷As they played, they sang,

> "Saul has killed thousands of his enemies.
>   But David has killed tens of thousands!"

⁸The women's song upset Saul, and he became very angry. He thought, "The women say David has killed tens of thousands of enemies. But they say I killed only thousands of enemies. The only thing left for him to have is the kingdom!" ⁹So Saul watched David closely from then on. He was jealous of him.

¹⁰The next day an evil spirit from God entered Saul with power. And he prophesied in his house. David was playing the harp as he usually did. But Saul had a spear in his hand. ¹¹He raised the spear and thought, "I'll pin David to the wall." But David got away from him two times.

¹²The Lord was with David but had left Saul. So Saul was afraid of David. ¹³He sent David away from him. He made David commander of 1,000 soldiers. So David led them in battle. ¹⁴He had great success in everything he did because the Lord was with him. ¹⁵Saul saw that David was very successful. And he became even more afraid of David. ¹⁶But all the people of Israel and Judah loved David. This was because he led them well in battle.

³⁰The Philistine commanders continued to go out to fight the Israelites. But every time, David defeated them. He had more success than Saul's officers. And he became famous.

Prayer Starter: Father, don't let me become jealous toward others. May I be happy when others are successful.

Memory Verse: I go to bed and sleep . . .   *—Psalm 4:8*

Good Friends Part

Jonathan asked his father, "Why should David be killed? What wrong has he done?" ³³Then Saul threw his spear at Jonathan, trying to kill him. So Jonathan knew that his father really wanted to kill David. ³⁴Jonathan was very angry and left the table. That second day of the month he refused to eat. He was upset about what his father wanted to do to David.

³⁵The next morning Jonathan went out to the field. He went to meet David as they had agreed. He had a young boy with him. ³⁶Jonathan said to the boy, "Run and find the arrows I shoot." When he ran, Jonathan shot an arrow beyond him. ³⁷The boy ran to the place where Jonathan's arrow fell. But Jonathan called, "The arrow is beyond you!" ³⁸Then he shouted, "Hurry! Go quickly! Don't stop!" The boy picked up the arrow and brought it back to his master. ³⁹(The boy knew nothing about what this meant. Only Jonathan and David knew.) ⁴⁰Then Jonathan gave his weapons to the boy. He told him, "Go back to town."

⁴¹When the boy left, David came out from the south side of the rock. He bowed facedown on the ground before Jonathan. He did this three times. Then David and Jonathan kissed each other. They cried together, but David cried the most.

⁴²Jonathan said to David, "Go in peace. We have promised by the Lord that we will be friends. We said, 'The Lord will be a witness between you and me, and between our descendants forever.' " Then David left, and Jonathan went back to town.

Prayer Starter: Thank you, Lord, for my good friends. Please take care of them.

Memory Verse: I go to bed and sleep in peace. . . . —*Psalm 4:8*

Is That You?

Now Saul had chased the Philistines away. Then he was told, "David is in the desert of En Gedi." [2]So he chose 3,000 men from all Israel. He took these men and began looking for David and his men. They looked near the Rocks of the Wild Goats.

[3]Saul came to the sheep pens beside the road. A cave was there, and he went in to relieve himself. Now David and his men were hiding far back in the cave. [4]The men said to David, "Today is the day the Lord talked about! The Lord told you, 'I will give your enemy to you. You can do anything you want with him.'"

Then David crawled near Saul. He cut off a corner of Saul's robe. But Saul did not notice him. [5]Later David felt guilty because he had cut off a corner of Saul's robe. [6]He said to his men, "May the Lord keep me from doing such a thing to my master! Saul is the Lord's appointed king. I should not do anything against him, because he is the Lord's appointed king!" [7]David used these words to stop his men. He did not let them attack Saul. Then Saul left the cave and went his way.

[8]When David came out of the cave, he shouted to Saul, "My master and king!" Saul looked back, and David bowed facedown on the ground. [9]He said to Saul, "Why do you listen when people say, 'David plans to harm you'? [10]You have seen something with your own eyes today. You

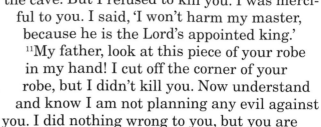

have seen how the Lord put you in my power in the cave. But I refused to kill you. I was merciful to you. I said, 'I won't harm my master, because he is the Lord's appointed king.' [11]My father, look at this piece of your robe in my hand! I cut off the corner of your robe, but I didn't kill you. Now understand and know I am not planning any evil against you. I did nothing wrong to you, but you are hunting me to kill me. [12]May the Lord judge between us. And may he punish you for the wrong you have done to me! But I won't fight you. [13]There is an old saying: 'Evil things come from evil people.' So I won't hurt you. [14]Whom is the king of Israel coming out against? Whom are you chasing? You're not chasing someone who will hurt you! It's as if you are chasing a dead dog or a flea. [15]May the Lord be our judge and decide between you and me. May the Lord support me and show that I am right. May he save me from you!"

[16]David finished saying these words. Then Saul asked, "Is that your voice, David my son?" And he cried loudly. [17]He said, "You are right, and I am wrong. You have been good to me. But I have done wrong to you. [18]You told me what good things you did. The Lord brought me to you, but you did not kill me. [19]If a man finds his enemy, he won't send him away with goodness, will he? May the Lord reward you because you were good to me today. [20]I know you will surely be king. You will rule the kingdom of Israel. [21]Now make a promise to me. Promise in the name of the Lord that you will not kill my descendants. Promise me that you won't wipe out my name from my father's family."

[22]So David made the promise to Saul. Then Saul went back home. David and his men went up to the protected place.

Prayer Starter: Bless the leaders of my country today, Lord. Give them wisdom.

Memory Verse: I go to bed and sleep in peace. Lord, only you . . .
—Psalm 4:8

The Spear and Water Jug

The people of Ziph went to see Saul at Gibeah. They said to him, "David is hiding on the hill of Hakilah opposite Jeshimon."

²So Saul went down to the Desert of Ziph. His 3,000 chosen men of Israel went with him. They looked for David in the Desert of Ziph. ³Saul made his camp on the hill of Hakilah, beside the road opposite Jeshimon. But David stayed in the desert. He heard Saul had followed him. ⁴So David sent out spies and learned that Saul had come to Hakilah.

⁵Then David went to the place where Saul had camped. He saw where Saul and Abner son of Ner were sleeping. Abner was the commander of Saul's army. Saul was sleeping in the middle of the camp with all the army around him.

⁶David talked to Ahimelech the Hittite and Abishai son of Zeruiah. Abishai was Joab's brother. He asked them, "Who will go down into Saul's camp with me?"

Abishai answered, "I'll go with you."

⁷So that night David and Abishai went into Saul's camp. Saul was asleep in the middle of the camp. His spear was stuck in the ground near his head. Abner and the army were sleeping around Saul. ⁸Abishai said to David, "Today God has let you defeat your enemy! Let me pin Saul to the ground with the spear. I'll only do it once! I won't hit him twice."

⁹But David said to Abishai, "Don't kill Saul! No one can harm the Lord's appointed king and still be innocent! ¹⁰As surely as the Lord lives, the Lord himself will punish Saul. Maybe Saul will die naturally. Or maybe he will go into battle and be killed. ¹¹But may the Lord keep me from harming his appointed king! Now pick up the spear and water jug that are near Saul's head. Then let's go."

¹²So David took the spear and water jug that were near Saul's head. They left, and no one saw them. No one knew about it or woke up. The Lord had made them stay asleep.

Prayer Starter: Lord, help me to respect and honor the people you have placed in authority over me.

Memory Verse: I go to bed and sleep in peace. Lord, only you keep me safe.
                                             —Psalm 4:8

The Spirit of Samuel

Later, the Philistines gathered their armies to fight against Israel. Achish said to David, "You understand that you and your men must join with me in my army."

²David answered, "Certainly! Then you can see for yourself what I, your servant, can do!"

Achish said, "Fine, I'll make you my bodyguard for life."

³Now Samuel was dead, and all the Israelites had shown their sadness for him. They had buried Samuel in his hometown of Ramah.

And Saul had forced out the mediums and fortune-tellers from the land of Israel.

⁴The Philistines came together and made camp at Shunem. Saul gathered all the Israelites and made camp at Gilboa. ⁵When he saw the Philistine army, he was afraid. His heart pounded with fear. ⁶He prayed to the Lord, but the Lord did not answer him through dreams, Urim or prophets. ⁷Then Saul said to his servants, "Find me a woman who is a medium. I'll go and ask her what will happen."

His servants answered, "There is a medium in Endor."

⁸Then Saul put on other clothes so no one would know who he was. At night Saul and two of his men went to see the woman. Saul said to her, "Talk to a spirit for me. Call up the person I name."

⁹But the woman said to him, "Surely you know what Saul has done. He has forced the mediums and fortune-tellers out from the land of Israel. You are trying to trap me and kill me."

¹⁰Saul made a promise to the woman in the name of the Lord. He said, "As surely as the Lord lives, you won't be punished for doing this."

¹¹The woman asked, "Whom do you want me to bring up for you?"

He answered, "Bring up Samuel."

¹²When the woman saw Samuel, she screamed loudly. She said, "Why have you tricked me? You are Saul!"

¹³The king said to the woman, "Don't be afraid! What do you see?"

The woman said, "I see a spirit coming up out of the ground."

¹⁴Saul asked, "What does he look like?"

The woman answered, "An old man wearing a coat is coming up."

Then Saul knew it was Samuel, and he bowed facedown on the ground. ¹⁵Samuel asked Saul, "Why have you disturbed me by bringing me up?"

Saul said, "I am greatly troubled. The Philistines are fighting against me. God has left me. He won't answer me anymore, either by prophets or in dreams. That's why I called you. I want you to tell me what to do."

¹⁶Samuel said, "The Lord has left you. He has become your enemy. So why do you call on me? ¹⁷He has done what he said he would do. He said these things through me. He has torn the kingdom out of your hands. He has given it to one of your neighbors, David."

Prayer Starter: Keep us safe from the devil, Father. Protect us from the evil one.

Memory Verse: Obey everything that the Lord commands. . . .

—*1 Kings 2:3a*

Saul and His Sons Die

The Philistines fought against Israel, and the Israelites ran away from them. Many Israelites were killed at Mount Gilboa. ²The Philistines fought hard against Saul and his sons. They killed his sons Jonathan, Abinadab and Malki-Shua. ³The fighting became bad around Saul. When the archers shot at him, he was badly wounded. ⁴He said to the officer who carried his armor, "Pull out your sword and kill me. Then those uncircumcised men won't make fun of me and kill me." But Saul's officer refused, because he was afraid. So Saul took his own sword and threw himself on it. ⁵The officer saw that Saul was dead. So he threw himself on his own sword. And he died with Saul. ⁶So Saul, his three sons and the officer who carried his armor died together that day.

⁷Now there were Israelites who lived on the other side of Jezreel Valley. And some lived across the Jordan River. They saw how the Israelite army had run away. And they saw that Saul and his sons were dead. So they left their cities and ran away. Then the Philistines came and lived there.

Prayer Starter: Dear Father, so many people are sad and afraid. Help me point them to Jesus.

Memory Verse: Obey everything that the Lord commands. Follow the commands . . .
—*1 Kings 2:3a*

David and the Holy Box

David again gathered all the chosen men of Israel. There were 30,000 of them. ²Then David and all his people went to Baalah in Judah." They took the Holy Box of God from Baalah in Judah and moved it to Jerusalem. The Holy Box is called by the Name, the name of the Lord of heaven's armies. His throne is between the gold creatures with wings that are on the Holy Box. ³David's men put the Holy Box of God on a new cart. Then they brought the Holy Box out of Abinadab's house on the hill. Uzzah and Ahio, sons of Abinadab, led the new cart. ⁴This cart had the Holy Box of God on

it. Ahio was walking in front of it. ⁵David and all the Israelites were playing all kinds of musical instruments before the Lord. They were made of pine wood. There were lyres, harps, tambourines, rattles and cymbals.

⁶When David's men came to the threshing floor of Nacon, the oxen stumbled. The Holy Box of God began to fall off the cart. So Uzzah reached out and took hold of it. ⁷The Lord was angry with Uzzah and killed him. Uzzah had not honored God when he touched the Holy Box. So Uzzah died there beside it. ⁸David was angry because the Lord had killed Uzzah. So that place is called The Punishment of Uzzah even today.

⁹David was afraid of the Lord that day. He said, "How can the Holy Box of the Lord come to me now?" ¹⁰So David would not move the Holy Box

of the Lord to be with him in Jerusalem. Instead, he took it to the house of Obed-Edom, a man from Gath. [11]The Holy Box of the Lord stayed in Obed-Edom's house for three months. And the Lord blessed Obed-Edom and all his family.

[12]The people told David, "The Lord has blessed the family of Obed-Edom. And all his things are blessed. This is because the Holy Box of God is there." So David went and brought it up from Obed-Edom's house to Jerusalem with joy. [13]When the men carrying the Holy Box of the Lord had walked six steps, David sacrificed a bull and a fat calf. [14]Then David danced with all his might before the Lord. He had on a holy linen vest. [15]David and all the Israelites shouted with joy. They blew the trumpets as they brought the Holy Box of the Lord to the city.

[16]Saul's daughter Michal was looking out the window. She watched as the Holy Box of the Lord came into the city. When she saw David jumping and dancing before the Lord, she hated him.

[17]David put up a tent for the Holy Box. Then the Israelites put it in its place inside the tent. David offered whole burnt offerings and fellowship offerings before the Lord. [18]When David finished offering the whole burnt offerings and the fellowship offerings, he blessed the people in the name of the Lord of heaven's armies. [19]David gave a loaf of bread, a cake of dates and a cake of raisins to everyone. He gave them to all the Israelites, both men and women. Then all the people went home.

[20]David went back to bless the people in his home. But Saul's daughter Michal came out to meet him. She said, "The king of Israel did not honor himself today! You took off your clothes in front of the servant girls of your officers. You were like a foolish man who takes off his clothes without shame!"

[21]Then David said to Michal, "I did it before the Lord. The Lord chose me, not your father. He didn't choose anyone from Saul's family. The Lord appointed me to be leader of his people, the Israelites. So I will celebrate in front of the Lord."

ⁿ**Baalah in Judah** Another name for Kiriath Jearim.

Prayer Starter: Sometimes I don't do the right thing, Lord, but please continue to show me how to follow you.

Mephibosheth

David asked, "Is there anyone still left in Saul's family? I want to show kindness to this person for Jonathan's sake!"

²Now there was a servant named Ziba from Saul's family. So David's servants called Ziba to him. King David said to him, "Are you Ziba?"

He answered, "Yes, I am Ziba, your servant.

³The king asked, "Is there anyone left in Saul's family? I want to show God's kindness to this person."

Ziba answered the king, "Jonathan has a son still living. He is crippled in both feet."

⁴The king asked Ziba, "Where is this son?"

Ziba answered, "He is at the house of Makir son of Ammiel in Lo Debar."

⁵Then King David had servants bring Jonathan's son from the house of Makir son of Ammiel in Lo Debar. ⁶Mephibosheth, Jonathan's son, came before David and bowed facedown on the floor.

David said, "Mephibosheth!"

Mephibosheth said, "I am your servant."

⁷David said to him, "Don't be afraid. I will be kind to you for your father Jonathan's sake. I will give you back all the land of your grandfather Saul. And you will always be able to eat at my table."

⁸Mephibosheth bowed to David again. Mephibosheth said, "You are being very kind to me, your servant! And I am no better than a dead dog!"

⁹Then King David called Saul's servant Ziba. David said to him, "I have given your master's grandson everything that belonged to Saul and his family. ¹⁰You, your sons and your servants will farm the land for Mephibosheth. You will harvest the crops. Then your master's grandson will have food to eat. But Mephibosheth, your master's grandson, will always be able to eat at my table."

(Now Ziba had 15 sons and 20 servants.) ¹¹Ziba said to King David, "I am your servant. I will do everything my master, the king, commands me."

So Mephibosheth ate at David's table as if he were one of the king's sons. ¹²Mephibosheth had a young son named Mica. Everyone in Ziba's family became Mephibosheth's servants. ¹³Mephibosheth was crippled in both feet. He lived in Jerusalem and always ate at the king's table.

Prayer Starter: Give us kind hearts toward one another, Lord, for you are kind toward us.

Memory Verse: Obey everything that the Lord commands. Follow the commands he has given us. Obey all his laws . . .   —*1 Kings 2:3a*

Obey the Lord

It was almost time for David to die. So he talked to Solomon and gave him his last commands. ²David said, "My time to die is near. Be a good and strong leader. ³Obey everything that the Lord commands. Follow the commands he has given us. Obey all his laws, and do what he told us. Obey what is written in the teachings of Moses. If you do these things, you will be successful in all you do and wherever you go. ⁴And if you obey the Lord, he will keep the promise he made to me. He promised: 'Your descendants must live as I tell them. They must have complete faith in me. If they do this, then a man from your family will always be king over the people of Israel.' "

¹⁰Then David died and was buried with his ancestors in Jerusalem. ¹¹He had ruled over Israel 40 years. Seven years were in Hebron, and 33 years were in Jerusalem.

3 King Solomon went to Gibeon to offer a sacrifice. He went there because it was the most important place of worship. He offered 1,000 burnt offerings on that altar. ⁵While he was at Gibeon, the Lord came to him in a dream during the night. God said, "Ask for anything you want. I will give it to you."

⁶Solomon answered, "You were very kind to your servant, my father David. He obeyed you. He was honest and lived right. And you showed great kindness to him when you allowed his son to be king after him. ⁷Lord my God, you have allowed me to be king in my father's place. But I am like a little child. I do not have the wisdom I need to do what I must do. ⁸I, your servant, am here among your chosen people. There are too many of them to count. ⁹So I ask that you give me wisdom. Then I can rule the people in the right way. Then I will know the difference between right and wrong. Without wisdom, it is impossible to rule this great people of yours."

¹⁰The Lord was pleased that Solomon had asked him for this. ¹¹So God said to him, "You did not ask for a long life. And you did not ask for riches for yourself. You did not ask for the death of your enemies. Since you asked for wisdom to make the right decisions, ¹²I will give you what you asked. I will give you wisdom and understanding. Your wisdom will be greater than anyone has had in the past. And there will never be anyone in the future like you."

Prayer Starter: Give me wisdom, dear Lord, and help me to think clearly.

Memory Verse: Obey everything that the Lord commands. Follow the commands he has given us. Obey all his laws, and do what he told us.
　　　　　　　　　　　　　　　　　　　　　—1 Kings 2:3a

The Two Mothers

One day two women who were prostitutes came to Solomon. They stood before him. [17]One of the women said, "My master, this woman and I live in the same house. I gave birth to a baby while she was there with me. [18]Three days later this woman also gave birth to a baby. No one else was in the house with us. There were only the two of us. [19]One night this woman rolled over on her baby, and it died. [20]So during the night she took my son from my bed while I was asleep. She carried him to her bed. Then she put the dead baby in my bed. [21]The next morning I got up to feed my baby. But I saw that he was dead! Then I looked at him more closely. I saw that he was not my son."

[22]But the other woman said, "No! The living baby is my son. The dead baby is yours!"

But the first woman said, "No! The dead baby is yours, and the living one is mine!" So the two women argued before the king.

[23]Then King Solomon said, "Each of you says the living baby is your own. And each of you says the dead baby belongs to the other woman."

[24]Then King Solomon sent his servants to get a sword. When they brought it to him, [25]he said, "Cut the living baby into two pieces. Give each woman half of the baby."

[26]The real mother of the living child was full of love for her son. She said to the king, "Please, my master, don't kill him! Give the baby to her!"

But the other woman said, "Neither of us will have him. Cut him into two pieces!"

[27]Then King Solomon said, "Give the baby to the first woman. Don't kill him. She is the real mother."

[28]When the people of Israel heard about King Solomon's decision, they respected him very much. They saw he had wisdom from God to make the right decisions.

Prayer Starter: Use me, dear Lord, to help others solve their problems. Make me wise.

Memory Verse: When a good man . . .   *—James 5:16b–17a*

The Queen of Sheba

Now the queen of Sheba heard about Solomon's fame. So she came to test him with hard questions. ²She traveled to Jerusalem with a very large group of servants. There were many camels carrying spices, jewels and much gold. She came to Solomon and talked with him about all that she had in mind. ³Solomon answered all her questions. Nothing was too hard for him to explain to her. ⁴The queen of Sheba learned that Solomon was very wise. She saw the palace he had built. ⁵She saw his many officers and the food on his table. She saw the palace servants and their good clothes. She was shown the servants who served him at feasts. And she was shown the whole burnt offerings he made in the Temple of the Lord. All these things amazed her.

⁶So she said to King Solomon, "I heard in my own country about your achievements and wisdom. And all of it is true. ⁷I could not believe it then. But now I have come and seen it with my own eyes. I was not told even half of it! Your wisdom and wealth are much greater than I had heard. ⁸Your men and officers are very lucky! In always serving you, they are able to hear your wisdom! ⁹Praise the Lord your God! He was pleased to make you king of Israel. The Lord has constant love for Israel. So he made you king to keep justice and to rule fairly."

¹⁰Then the queen of Sheba gave the king about 9,000 pounds of gold. She also gave him many spices and jewels. No one since that time has brought more spices into Israel than the queen of Sheba gave King Solomon.

¹¹(Hiram's ships brought gold from Ophir. They also brought from there very much juniper wood and jewels. ¹²Solomon used the juniper wood to build supports for the Temple of the Lord and the palace. He also used it to make harps and lyres for the musicians. Such fine juniper wood has not been brought in or seen since that time.)

¹³King Solomon gave the queen of Sheba many gifts. He gave her gifts that a king would give to another ruler. Then he gave her whatever else she wanted and asked for. After this, she and her servants went back to her own country.

Prayer Starter: Thank you for all you give us, dear Lord. Thanks for my home, my bed, my clothes, my food.

Memory Verse: When a good man prays . . .   —*James 5:16b–17a*

Fed by Ravens

Ahab son of Omri became king of Israel. This was during Asa's thirty-eighth year as king of Judah. Ahab ruled Israel in the town of Samaria for 22 years. ³⁰Ahab did many things that the Lord said were wrong. He did more evil than any of the kings before him. ³¹He sinned in the same ways that Jeroboam son of Nebat had sinned. But he did even worse things. He married Jezebel daughter of Ethbaal. (Ethbaal was king of the city of Sidon.) Then Ahab began to serve Baal and worship him. ³²He built a temple in Samaria for worshiping Baal. And he put an altar there for Baal. ³³Ahab also made an idol for worshiping Asherah. He did more things to make the Lord, the God of Israel, angry than all the other kings before him.

³⁴During the time of Ahab, Hiel from Bethel rebuilt the town of Jericho. It cost Hiel the life of Abiram, his oldest son, to begin work on the city. And it cost the life of Segub, his youngest son, to build the city gates. The Lord had said, through Joshua, that this would happen.ⁿ (Joshua was the son of Nun.)

17 Now Elijah was a prophet from the town of Tishbe in Gilead. Elijah said to King Ahab, "I serve the Lord, the God of Israel. As surely as the Lord lives, I tell you the truth. No rain or dew will fall during the next few years unless I command it."

²Then the Lord spoke his word to Elijah: ³"Leave this place. Go east and hide near Kerith Ravine. It is east of the Jordan River. ⁴You may drink from the brook. And I have commanded ravens to bring you food there." ⁵So Elijah did what the Lord told him to do. He went to Kerith Ravine, east of the Jordan, and lived there. ⁶The birds brought Elijah bread and meat every morning and every evening. And he drank water from the brook.

ⁿ**The Lord . . . happen** When Joshua destroyed Jericho, he said whoever rebuilt the city would lose his oldest and youngest sons.

Prayer Starter: Thank you for the stories in the Bible, Father. Help me to pray like Elijah.

Memory Verse: When a good man prays, great things happen. . . .
—*James 5:16b–17a*

A Handful
of Flour

After a while the brook dried up because there was no rain. ⁸Then the Lord spoke his word to Elijah, ⁹"Go to Zarephath in Sidon. Live there. I have commanded a widow there to take care of you."

¹⁰So Elijah went to Zarephath. When he reached the town gate, he saw a widow there. She was gathering wood for a fire. Elijah asked her, "Would you bring me a little water in a cup? I would like to have a drink." ¹¹As she was going to get his water, Elijah said, "Please bring me a piece of bread, too."

¹²The woman answered, "As surely as the Lord your God lives, I tell you the truth. I have no bread. I have only a handful of flour in a jar. And I have only a little olive oil in a jug. I came here to gather some wood. I will take it home and cook our last meal. My son and I will eat it and then die from hunger."

¹³Elijah said to her, "Don't worry. Go home and cook your food as you have said. But first make a small loaf of bread from the flour you have. Bring it to me. Then cook something for yourself and your son. ¹⁴The Lord, the God of Israel, says, 'That jar of flour will never become empty. The jug will always have oil in it. This will continue until the day the Lord sends rain to the land.'"

¹⁵So the woman went home. And she did what Elijah told her to do. So Elijah, the woman and her son had enough food every day. ¹⁶The jar of flour and the jug of oil were never empty. This happened just as the Lord, through Elijah, said it would.

[17]Some time later the son of the woman who owned the house became sick. He grew worse and worse. Finally he stopped breathing. [18]So the woman said to Elijah, "You are a man of God. What have you done to me? Did you come here to remind me of my sin? Did you come here to kill my son?"

[19]Elijah said to her, "Give me your son." So Elijah took the boy from her and carried him upstairs. Elijah laid the boy on the bed in the room where he was staying. [20]Then he prayed to the Lord. He said, "Lord my God, this widow is letting me stay in her house. Why have you done this terrible thing to her? Why have you caused her son to die?" [21]Then Elijah lay on top of the boy three times. Elijah prayed to the Lord, "Lord my God, let this boy live again!"

[22]The Lord answered Elijah's prayer. The boy began breathing again, and he was alive. [23]Elijah carried the boy downstairs. He gave the boy to his mother and said, "See! Your son is alive!"

[24]The woman said to Elijah, "Now I know you really are a man from God. I know that the Lord truly speaks through you!"

Prayer Starter: Give me a generous heart, O Lord, and make me willing to share.

Memory Verse: When a good man prays, great things happen. Elijah was a man . . .   —*James 5.16b–17a*

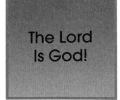

The Lord
Is God!

Elijah said to the prophets of Baal, "There are many of you. So you go first. Choose a bull and prepare it. Pray to your god, but don't start the fire." ²⁶So they took the bull that was given to them and prepared it. They prayed to Baal from morning until noon. They shouted, "Baal, answer us!" But there was no sound. No one answered. They danced around the altar they had built.

²⁷At noon Elijah began to make fun of them. He said, "Pray louder! If Baal really is a god, maybe he is thinking. Or maybe he is busy or traveling! Maybe he is sleeping so you will have to wake him!" ²⁸So the prophets prayed louder. They cut themselves with swords and spears until their blood flowed. (This was the way they worshiped.) ²⁹The afternoon passed, and the prophets continued to act wildly. They continued until it was time for the evening sacrifice. But no voice was heard. Baal did not answer. No one paid attention.

³⁰Then Elijah said to all the people, "Now come to me." So they gathered around him. Elijah rebuilt the altar of the Lord because it had been torn down. ³¹He took 12 stones. He took 1 stone for each of the 12 tribes. These 12 tribes were named for the 12 sons of Jacob. (Jacob was the man the Lord had called Israel.) ³²Elijah used these stones to rebuild the altar in honor of the Lord. Then he dug a small ditch around it. It was big enough to hold about 13 quarts of seed. ³³Elijah put the wood on the altar. He cut the bull into pieces and laid them on the wood. Then he said, "Fill four jars with water. Put the water on the meat and on the wood."

³⁴Then Elijah said, "Do it again." And they did it again.

Then he said, "Do it a third time." And they did it the third time. ³⁵So the water ran off of the altar and filled the ditch.

³⁶It was time for the evening sacrifice. So the prophet Elijah went near the altar. He prayed, "Lord, you are the God of Abraham, Isaac and Israel. I ask you now to prove that you are the God of Israel. And prove that I am your servant. Show these people that you commanded me to do all these things. ³⁷Lord, answer my prayer. Show these people that you, Lord, are God. Then the people will know that you are bringing them back to you."

³⁸Then fire from the Lord came down. It burned the sacrifice, the wood, the stones and the ground around the altar. It also dried up the water in the ditch. ³⁹When all the people saw this, they fell down to the ground. They cried, "The Lord is God! The Lord is God!"

Prayer Starter: I want to be true to you, Lord, even if I'm the only Christian in my group. Keep me faithful.

Memory Verse: When a good man prays, great things happen. Elijah was a man just like us.
—*James 5:16b–17a*

Chariot of Fire

It was near the time for the Lord to take Elijah. He was going to take him by a whirlwind up into heaven. Elijah and Elisha were at Gilgal. [2]Elijah said to Elisha, "Please stay here. The Lord has told me to go to Bethel."

But Elisha said, "As the Lord lives, and as you live, I won't leave you." So they went down to Bethel. [3]A group of the prophets at Bethel came to Elisha. They said to him, "Do you know the Lord will take your master away from you today?"

Elisha said, "Yes, I know. But don't talk about it."

[4]Elijah said to him, "Stay here, because the Lord has sent me to Jericho."

But Elisha said, "As the Lord lives, and as you live, I won't leave you."

So they went to Jericho. [5]A group of the prophets at Jericho came to Elisha. They said, "Do you know that the Lord will take your master away from you today?"

Elisha answered, "Yes, I know. But don't talk about it."

[6]Elijah said to Elisha, "Stay here. The Lord has sent me to the Jordan River."

Elisha answered, "As the Lord lives, and as you live, I won't leave you."

So the two of them went on. [7]Fifty men from a group of the prophets came. They stood far from where Elijah and Elisha were by the Jordan. [8]Elijah took off his coat. Then he rolled it up and hit the water. The water divided to the right and to the left. Then Elijah and Elisha crossed over on dry ground.

[9]After they had crossed over, Elijah said to Elisha, "What can I do for you before I am taken from you?"

Elisha said, "Leave me a double share of your spirit."[n]

[10]Elijah said, "You have asked a hard thing. But if you see me when I am taken from you, it will be yours. If you don't, it won't happen."

[11]Elijah and Elisha were still walking and talking. Then a chariot and horses of fire appeared. The chariot and horses of fire separated Elijah from Elisha. Then Elijah went up to heaven in a whirlwind. [12]Elisha saw it and shouted, "My father! My father! The chariots of Israel and their horsemen!" Elisha did not see him anymore. Elisha grabbed his own clothes and tore them to show how sad he was.

[n]**Leave . . . spirit** By law, the first son in a family would inherit a double share of his father's possessions. Elisha is asking to inherit a share of his master's power. He is not asking for twice as much power as Elijah had.

Prayer Starter: I praise you, Lord, for eternal life. Thank you for all the Bible says about heaven.

Memory Verse: God says, "Be quiet . . ."   *—Psalm 46:10*

Naaman's Skin Disease

Naaman was commander of the army of the king of Aram. He was a great man to his master. He had much honor because the Lord had used him to give victory to Aram. He was a mighty and brave man. But he had a harmful skin disease.

²The Arameans had gone out to steal from the Israelites. And they had taken a little girl as a captive from Israel. This little girl served Naaman's wife. ³She said to her mistress, "I wish that my master would meet the prophet who lives in Samaria. He would heal Naaman of his disease."

⁴Naaman went to the king. He told him what the girl from Israel had said. ⁵The king of Aram said, "Go now. And I will send a letter to the king of Israel." So Naaman left and took about 750 pounds of silver. He also took about 150 pounds of gold and ten changes of clothes with him. ⁶He brought the letter to the king of Israel. It read, "I am sending my servant Naaman to you. I'm sending him so you can heal him of his skin disease."

⁷The king of Israel read the letter. Then he tore his clothes to show how upset he was. He said, "I'm not God! I can't kill and make alive again! Why does this man send someone with a harmful skin disease for

me to heal? You can see that the king of Aram is trying to start trouble with me!"

⁸Elisha, the man of God, heard that the king of Israel had torn his clothes. So he sent a message to the king. It said, "Why have you become so upset that you tore your clothes? Let Naaman come to me. Then he will know there is a prophet in Israel!" ⁹So Naaman went with his horses and chariots to Elisha's house. And he stood outside the door.

¹⁰Elisha sent a messenger to Naaman. The messenger said, "Go and wash in the Jordan River seven times. Then your skin will be healed, and you will be clean."

¹¹Naaman became angry and left. He said, "I thought Elisha would surely come out and stand before me. I thought he would call on the name of the Lord his God. I thought he would wave his hand over the place and heal the disease! ¹²Abana and Pharpar, the rivers of Damascus, are better than all the waters of Israel! Why can't I wash in them and become clean?" So Naaman went away very angry.

¹³But Naaman's servants came near and talked to him. They said, "My father, if the prophet had told you to do some great thing, wouldn't you have done it? Doesn't it make more sense just to do it? After all, he only told you, 'Wash, and you will be clean.'" ¹⁴So Naaman went down and dipped in the Jordan seven times. He did just as Elisha had said. Then Naaman's skin became new again. It was like the skin of a little boy. And Naaman was clean!

¹⁵Naaman and all his group came back to Elisha. He stood before Elisha and said, "Look. I now know there is no God in all the earth except in Israel! Now please accept a gift from me."

¹⁶But Elisha said, "I serve the Lord. As surely as the Lord lives, I won't accept anything." Naaman urged him to take the gift, but he refused.

Prayer Starter: Make me clean on the inside, dear God. May my mind and my spirit be holy.

Memory Verse: God says, "Be quiet and know that I am God. . . ."
—*Psalm 46:10*

Horses and Chariots of Fire

The king of Aram was at war with Israel. He had a council meeting with his officers. He said, "I will set up my camp in this place."

⁹But Elisha sent a message to the king of Israel. It said, "Be careful! Don't pass that place. The Arameans are going down there!"

¹⁰The king of Israel checked the place about which Elisha had warned him. Elisha warned him several times. So the king added guards in those places.

¹¹The king of Aram was angry about this. He called his officers together. He said to them, "Tell me who of us is working for the king of Israel."

¹²One of the officers of the king of Aram said, "No, my master and king. It's Elisha, the prophet from Israel. He can tell you what you speak in your bedroom."

¹³The king said, "Go and find him. Then I can send men and catch him." The servants came back and reported, "He is in Dothan."

¹⁴Then the king sent horses, chariots and a large army to Dothan. They arrived at night and surrounded the city.

¹⁵The servant of Elisha got up early. When he went out, he saw an army with horses and chariots all around the city. The servant said to Elisha, "Oh, my master, what can we do?"

¹⁶Elisha said, "Don't be afraid. The army that fights for us is larger than the one against us."

¹⁷Then Elisha prayed, "Lord, open my servant's eyes. Let him see."

The Lord opened the eyes of the young man. And he saw that the mountain was full of horses and chariots of fire all around Elisha.

¹⁸As the enemy came down toward Elisha, he prayed to the Lord. He said, "Make these people blind." So the Lord made the Aramean army blind, as Elisha had asked.

¹⁹Elisha said to them, "This is not the right road. This is not the right city. Follow me. I'll take you to the man you are looking for." Then Elisha led them to Samaria.

²⁰After they entered Samaria, Elisha said, "Lord, open these men's eyes so they can see." So the Lord opened their eyes. And the Aramean army saw that they were inside the city of Samaria!

²¹The king of Israel saw the Aramean army. He said to Elisha, "My father, should I kill them? Should I kill them?"

²²Elisha answered, "Don't kill them. You wouldn't kill people whom you captured with your sword and bow. Give them food and water. And let them eat and drink. Then let them go home to their master."

Prayer Starter: Keep your angels around, heavenly Father. Keep us safe wherever we go.

Memory Verse: God says, "Be quiet and know that I am God. I will be supreme . . ."
—*Psalm 46:10*

Jezebel

Elisha called a man from the group of the prophets. Elisha said, "Tighten your clothes around you. And take this small bottle of olive oil in your hand. Go to Ramoth in Gilead. ²When you arrive, find Jehu son of Jehoshaphat. Jehoshaphat is the son of Nimshi. Go in and make Jehu get up from among his brothers. Take him to an inner room. ³Take the bottle and pour the oil on Jehu's head. Say, 'This is what the Lord says: I have appointed you king over Israel.' Then open the door and run away. Don't wait!"

[4]So the young man, the prophet, went to Ramoth in Gilead. [5]When he arrived, he saw the officers of the army sitting together. He said, "Commander, I have a message for you."

Jehu asked, "For which one of us?"

The young man said, "For you, commander."

[6]Jehu got up and went into the house. Then the young prophet poured the olive oil on Jehu's head. He said to Jehu, "This is what the Lord of Israel says: 'I have appointed you king over the Lord's people, Israel. [7]You must destroy the family of Ahab your master. I will punish Jezebel for the deaths of my servants the prophets. And I will punish her for all the Lord's servants who were murdered.' "

[30]When Jehu came to Jezreel, Jezebel heard about it. She put paint on her eyes and fixed her hair. Then she looked out the window. [31]Jehu entered the city gate. And Jezebel said, "Have you come in peace, you Zimri,ⁿ you who killed your master?"

[32]Jehu looked up at the window. He said, "Who is on my side? Who?" Two or three eunuchs looked out from the window at Jehu. [33]Jehu said to them, "Throw her down!" So they threw Jezebel down. And the horses ran over her body. Some of her blood splashed on the wall and on the horses.

[34]Jehu went into the house and ate and drank. Then he said, "Now see about this cursed woman. Bury her, because she is a king's daughter."

[35]The men went to bury Jezebel. But they could not find her body. They could only find the skull, feet and palms of her hands. [36]So they came back and told Jehu. Then Jehu said, "The Lord said this through his servant Elijah the Tishbite: 'The dogs will eat the body of Jezebel in the portion of land at Jezreel. [37]Her body will be like manure on the field in the land at Jezreel. Then people cannot say that the body is Jezebel.' "

ⁿ**Zimri** He was the man who killed Elah and the family of Baasha.

Prayer Starter: Some people are hard and cruel, dear Lord. Help me to leave them in your hands. Make me kind and strong.

Memory Verse: God says, "Be quiet and know that I am God. I will be supreme over all the nations. . . ."   —*Psalm 46:10*

Hezekiah Prays

The king received a report that Tirhakah was coming to attack him. Tirhakah was the Cushite king of Egypt. When the king of Assyria heard this, he sent messengers to Hezekiah. The king said: [10]"Say this to Hezekiah king of Judah: Don't be fooled by the god you trust. Don't believe him when he says Jerusalem will not be defeated by the king of Assyria. [11]You have heard what the kings of Assyria have done. They have completely defeated every country. Do not think you will be saved."

[14]Hezekiah received the letter from the messengers and read it. Then he went up to the Temple of the Lord. Hezekiah spread the letter out before the Lord. [15]And he prayed to the Lord: "Lord, God of Israel, your throne is between the gold creatures with wings! Only you are God of all the kingdoms of the earth. You made the heavens and the earth. [16]Hear, Lord, and listen. Open your eyes, Lord, and see. Listen to the word Sennacherib has said to insult the living God. [17]It is true, Lord. The kings of Assyria have destroyed these countries and their lands. [18]These kings have thrown the gods of these nations into the fire. But they were only wood and rock statues that men made. So the kings have destroyed them. [19]Now, Lord our God, save us from the king's power. Then all the kingdoms of the earth will know that you, Lord, are the only God."

[35]That night the angel of the Lord went out. He killed 185,000 men in the Assyrian camp. The people got up early the next morning. And they saw all the dead bodies! [36]So Sennacherib king of Assyria left. He went back to Nineveh and stayed there.

Prayer Starter: Protect our nation, dear Lord, and bless our country. Keep us safe from war.

Memory Verse: God says, "Be quiet and know that I am God. I will be supreme over all the nations. I will be supreme in the earth." —*Psalm 46:10*

Hezekiah's Guests

At that time Hezekiah became very sick. He was almost dead. The prophet Isaiah son of Amoz went to see him. Isaiah told him, "This is what the Lord says: You are going to die. So you should give your last orders to everyone. You will not get well."

²Hezekiah turned toward the wall and prayed to the Lord. He said, ³"Lord, please remember that I have always obeyed you. I have given myself completely to you. I have done what you said was right." And Hezekiah cried loudly.

⁴Before Isaiah had left the middle courtyard, the Lord spoke his word to Isaiah: ⁵"Go back and tell Hezekiah, the leader of my people: 'This is what

the Lord, the God of your ancestor David, says: I have heard your prayer. And I have seen your tears. So I will heal you. Three days from now you will go up to the Temple of the Lord. ⁶I will add 15 years to your life. I will save you and this city from the king of Assyria. And I will protect the city for myself and for my servant David.' "

⁷Then Isaiah said, "Make a paste from figs." So they made it and put it on Hezekiah's boil. And he got well.

⁸Hezekiah asked Isaiah, "What will be the sign that the Lord will heal me? What is the sign that I will go up to the Temple of the Lord on the third day?"

⁹Isaiah said, "The Lord will do what he says. This is the sign from the Lord to show you: Do you want the shadow to go forward ten steps? Or do you want it to go back ten steps?"

¹⁰Hezekiah answered, "It's easy for the shadow to go forward ten steps. Instead, let it go back ten steps."

¹¹Then Isaiah the prophet called to the Lord. And the Lord brought the shadow back ten steps. It went back up the stairway of Ahaz that it had gone down.

¹²At that time Merodach-Baladan, son of Baladan, was king of Babylon. He sent letters and a gift to Hezekiah. He did this because he had heard that Hezekiah had been sick. ¹³Hezekiah was happy to see the messengers. So he showed them what was in his storehouses: the silver, gold, spices and expensive perfumes. He showed them his swords and shields. He showed them all his wealth. He showed them everything in his palace and his kingdom.

¹⁴Then Isaiah the prophet went to King Hezekiah. Isaiah asked him, "What did these men say? Where did they come from?"

Hezekiah said, "They came from a faraway country. They came to me from Babylon."

¹⁵So Isaiah asked him, "What did they see in your palace?"

Hezekiah said, "They saw everything in my palace. I showed them all my wealth."

¹⁶Then Isaiah said to Hezekiah, "Listen to the words of the Lord: ¹⁷In the future everything in your palace will be taken away to Babylon. Everything your ancestors have stored up until this day will be taken away. Nothing will be left,' says the Lord. ¹⁸Some of your own children will be taken away. Those who will be born to you will be taken away. And they will become eunuchs in the palace of the king of Babylon.' "

¹⁹Hezekiah told Isaiah, "These words from the Lord are good." He said this because he thought, "There will be peace and security while I am king."

Prayer Starter: You know the future, Lord. Guide me day by day.

Memory Verse: The Lord searches . . .   —*2 Chronicles 16:9a*

**The Book
of the
Agreement**

The king [Josiah] gathered all the older leaders of Judah and Jerusalem together. ²He went up to the Temple of the Lord. All the men from Judah and Jerusalem went with him. The priests, prophets and all the people—from the least important to the most important—went with him. He read to them all the words of the Book of the Agreement. That book was found in the Temple of the Lord. ³The king stood by the pillar. He made an agreement in the presence of the Lord. He agreed to follow the Lord and obey his commands, rules and laws with his whole being. He agreed to do what was written in this book. Then all the people promised to obey the agreement.

⁴The king gave a command to Hilkiah the high priest. He also gave it to the priests of the next rank and the gatekeepers. He told them to bring out of the Temple of the Lord everything made for Baal, Asherah and all the stars of heaven. Then Josiah burned them outside Jerusalem in the fields of the Kidron Valley. And he carried the ashes to Bethel.

²⁴Josiah destroyed the mediums, fortune-tellers, house gods and idols. He destroyed all the hated gods seen in the land of Judah and Jerusalem. He did this to obey the words of the teachings. They were written in the book Hilkiah the priest had found in the Temple of the Lord.

²⁵There was no king like Josiah before or after him. He obeyed the Lord with all his heart, soul and strength. He followed all the Teachings of Moses.

Prayer Starter: Help me to obey your Word, dear Lord. And give me strength to live a holy life.

Memory Verse: The Lord searches all the earth for people . . .

—*2 Chronicles 16:9a*

The Three Warriors

David made his home in the strong, walled city. That is why it was named the City of David. [8]David rebuilt the city. He started where the land was filled in and went to the wall that was around the city. Joab repaired the other parts of the city. [9]David became more and more powerful. And the Lord of heaven's armies was with him.

[10]This is a list of the leaders over David's warriors. These warriors helped make David's kingdom strong. All the people of Israel also supported David's kingdom. These heroes and all the people of Israel made David king. This happened as the Lord had promised.

[11]This is a list of David's warriors:

Jashobeam was from the Hacmonite people. He was the leader of the Three,[n] David's most powerful soldiers. He used his spear to fight 300 men at one time. And he killed them all.

[12]Next was Eleazar. He was one of the Three. Eleazar was Dodai's son. Dodai was from the Ahohite people. [13]Eleazar was with David at Pas-Dammim. The Philistines came there to fight the Israelites. There was a field of barley at that place. The Israelites ran away from the Philistines. [14]But they stopped in the middle of that field and fought the Philistines. And they killed the Philistines. The Lord gave Israel a great victory.

[15]Three of the 30 leaders went to David. He was at the rock by the cave near Adullam. At the same time a group from the Philistine army was camped in the Valley of Rephaim.

[16]David was in a protected place at that time. The Philistine army was staying in the town of Bethlehem. [17]David had a strong desire for some water. He said, "Oh, I wish someone would get me water from the well near the city gate of Bethlehem!" [18]So the Three fought their way through the Philistine army. And they took water out of the well near the city gate in Bethlehem. Then they took it back to David. But he refused to drink it. He poured it out before the Lord. [19]David said, "May God keep me from drinking this water! It would be like drinking the blood of the men who risked their lives to bring me this water." So David refused to drink it.

These were the brave things the Three did.

[n]**Three** Or maybe "Thirty." These were David's most powerful soldiers.

Prayer Starter: You are so strong, dear Lord, that I can be brave when you are near me. I love you. I thank you.

Memory Verse: The Lord searches all the earth for people who have given themselves . . .   *—2 Chronicles 16:9a*

Solomon's Wealth

K ing Solomon made 200 large shields from hammered gold. Each shield contained about 7½ pounds of hammered gold. ¹⁶Solomon also made 300 small shields of hammered gold. Each shield contained about 4 pounds of gold. King Solomon put them in the Palace of the Forest of Lebanon.

¹⁷Then he built a large throne of ivory. And he covered it with pure gold. ¹⁸The throne had six steps on it. And it had a gold footstool on it. There were armrests on both sides of the chair. And beside each armrest was a statue of a lion. ¹⁹Twelve lions stood on the six steps. There was one lion at each end of each step. Nothing like this had ever been made for any other kingdom. ²⁰All King Solomon's drinking cups were made of gold. All of the dishes in the Palace of the Forest of Lebanon were pure gold. In Solomon's time people did not think silver was valuable. So nothing was made of silver. ²¹King Solomon had many ships that he sent out to trade. Hiram's men sailed Solomon's ships. Every three years the ships returned. They brought back gold, silver, ivory, apes and baboons.

²²King Solomon had more riches and wisdom than all the other kings on earth. ²³All the kings of the earth came to see Solomon. They wanted to hear the wisdom God had given him. ²⁴Every year everyone who came brought a gift. They brought things made of silver and gold, clothes, weapons, spices, horses and mules.

Prayer Starter: Keep me from loving money too much, Lord. Teach me to love your Word more.

Memory Verse: The Lord searches all the earth for people who have given themselves completely to him. . . .   —*2 Chronicles 16:9a*

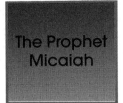

The Prophet Micaiah

Jehoshaphat had much wealth and honor. He made an agreement with King Ahab through marriage.ⁿ ²A few years later Jehoshaphat visited Ahab in Samaria. Ahab sacrificed many sheep and cattle as a great feast to honor Jehoshaphat and the people with him. He encouraged Jehoshaphat to attack Ramoth in Gilead. ³Ahab king of Israel asked Jehoshaphat king of Judah, "Will you go with me to attack Ramoth in Gilead?"

Jehoshaphat answered, "I will be with you. And my soldiers will be like your own soldiers. We will join you in the battle." ⁴Jehoshaphat also said to Ahab, "But first we should ask the Lord to guide us."

⁵So King Ahab called a meeting of the prophets. There were 400 men. Ahab asked them, "Should we go to war against Ramoth in Gilead or not?"

They answered, "Go, because God will let you defeat it."

⁶But Jehoshaphat asked, "Is there a prophet of the Lord here? If there is, let's ask him what we should do."

⁷Then King Ahab said to Jehoshaphat, "There is one other prophet. We could ask the Lord through him. But I hate him. When he prophesies, he never says anything good about me. He always says something bad. He is Micaiah, Imlah's son."

Jehoshaphat said, "King Ahab, you shouldn't say that."

⁸So King Ahab told one of his officers to bring Micaiah to him at once.

⁹King Ahab of Israel and King Jehoshaphat of Judah had on their royal robes. They were sitting on their thrones at the threshing floor. This was near the entrance to the gate of Samaria. All the prophets were speaking messages in front of the two kings. ¹⁰One of the prophets was Zedekiah son of Kenaanah. He had made some iron horns. He said to Ahab, "This is what the Lord says: 'You will use these horns to fight the Arameans. And you will destroy them.' "

¹¹All the other prophets said the same thing. They said, "Attack Ramoth in Gilead and win. The Lord will let you defeat the Arameans."

¹²The messenger who had gone to get Micaiah found him. He said to Micaiah, "All the other prophets are saying the same thing. They are saying that King Ahab will win against the Arameans. You had better agree with them. Give the king a good answer."

¹³But Micaiah said, "As surely as the Lord lives, I can tell him only what my God says."

¹⁴Then Micaiah came to King Ahab. The king asked him, "Micaiah, should we attack Ramoth in Gilead or not?"

Micaiah answered, "Attack and win. You will defeat it."

¹⁵King Ahab said to Micaiah, "Tell me only the truth by the power of the Lord. How many times do I have to tell you this?"

¹⁶Then Micaiah answered, "I saw the army of Israel. They were scattered over the hills like sheep without a shepherd. The Lord said, 'They have no leaders. Let each one go home and not fight.' "

¹⁷Then King Ahab of Israel said to Jehoshaphat, "I told you! This prophet never says anything good about me. He only says bad things about me."

ⁿ**agreement . . . through marriage** Jehoshaphat's son Jehoram married Athaliah, Ahab's daughter.

Prayer Starter: Help me to be truthful, dear God. Make me honest, and keep me from telling lies.

Memory Verse: The Lord searches all the earth for people who have given themselves completely to him. He wants to make them strong.
—2 Chronicles 16:9a

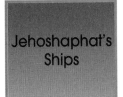

Jehoshaphat's Ships

Jehoshaphat ruled over the country of Judah. He was 35 years old when he began to rule. And he ruled 25 years in Jerusalem. His mother's name was Azubah daughter of Shilhi. ³²Jehoshaphat lived as his father Asa had lived. He followed what Asa had done. He did what the Lord said was right. ³³But the places where false gods were worshiped were not removed. And the people did not strongly desire to follow the God their ancestors had followed.

³⁴The other things Jehoshaphat did as king, from the beginning to the end, are written down. They are in the writings of Jehu son of Hanani. These writings are in the book of the kings of Israel.

³⁵Later, Jehoshaphat king of Judah made an agreement with Ahaziah king of Israel. It was wrong for him to do this. ³⁶Jehoshaphat agreed with Ahaziah to build trading ships. They built them in the town of Ezion Geber. ³⁷Then Eliezer son of Dodavahu spoke against Jehoshaphat. Eliezer was from the town of Mareshah. He said, "Jehoshaphat, because you joined with Ahaziah, the Lord will destroy what you have made." The ships were wrecked. So Jehoshaphat and Ahaziah could not send them out to trade.

21 Then Jehoshaphat died and was buried with his ancestors in Jerusalem. Jehoshaphat's son Jehoram became king in his place.

Prayer Starter: God, I know you are Lord of the winds and waves and storms. Thank you for your mighty power.

Memory Verse: Lord, God of heaven, you are the great God . . .
—*Nehemiah 1:5*

Joash was seven years old when he became king. And he ruled 40 years in Jerusalem. His mother's name was Zibiah. She was from Beersheba. ²Joash did what the Lord said was right as long as Jehoiada the priest was alive. ³Jehoiada chose two wives for Joash. And Joash had sons and daughters.

Repairing the Temple

⁴Later, Joash decided to repair the Temple of the Lord. ⁵He called the priests and the Levites together. He said to them, "Go to the towns of Judah. Gather the money all the Israelites have to pay every year. Use it to repair the Temple of your God. Do this now." But the Levites did not hurry.

⁶So King Joash called Jehoiada the leading priest. Joash said to him, "Why haven't you made the Levites bring in the tax money from Judah and Jerusalem? Moses the Lord's servant and the people of Israel used that money for the Holy Tent."

⁷In the past the sons of wicked Athaliah had broken into the Temple of God. They had used its holy things for worshiping the Baal idols.

⁸King Joash commanded that a box for contributions be made. It was to be put outside, at the gate of the Temple of the Lord. ⁹Then the Levites made an announcement in Judah and Jerusalem. They told the people to

bring the tax money to the Lord. Moses the servant of God had made the Israelites give it while they were in the desert. ¹⁰All the officers and people were happy to give their money. They put it in the box until the box was full. ¹¹Then the Levites would take the box to the king's officers. They would see that it was full of money. Then the king's royal assistant and the leading priest's officer would come and take out the money. Then they would take the box back to its place. They did this often and gathered much money. ¹²King Joash and Jehoiada gave the money to the people who worked on the Temple of the Lord. And they hired stoneworkers and carpenters to repair the Temple of the Lord. They also hired people to work with iron and bronze to repair the Temple.

¹³The people worked hard. And the work to repair the Temple went well. They rebuilt the temple of God to be as it was before. And they made it stronger. ¹⁴When the workers finished, they brought the money that was left to King Joash and Jehoiada. They used that money to make things for the Temple of the Lord. They made things for the service in the Temple and for the burnt offerings. They also made bowls and other things from gold and silver. Burnt offerings were given every day in the Temple of the Lord while Jehoiada was alive.

¹⁵Jehoiada grew old. He had lived many years. Then he died when he was 130 years old. ¹⁶Jehoiada was buried in Jerusalem with the kings. He was buried there because he had done much good in Israel for God and his Temple.

Prayer Starter: Thank you for our church, dear Lord. Please give wise and godly hearts to our church members.

Memory Verse: Lord, God of heaven, you are the great God who is to be respected. . . .   *—Nehemiah 1:5*

Uzziah

Then all the people of Judah chose Uzziah[n] to be king. He became king in place of Amaziah, his father. Uzziah was 16 years old. [2]He rebuilt the town of Elath and made it part of Judah again. He did this after Amaziah died.

[3]Uzziah was 16 years old when he became king. And he ruled 52 years in Jerusalem.

[15]Uzziah became famous in faraway places. He had much help until he became powerful.

[16]But when Uzziah became strong, his pride caused him to be destroyed. He was unfaithful to the Lord his God. He went into the Temple of the Lord to burn incense on the altar for incense. [17]Azariah and 80 other brave priests who served the Lord followed Uzziah into the Temple. [18]They told Uzziah he was wrong. They said to him, "You don't have the right to burn incense to the Lord. Only the priests, Aaron's descendants, should burn the incense. They have been made holy for the Lord to do this special duty. Leave this holy place. You have been unfaithful to God. The Lord God will not honor you for this."

[19]Uzziah was standing beside the altar for incense in the Temple of the Lord. He had in his hand a pan for burning incense. He was very angry with the priests. As he was standing in front of the priests, a harmful skin disease broke out on his forehead. [20]Azariah the leading priest and all the other priests looked at him. They could see the harmful skin disease on his forehead. So they hurried him out of the Temple. Uzziah rushed out, because the Lord had punished him. [21]So King Uzziah had the skin disease until the day he died. He had to live in a separate house. He could not enter the Temple of the Lord. His son Jotham was in charge of the palace. He governed the people of the land.

[n]**Uzziah** Also called Azariah in 2 Kings.

Prayer Starter: Lord, keep me from becoming proud and thinking too highly of myself. May I always put you first.

Memory Verse: Lord, God of heaven, you are the great God who is to be respected. You keep your agreement of love . . .   —*Nehemiah 1:5*

Ahaz Closes the Temple Doors

Ahaz was 20 years old when he became king. And he ruled 16 years in Jerusalem. He was not like his ancestor David. He did not do what the Lord said was right. ²Ahaz did the same things the kings of Israel had done. He made metal idols to worship Baal. ³He burned incense in the Valley of Ben Hinnom. He sacrificed his own sons by burning them in the fire. He did the same terrible sins as the other nations had done. And the Lord had forced these nations out of the land ahead of the Israelites. ⁴Ahaz offered sacrifices and burned incense at the places where false gods were worshiped. And he did this on the hills and under every green tree.

²²In Ahaz's troubles he was even more unfaithful to the Lord. ²³He offered sacrifices to the gods the people of Damascus worshiped. These people had defeated him. So he thought, "The gods of the kings of Aram helped them. If I offer sacrifices to them, they will help me also." But this brought ruin to Ahaz and all Israel.

²⁴Ahaz gathered the things from the Temple of God and broke them into pieces. Then he closed the doors of the Temple of the Lord. He made altars and put them on every street corner in Jerusalem.

Prayer Starter: The doors of my heart are open to you, O Lord. Never let them close.

Memory Verse: Lord, God of heaven, you are the great God who is to be respected. You keep your agreement of love with those who love you . . .
—*Nehemiah 1:5*

Nehemiah Before the King

It was the month of Nisan. It was in the twentieth year King Artaxerxes was king. He wanted some wine. So I [Nehemiah] took some and gave it to the king. I had not been sad in his presence before. ²So the king said, "Why does your face look sad? You are not sick. Your heart must be sad."

Then I was very afraid. ³I said to the king, "May the king live forever! My face is sad because the city where my ancestors are buried lies in ruins. And its gates have been destroyed by fire."

⁴Then the king said to me, "What do you want?"

First I prayed to the God of heaven. ⁵Then I answered the king, "Send me to the city in Judah where my ancestors are buried. I will rebuild it. Do this if you are willing and if I have pleased you."

⁶The queen was sitting next to the king. He asked me, "How long will your trip take? When will you get back?" It pleased the king to send me. So I set a time.

⁷I also said to him, "If you are willing, give me letters for the governors west of the Euphrates River. Tell them to let me pass safely through their lands on my way to Judah. ⁸And may I have a letter for Asaph? He is the keeper of the king's forest. Tell him to give me timber. I will need it to make boards for the gates of the palace. It is by the Temple. The wood is also for the city wall and the house I will live in." So the king gave me the letters. This was because God was showing kindness to me. ⁹So I went to the governors west of the Euphrates River. I gave them the king's letters. The king had also sent army officers and soldiers on horses with me.

Prayer Starter: Lord God of heaven, you are great, and you faithfully keep your promises.

Memory Verse: Lord, God of heaven, you are the great God who is to be respected. You keep your agreement of love with those who love you and obey your commands.
—*Nehemiah 1:5*

Rebuilding Jerusalem's Walls

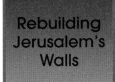

I went to Jerusalem and stayed there three days. [12]Then at night I started out with a few men. I had not told anyone what God had caused me to do for Jerusalem. There were no animals with me except the one I was riding.

[13]It was night. I went out through the Valley Gate. I rode toward the Dragon Well and the Trash Gate. I was inspecting the walls of Jerusalem. They had been broken down. And the gates had been destroyed by fire. [14]Then I rode on toward the Fountain Gate and the King's Pool. But there was not enough room for the animal I was riding to get through. [15]So I went up the valley at night. I was inspecting the wall. Finally, I turned and went back in through the Valley Gate. [16]The officers did not know where I had gone or what I was doing. I had not yet said anything to the Jews, the priests, the important men or the officers. I had not said anything to any of the others who would do the work.

[17]Then I said to them, "You can see the trouble we have here. Jerusalem is a pile of ruins. And its gates have been burned. Come, let's rebuild the wall of Jerusalem. Then we won't be full of shame any longer." [18]I also told them how God had been kind to me. And I told them what the king had said to me.

Then they answered, "Let's start rebuilding." So they began to work hard.

Prayer Starter: Make me a hard worker, dear Lord.

Memory Verse: You must give . . .   *—Job 11:13*

Queen Esther

Mordecai had a cousin named Hadassah, who had no father or mother. So Mordecai took care of her. Hadassah was also called Esther, and she had a very pretty figure and face. Mordecai had adopted her as his own daughter when her father and mother died.

⁸The king's command and order had been heard. And many girls had been brought to the palace in Susa. They had been put under the care of Hegai. When this happened, Esther was also taken to the king's palace. She was put into the care of Hegai, who was in charge of the women. ⁹Esther pleased Hegai, and he liked her. So Hegai quickly began giving Esther her beauty treatments and special food. He gave her seven servant girls chosen from the king's palace. Then Hegai moved Esther and her seven servant girls to the best part of the women's quarters.

¹⁰Esther did not tell anyone about her family or who her people were. Mordecai had told her not to. ¹¹Every day Mordecai walked back and forth near the courtyard. This was where the king's women lived. He wanted to find out how Esther was and what was happening to her.

¹²Before a girl could take her turn with King Xerxes, she had to complete 12 months of beauty treatments. These were ordered for the women. For 6 months she was treated with oil and myrrh. And she spent 6 months with perfumes and cosmetics.

¹⁵Esther daughter of Abihail, Mordecai's uncle, had been adopted by Mordecai. The time came for Esther to go to the king. She asked for only what Hegai suggested she should take. (Hegai was the king's eunuch who was in charge of the women.) And everyone who saw Esther liked her. ¹⁶So Esther was taken to King Xerxes in the royal palace. This happened in the tenth month, the month of Tebeth. It was in Xerxes' seventh year as king.

¹⁷And the king was pleased with Esther more than with any of the other girls. And he liked her more than any of the other virgins. So King Xerxes put a royal crown on Esther's head. And he made her queen in place of Vashti. ¹⁸Then the king gave a great banquet for Esther. He invited all his important men and royal officers. He announced a holiday in all the empire. And he was generous and gave everyone a gift.

Prayer Starter: Heavenly Father, I believe you guide world rulers even when they don't know it. Bless our nation and our leaders today.

Memory Verse: You must give your whole heart . . .   —*Job 11:13*

Let My People Live

Then Mordecai told Hathach everything that had happened to him. And he told Hathach about the amount of money Haman had promised to pay into the king's treasury for the killing of the Jews. ⁸Mordecai also gave him a copy of the order to kill the Jews, which had been given in Susa. He wanted Hathach to show it to Esther and to tell her about it. And Mordecai told him to order Esther to go into the king's presence. He wanted her to beg for mercy and to plead with him for her people.

⁹Hathach went back and reported to Esther everything Mordecai had said. ¹⁰Then Esther told Hathach to say to Mordecai, ¹¹"All the royal officers and people of the royal areas know this: No man or woman may go to the king in the inner courtyard without being called. There is only one law about this. Anyone who enters must be put to death. But if the king holds out his gold scepter, that person may live. And I have not been called to go to the king for 30 days."

¹²And Esther's message was given to Mordecai. ¹³Then Mordecai gave orders to say to Esther: "Just because you live in the king's palace, don't think that out of all the Jews you alone will escape. ¹⁴You might keep quiet at this time. Then someone else will help and save the Jews. But you and your father's family will all die. And who knows, you may have been chosen queen for just such a time as this."

5 On the third day Esther put on her royal robes. Then she stood in the inner courtyard of the king's palace, facing the king's hall. The king was sitting on his royal throne in the hall, facing the doorway. ²The king saw Queen Esther standing in the courtyard. When he saw her, he was very pleased. He held out to her the gold scepter that was in his hand.

7 So the king and Haman went in to eat with Queen Esther. ²They were drinking wine. And the king said to Esther on this second day also, "What are you asking for? I will give it to you. What is it you want? I will give you as much as half of my kingdom."

³Then Queen Esther answered, "My king, I hope you are pleased with me. If it pleases you, let me live. This is what I ask. And let my people live, too. This is what I want. ⁴I ask this because my people and I have been sold to be destroyed. We are to be killed and completely wiped out. If we had been sold as male and female slaves, I would have kept quiet. That would not be enough of a problem to bother the king."

⁵Then King Xerxes asked Queen Esther, "Who is he? Where is he? Who has done such a thing?"

Prayer Starter: Please help me, Lord, to do the right thing always, especially during times when I am afraid.

Memory Verse: You must give your whole heart to him. . . . —*Job 11:13*

⁶Esther said, "A man who is against us! Our enemy is this wicked Haman!"

Then Haman was filled with terror before the king and queen. ⁷The king was very angry. He got up, left his wine and went out into the palace garden. But Haman stayed inside to beg Queen Esther to save his life. He could see that the king had already decided to kill him.

Job Loses Everything

Aman named Job lived in the land of Uz. He was an honest man and innocent of any wrong. He honored God and stayed away from evil. ²Job had seven sons and three daughters. ³He owned 7,000 sheep, 3,000 camels, 500 pairs of oxen and 500 female donkeys. And he had a large number of servants. He was the greatest man among all the people of the East.

2On another day the angels came to show themselves before the Lord. And Satan also came with them. ²The Lord said to Satan, "Where have you come from?"

Satan answered the Lord, "I have been wandering around the earth. I have been going back and forth in it."

³Then the Lord said to Satan, "Have you noticed my servant Job? No one else on earth is like him. He is an honest man, innocent of any wrong. He honors God and stays away from evil. You caused me to ruin him for no good reason. But he continues to be without blame."

⁴"One skin for another!" Satan answered. "A man will give all he has to save his own life. ⁵But reach out your hand and destroy his own flesh and bones. Then he will curse you to your face."

⁶The Lord said to Satan, "All right, then. Job is in your power. But you must let him live."

⁷So Satan left the Lord's presence. And he put painful sores all over Job's body. They went from the top of his head to the soles of his feet. ⁸Then Job took a piece of broken pottery. And he used it to scrape himself. He sat in ashes to show how upset he was.

⁹Job's wife said to him, "Are you still trying to stay innocent? You should just curse God and die!"

¹⁰Job answered, "You are talking like a foolish woman. Should we take only good things from God and not trouble?" In all this Job did not sin in what he said.

Prayer Starter: Keep me from being a complainer, Lord. Give me a good attitude in everything.

Memory Verse: You must give your whole heart to him. You must hold out your hands . . .
—*Job 11:13*

God Speaks
from a
Storm

The Lord answered Job from the storm. He said:

2 "Who is this that makes my purpose unclear
    by saying things that are not true?
3 Be strong like a man
    I will ask you questions,
and you must answer me.
4 Where were you when I made the earth's foundation?
    Tell me, if you understand.
5 Who marked off how big it should be?
    Surely you know!
6 What were the earth's foundations set on?
    Or who put its cornerstone in place?

7 Who did all this while the morning stars sang together?
   Who did this while the angels shouted with joy?

8 "Who shut the doors to keep the sea in
   when it broke through and was born?
9 This was when I made the clouds like a coat for the sea.
   And I wrapped the sea in dark clouds.
10 It was when I put limits on the sea.
   And I put its doors and bars in place.
11 It was when I said to the sea, 'You may come this far,
      but no farther.
   This is where your proud waves must stop.'

12 "Have you ever given orders for morning to begin?
   Or have you shown the dawn where its
      place was?

16 "Have you ever gone to where the sea begins?
   Or have you walked in the valleys under
      the sea?

34 "Can you shout an order to the clouds
   and cover yourself with a flood of water?
35 Can you send lightning bolts on their way?
   Do the flashes of lightning report to you and say, 'Here we are'?
36 Who put wisdom inside the mind?
   Or who put understanding in the heart?
37 Who has the wisdom to count the clouds?
   Who can pour water from the jars of heaven?
38 Who can do this when the dust becomes hard
   and the clumps of dirt stick together?"

40 The Lord said to Job:
2"Will the person who argues with God All-Powerful correct him?
   Let the person who accuses God answer him!"

3 Then Job answered the Lord:
4 "I am not worthy. I cannot answer you anything.
   I will put my hand over my mouth."

Prayer Starter: Thank you for the thunder and lightning and wind and storms—signs of your power, dear Lord.

Memory Verse: You must give your whole heart to him. You must hold out your hands to him for help.   —*Job 11:13*

Lord, Rise Up

L ord, why are you so far away?
    Why do you hide when there is trouble?
² Proudly the wicked chase down those who suffer.
    The wicked set traps to catch them.
³ They brag about the things they want.
    They bless the greedy but hate the Lord.
⁴ The wicked people are too proud.
They do not look for God.
There is no room for God in their thoughts.
⁵ They always succeed.
    They are far from keeping your laws.
    They make fun of their enemies.
⁶ They say to themselves, "Nothing bad will ever happen to me.
    I will never be ruined."
⁷ Their mouths are full of curses, lies and threats.

They use their tongues for sin and evil.
8 They hide near the villages.
    They look for innocent people to kill.
    They watch in secret for the helpless.
9 They wait in hiding like a lion.
    They wait to catch poor people.
    They catch the poor in nets.
10 The poor are thrown down and crushed.
    They are defeated because the others are stronger.
11 The wicked think,
    "God has forgotten us.
    He doesn't see what is happening."

12 Lord, rise up and punish the wicked.
    Don't forget those who need help.
13 Why do wicked people hate God?
    They say to themselves, "God won't punish us."
14 Lord, surely you see these cruel and evil things.
    Look at them and do something.
  People in trouble look to you for help.
    You are the one who helps the orphans.
15 Break the power of wicked men.
    Punish them for the evil they have done.

16 The Lord is King forever and ever.
    Remove from your land those nations that do not worship you.
17 Lord, you have heard what the poor people want.
    Do what they ask. Listen to them.
18 Protect the orphans. Put an end to suffering.
    Then they will no longer be afraid of evil people.

Prayer Starter: Lord, please do something to help those in need.

Memory Verse: The Lord is my shepherd. . . .   —*Psalm 23:1–2*

My Shepherd

T he Lord is my shepherd.
　　I have everything I need.
[2] He gives me rest in green pastures.
　　　He leads me to calm water.
[3] 　　He gives me new strength.
　　For the good of his name,
　　　he leads me on paths that are right.

[4] Even if I walk
　　　through a very dark valley,
　I will not be afraid
　　　because you are with me.
　Your rod and your walking stick[n] comfort me.

[5] You prepare a meal for me
　　　in front of my enemies.
　You pour oil on my head.[n]
　　　You give me more than I can hold.
[6] Surely your goodness and love will be with me
　　　all my life.
　And I will live in the house of the Lord forever.

[n]**walking stick** The stick a shepherd uses to guide and protect his sheep.
[n]**pour oil . . . head** This can mean that God gave him great wealth and blessed him.

Prayer Starter: Thank you for being my shepherd, O Lord. May your kindness and love always be with me.

Memory Verse: The Lord is my shepherd. I have everything I need. . . .
　　　　　　　　　　　　　　　　　　—Psalm 23:1–2

My Hiding
Place

Happy is the person whose sins are forgiven,
whose wrongs are pardoned.
2 Happy is the person
whom the Lord does not consider guilty.
In that person there is nothing false.

3 When I kept things to myself,
I felt weak deep inside me.
I moaned all day long.
4 Day and night
you punished me.
My strength was gone
as in the summer heat.   *Selah*
5 Then I confessed my sins to you.
I didn't hide my guilt.
I said, "I will confess my sins to the Lord."
And you forgave my guilt.   *Selah*

6 For this reason, all who obey you
should pray to you while they still can.

⁷ You are my hiding place.
    You protect me from my troubles.
    You fill me with songs of salvation.   *Selah*

⁸ The Lord says, "I will make you wise. I will show you where to go.
    I will guide you and watch over you.
⁹ So don't be like a horse or donkey.
    They don't understand.
They must be led with bits and reins,
    or they will not come near you."

¹⁰ Wicked people have many troubles.
    But the Lord's love surrounds those who trust him.
¹¹ Good people, rejoice and be happy in the Lord.
    All you whose hearts are right, sing.

Prayer Starter: Forgive my sins today, O Lord, and wipe them away. Please guide me and watch over me.

Memory Verse: The Lord is my shepherd. I have everything I need. He gives me rest . . .
    —Psalm 23:1–2

Thirsty for God

A deer thirsts for a stream of water.
    In the same way, I thirst for you, God.
² I thirst for the living God.
    When can I go to meet with him?
³ Day and night, my tears have been my food.
    People are always saying,
        "Where is your God?"

⁴ When I remember these things,
    I speak with a broken heart.
I used to walk with the crowd.
    I led the happy crowd to God's Temple,
    with songs of praise.

⁵ Why am I so sad?
    Why am I so upset?
I should put my hope in God.
    I should keep praising him,
    My Savior and ⁶my God.

⁷ Troubles have come again and again.
    They sound like waterfalls.
Your waves are crashing
    all around me.
⁸ The Lord shows his true love every day.
    At night I have a song,
    and I pray to my living God.
⁹ I say to God, my Rock,
    "Why have you forgotten me?
Why am I sad
    and troubled by my enemies?"
¹⁰ My enemies' insults make me feel
    as if my bones were broken.
They are always saying,
    "Where is your God?"

¹¹ Why am I so sad?
    Why am I so upset?
I should put my hope in God.
    I should keep praising him,
    my Savior and my God.

Prayer Starter: Make me thirsty for you, Lord, like a deer by streams of water.

Memory Verse: The Lord is my shepherd. I have everything I
need. He gives me rest in green pastures. . . .
        —*Psalm 23:1–2*

You Hear Our Prayers

God, you will be praised in Jerusalem.
We will keep our promises to you.
2   You hear our prayers.
All people will come to you.
3   Our guilt overwhelms us.
But you forgive our sins.
4   Happy are the people you choose.
You have them stay in your courtyards.
We are filled with good things in your house,
your holy Temple.

5   You answer us in amazing ways,
God our Savior.
People everywhere on the earth
and beyond the sea trust you.
6   You made the mountains by your strength.
You have great power.
7   You stopped the roaring seas,
the roaring waves and the uproar of the nations.
8   Even those people at the ends of the earth fear your miracles.
You are praised from where the sun rises to where it sets.

9   You take care of the land and water it.
You make it very fertile.
The rivers of God are full of water.
Grain grows because you make it grow.
10   You cause rain to fall on the plowed fields.
You soak them with water.
You soften the ground with rain.
And then you bless it.
11   You give the year a good harvest.
You load the wagons with many crops.
12   The desert is covered with grass.
The hills are covered with happiness.
13   The pastures are full of sheep.
The valleys are covered with grain.
Everything shouts and sings for joy.

Prayer Starter: I praise you, Father, for hearing and answering my prayers and meeting all my needs.

Memory Verse: The Lord is my shepherd. I have everything I need. He gives me rest in green pastures. He leads me to calm water.
—*Psalm 23:1–2*

The Lord Shows Mercy

M y whole being, praise the Lord.
   All my being, praise his holy name.
2 My whole being, praise the Lord.
      Do not forget all his kindnesses.
3 The Lord forgives me for all my sins.
      He heals all my diseases.
4 He saves my life from the grave.
   He loads me with love and mercy.
5 He satisfies me with good things.
   He makes me young again, like the eagle.

6 The Lord does what is right and fair
      for all who are wronged by others.
7 He showed his ways to Moses
      and his miracles to the people of Israel.
8 The Lord shows mercy and is kind.
      He does not become angry quickly, and he has great love.
9 He will not always scold us.
      He will not be angry forever.
10 He has not punished us as our sins should be punished.
      He has not repaid us for the evil we have done.
11 As high as the sky is above the earth,
      so great is his love for those who respect him.
12 He has taken our sins away from us
      as far as the east is from the west.
13 The Lord has mercy on those who fear him,
      as a father has mercy on his children.
14 He knows how we were made.
      He remembers that we are dust.

15 Human life is like grass.
      We grow like a flower in the field.
16 After the wind blows, the flower is gone.
      There is no sign of where it was.
17 But the Lord's love for those who fear him
      continues forever and ever.
      And his goodness continues to their grandchildren
18 and to those who keep his agreement
      and who remember to obey his orders.

Prayer Starter: With all my heart I praise you, Lord, and with my whole being I praise your holy name.

Memory Verse: My whole being . . .   *—Psalm 103:1*

Teach Me Your Rules

Happy are the people who live pure lives.
　　They follow the Lord's teachings.
2　Happy are the people who keep his rules.
　　They ask him for help with their whole heart.
3　They don't do what is wrong.
　　They follow his ways.
4　Lord, you gave your orders
　　to be followed completely.
5　I wish I were more loyal
　　in meeting your demands.
6　Then I would not be ashamed
　　when I think of your commands.
7　When I learned that your laws are fair,
　　I praised you with an honest heart.
8　I will meet your demands.
　　So please don't ever leave me.

9　How can a young person live a pure life?
　　He can do it by obeying your word.
10　With all my heart I try to obey you, God.
　　Don't let me break your commands.
11　I have taken your words to heart
　　so I would not sin against you.
12　Lord, you should be praised.
　　Teach me your demands.
13　My lips will tell about
　　all the laws you have spoken.
14　I enjoy living by your rules
　　as people enjoy great riches.
15　I think about your orders
　　and study your ways.
16　I enjoy obeying your demands.
　　And I will not forget your word.

17　Do good to me, your servant, so I can live,
　　so I can obey your word.
18　Open my eyes to see the wonderful things
　　in your teachings.

Prayer Starter: Lord, help me to treasure your words above all else, so that I will not sin against you.

Memory Verse: My whole being, praise the Lord. . . .　　—*Psalm 103:1*

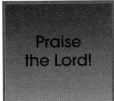

Praise the Lord!

Praise the Lord!

Praise the Lord from the heavens.
Praise him high above the earth.
2 Praise him, all you angels.
Praise him, all you armies of heaven.

3 Praise him, sun and moon.
Praise him, all you shining stars.
4 Praise him, highest heavens
and you waters above the sky.
5 Let them praise the Lord
because they were created by his command.
6 He set them in place forever and ever.
He made a law that will never end.

7 Praise the Lord from the earth.
Praise him, you large sea animals and all the oceans.

8 Praise him, lightning and hail, snow and clouds,
    and stormy winds that obey him.
9 Praise him, mountains and all hills,
    fruit trees and all cedar trees.
10 Praise him, you wild animals and all cattle,
    small crawling animals and birds.
11 Praise him, you kings of the earth and all nations,
    princes and all rulers of the earth.
12 Praise him, you young men and women,
    old people and children.

13 Praise the Lord.
    He alone is great.
    He is greater than heaven and earth.

Prayer Starter: Thank you, Lord, that the sun, moon, and stars display your majesty and power.

Memory Verse: My whole being, praise the Lord. All my being . . .
—*Psalm 103:1*

Rejoice in His Glory

Praise the Lord!

Sing a new song to the Lord.
Sing his praise in the meeting of his people.

² Let the Israelites be happy because of God,
their Maker.
Let the people of Jerusalem rejoice because of their King.
³ They should praise him with dancing.
They should praise him with tambourines and harps.
⁴ The Lord is pleased with his people.
He saves those who are not proud.
⁵ Let those who worship him rejoice in his glory.
Let them sing for joy even in bed!

⁶ Let them shout his praise
with their two-edged swords in their hands.
⁷ They will punish the nations.
They will defeat the people.
⁸ They will put those kings in chains
and those important men in iron bands.
⁹ They will punish them as God has written.
God is honored by all who worship him.

Praise the Lord!

150 Praise the Lord!

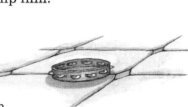

Praise God in his Temple.
Praise him in his mighty heaven.
² Praise him for his strength.
Praise him for his greatness.
³ Praise him with trumpet blasts.
Praise him with harps and lyres.
⁴ Praise him with tambourines and dancing.
Praise him with stringed instruments and flutes.
⁵ Praise him with loud cymbals.
Praise him with crashing cymbals.
⁶ Let everything that breathes praise the Lord.

Praise the Lord!

Prayer Starter: I rejoice in your glory, Lord, and I praise you for your strength and greatness.

Memory Verse: My whole being, praise the Lord. All my being, praise . . .
—*Psalm 103:1*

The Wise Words of Solomon

These are the wise words of Solomon son of David. Solomon was king of Israel.

² They teach wisdom and self-control.
    They give understanding.
³ They will teach you how to be wise and self-controlled.
    They will teach you what is honest and fair and right.
⁴ They give the ability to think to those with little knowledge.
    They give knowledge and good sense to the young.
⁵ Wise people should also listen to them and learn even more.
    Even smart people will find wise advice in these words.
⁶ Then they will be able to understand wise words and stories.
    They will understand the words of wise men and their riddles.

⁷ Knowledge begins with respect for the Lord.
    But foolish people hate wisdom and self-control.

⁸ My child, listen to your father's teaching.
    And do not forget your mother's advice.
⁹ Their teaching will beautify your life.
    It will be like flowers in your hair or a chain around your neck.
¹⁰ My child, sinners will try to lead you into sin.
    But do not follow them.
¹¹ They might say, "Come with us.

Let's ambush and kill someone.
Let's attack some harmless person just for fun.
¹² Let's swallow them alive, as death does.
Let's swallow them whole, as the grave does.
¹³ We will take all kinds of valuable things.
We will fill our houses with what we steal.
¹⁴ Come join us,
and we will share with you what we steal."
¹⁵ My child, do not go along with them.
Do not do what they do.
¹⁶ They run to do evil.
They are quick to kill.
¹⁷ It is useless to spread out a net
right where the birds can see it!
¹⁸ These men are setting their own trap.
They will only catch themselves!
¹⁹ All greedy people end up this way.
Greed takes away the life of the greedy person.

3 My child, do not forget my teaching.
Keep my commands in mind.
² Then you will live a long time.
And your life will be successful.

³ Don't ever stop being kind and truthful.
Let kindness and truth show in all you do.
Write them down in your mind as if on a tablet.
⁴ Then you will be respected
and pleasing to both God and men.

⁵ Trust the Lord with all your heart.
Don't depend on your own understanding.
⁶ Remember the Lord in everything you do.
And he will give you success.

⁷ Don't depend on your own wisdom.
Respect the Lord and refuse to do wrong.
⁸ Then your body will be healthy.
And your bones will be strong.

Prayer Starter: Cause us to respect and obey you, Lord, that we may be wise.

Memory Verse: My whole being, praise the Lord. All my being, praise his holy name.
—*Psalm 103:1*

T he Lord can control a king's mind
as easily as he controls a river.
He can direct it as he pleases.

² A person may believe he is doing right.
But the Lord judges his reasons.

³ Do what is right and fair.
That is more important to the Lord than animal sacrifices.

⁴ Proud looks, proud thoughts
and evil actions are sin.

⁵ Those who plan and work hard earn a profit.
But those who act too quickly become poor.

⁶ Wealth that comes from telling lies
vanishes like a mist and leads to death.

⁷ The violence of the wicked will destroy them
because they refuse to do what is right.

⁸ Guilty people live dishonest lives.
But honest people do what is right.

⁹ It is better to live in a corner on the roof[h]
than inside the house with a quarreling wife.

¹⁰ An evil person only wants to harm others.
　　His neighbor will get no mercy from him.

¹¹ Punish a person who makes fun of wisdom, and he will become wise.
　　But just teach a wise person, and he will get knowledge.

¹² God, who is always right, sees the house of the wicked.
　　And he brings about the ruin of every evil person.

¹³ If you ignore the poor when they cry for help,
　　you also will cry for help and not be answered.

¹⁴ A gift given secretly will calm an angry man.
　　A present given in secrecy will calm even great anger.

¹⁵ When things are done fairly, good people are happy,
　　but evil people are frightened.

¹⁶ A person who does not use understanding
　　will join the dead.

¹⁷ Whoever loves pleasure will become poor.
　　Whoever loves wine and rich food will never be wealthy.

¹⁸ Wicked people will suffer instead of good people.
　　And those who cannot be trusted will suffer
　　　　instead of those who can.

¹⁹ It is better to live alone in the desert
　　than with a quarreling and complaining wife.

²⁰ Wise people store up the best foods and olive oil.
　　But a foolish person eats up everything he has.

²¹ A person who tries to live right and be loyal
　　finds life, success and honor.

"**roof** In Bible times houses were built with flat roofs. The roof was used for drying things such as flax and fruit. And it was used as an extra room, as a place for worship and as a place to sleep in the summer.

Prayer Starter: Dear Lord, help me to seek wisdom from your word each day.

Memory Verse: Charm can fool you . . .　　　　　—*Proverbs 31:30*

Control Yourself

I f you sit down to eat with a ruler,
    notice the food that is in front of you.
² Control yourself
    if you have a big appetite.
³ Don't be greedy for his fine foods.
    He might use that rich food to trick you.

⁴ Don't wear yourself out trying to get rich.
    Be wise enough to
        control yourself.
⁵ Wealth can vanish in
    the wink of an eye.
It seems to grow
    wings
and fly away like
    an eagle in the
    sky.

⁶ Don't eat the food of a
    selfish person.
Don't be greedy for
    his fine foods.
⁷ A selfish person is
    always worrying
about how much the
    food costs.
He tells you, "Eat and
    drink."
But he doesn't really mean it.
⁸ So you will feel like throwing up the little bit you have eaten.
    And you will have wasted your kind words.

⁹ Don't speak to a foolish person.
    He will only ignore your wise words.

¹⁰ Don't move an old stone that shows where somebody's land is.
    And don't take fields that belong to orphans.
¹¹ God, their defender, is strong.
    He will take their side against you.

Prayer Starter: Lord, help me to learn to control myself in everything I do. May I bring honor to you.

Memory Verse: Charm can fool you, and beauty can trick you . . .
—Proverbs 31:30

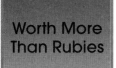

Worth More Than Rubies

I t is hard to find an excellent wife.
  She is worth more than rubies.
11 Her husband trusts her completely.
  With her, he has everything he needs.
12 She does him good and not harm
    for as long as she lives.
13 She looks for wool and linen.
  She likes to work with her hands.
14 She is like a trader's ship.
  She goes far to get food.
15 She gets up while it is still dark.
  She prepares food for her family.
  She also feeds her servant girls.
16 She looks at a field and buys it.
  With money she has earned, she plants a vineyard.
17 She does her work with energy.
  Her arms are strong.
18 She makes sure that what she makes is good.
  She works by her lamp late into the night.
19 She makes thread with her hands
  and weaves her own cloth.
20 She welcomes the poor.
  She helps the needy.
21 She does not worry about her family when it snows.
  They all have fine clothes to keep them warm.
22 She makes coverings for her bed.
  Her clothes are made of linen and other expensive material.
23 Her husband is recognized at the city meetings.
  He makes decisions as one of the leaders of the land.
24 She makes linen clothes and sells them.
  She provides belts to the merchants.
25 She is strong and is respected by the people.
  She looks forward to the future with joy.
26 She speaks wise words.
  And she teaches others to be kind.
27 She watches over her family.
  And she is always busy.
28 Her children bless her.
  Her husband also praises her.

Prayer Starter: Teach me, Lord, that loving you is more important than being beautiful.

Memory Verse: Charm can fool you, and beauty can trick you. But a woman who respects . . .
—*Proverbs 31:30*

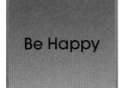

Be Happy

I saw the hard work God has given us to do. [11]God has also given us a desire to know the future. God certainly does everything at just the right time. But we can never completely understand what he is doing. [12]So I realize that the best thing for people is to be happy. They should enjoy themselves as long as they live. [13]God wants everyone to eat and drink and be happy in his work. These are gifts from God. [14]I know anything God does will continue forever. People cannot add anything to what God has done. And they cannot take anything away from it. God does it this way to cause people to honor him.

4 Two people are better than one.
They get more done by working together.
[10] If one person falls,
the other can help him up.
But it is bad for the person who is alone when he falls.
No one is there to help him.
[11] If two lie down together, they will be warm.
But a person alone will not be warm.
[12] An enemy might defeat one person,
but two people together can defend themselves.
A rope that has three parts wrapped together
is hard to break.

Prayer Starter: Thank you for being my best friend, dear Lord. Help me to be a good friend to others.

Memory Verse: Charm can fool you, and beauty can trick you. But a woman who respects the Lord . . .   *—Proverbs 31:30*

Solomon's Greatest Song

Solomon's Greatest Song.

The Woman Speaks to the Man She Loves

² Kiss me with the kisses of your mouth!
  Your love is better than wine.
³ The smell of your perfume is pleasant.
Your name is pleasant like expensive perfume!
That's why the young women love you.
⁴ Take me with you; let's run.
The king takes me into his rooms.

Friends Speak to the Man

We will rejoice and be happy with you.
  We praise your love more than wine.

The Woman Speaks

With good reason, the young women love you, my lover.
⁵ I'm dark but lovely,
    women of Jerusalem.
  I'm dark like the tents of Kedar,
  like the curtains of Solomon.
⁶ Don't look at how dark I am,
    at how dark the sun has made me.
  My brothers were angry with me.
    They made me tend the vineyards.
    So I haven't tended my own vineyard!
⁷ Tell me, you whom I love,
    where do you feed your sheep?
    Where do you make them rest at noon?
  Why should I look for you near your friend's sheep?
    Am I like a woman who wears a veil?ⁿ

The Man Speaks

¹⁵ My darling, you are beautiful!
     Oh, you are beautiful!
     Your eyes are like doves!

ⁿ**veil** This was the way a prostitute usually dressed.

Prayer Starter: Thank you for loving me, Lord, and for helping me to love others.

Memory Verse: Charm can fool you, and beauty can trick you. But a woman who respects the Lord should be praised.   —*Proverbs 31:30*

A Lily Among Thorns

The Woman Speaks Again

I am a rose in the Plain of Sharon.
I am a lily in the valleys.

The Man Speaks Again

2 Among the young women, my darling
is like a lily among thorns!

The Woman Answers

3 Among young men, my lover
is like an apple tree among the trees in the woods!
I enjoy siting in his shadow.
His fruit is sweet to my taste.

4 He brought me to the banquet room.
His banner over me is love.

5 Strengthen me with raisins.
Refresh me with apples,
because I am weak with love.

6 My lover's left hand is under my head.
And his right arm holds me tight!

The Woman Speaks to the Friends

7 Women of Jerusalem, promise me
by the gazelles and the deer.
Promise not to wake love.
Don't excite my feelings of love
until I'm ready.

The Woman Speaks Again

8 I hear my lover's voice.
He comes jumping across the mountains.
He comes skipping over the hills!

9 My lover is like a gazelle or a young deer.
Look, he stands behind our wall.
He stares in through the windows,
looking through the blinds.

10 My lover spoke. He said to me,
"Get up, my darling.
Let's go away, my beautiful one.

11 Look, the winter is past.
The rains are over and gone."

Prayer Starter: Lord, you are as beautiful to me as a rose from Sharon, as a lily from the valley. I love you.

Memory Verse: The Lord says, "Come, we will talk these things over. . . ."
—*Isaiah 1:18*

Isaiah's Message

This is the vision Isaiah son of Amoz saw. God showed Isaiah what would happen to Judah and Jerusalem. Isaiah saw these things while Uzziah, Jotham, Ahaz and Hezekiah were kings of Judah.

2 Heaven and earth, listen,
     because the Lord is speaking:
"I raised my children and helped them grow.
     But they have turned against me.
3 An ox knows its master.
     And a donkey knows where its owner feeds it.
But the people of Israel do not know me.
     My people do not understand."

4 Terrible times are coming for Israel, a nation of sin.
     The people are loaded down with guilt.
They are like a group of children doing evil.
     They are full of evil.
They have left the Lord.
     They hate God, the Holy One of Israel.
     They have turned away from him.

5 Why should you continue to be punished?
     Why do you continue to turn against him?
Your whole head is hurt.
     And your whole heart is sick.
6 There is no healthy spot
     from the bottom of your foot to the top of your head.
     You are covered with wounds, hurts and open sores.
Your wounds are not cleaned and covered.
     No medicine takes away the pain.

7 Your land is ruined.
     Your cities have been burned with fire.
While you watch,
     your enemies are stealing everything from your land.
     Your land is ruined like a country destroyed by enemies.
8 Jerusalem is left alone
     like an empty shelter in a vineyard.
It is like a hut left in a field of melons.
     It is like a city surrounded by enemies.
9 The Lord of heaven's armies
     allowed a few of our people to live.
     Otherwise we would have been completely destroyed
     like the cities of Sodom and Gomorrah.

¹⁰ Jerusalem, your rulers are like those of Sodom.
     Your people are like those of Gomorrah.
Hear the word of the Lord.
     Listen to the teachings of our God!

¹¹ The Lord says,
     "I do not want all these sacrifices you give me.
I have had enough of your sacrifices
     of male sheep and fat from fine animals.
I am not pleased
     by the blood of bulls, sheep and goats.

¹⁵ You will raise your arms in prayer to me.
     But I will refuse to look at you.
Even if you say many prayers,
     I will not listen to you.
It's because your hands are full of blood.

¹⁶ Wash yourselves and make yourselves clean.
     Stop doing the evil things I see you do.
Stop doing wrong!

¹⁷   Learn to do good.
Be fair to other people.
     Punish those who hurt others.
Help the orphans.
     Stand up for the rights of widows."

¹⁸ The Lord says,
     "Come, we will talk these things over.
Your sins are red like deep red cloth.
     But they can be as white as snow.
Your sins are bright red.
     But you can be white like wool."

Prayer Starter: Heavenly Father, thank you for Jesus who died on the cross that my sins could become whiter than snow.

Memory Verse: The Lord says, "Come, we will talk these things over. Your sins are red like deep red cloth. . . ."   *—Isaiah 1:18*

Holy,
Holy, Holy

In the year that King Uzziah died, I saw the Lord. He was sitting on a very high throne. His long robe filled the Temple. ²Burning heavenly creatures stood above him. Each creature had six wings. They used two wings to cover their faces. They used two wings to cover their feet. And they used two wings for flying. ³Each creature was calling to the others:

"Holy, holy, holy is the Lord of heaven's armies.
　　His glory fills the whole earth."

⁴Their voices cause the frame around the door to shake. The Temple filled with smoke.

⁵I said, "Oh, no! I will be destroyed. I am not pure. And I live among people who are not pure. But I have seen the King, the Lord of heaven's armies."

⁶On the altar there was a fire. One of the burning heavenly creatures used a pair of tongs to take a hot coal from the fire. Then he flew to me with the hot coal in his hand. ⁷The creature touched my mouth with the hot coal. Then he said, "Look. Your guilt is taken away because this hot coal has touched your lips. Your sin is taken away."

⁸Then I heard the Lord's voice. He said, "Whom can I send? Who will go for us?"

So I said, "Here I am. Send me!"

⁹Then the Lord said, "Go and tell this to the people:
　　'You will listen and listen, but you will not understand.
　　　　You will look and look, but you will not learn.'
¹⁰　Make these people stubborn.
　　　　Make them not able to understand what they hear and see.
　　Otherwise, they might really understand
　　　　what they see with their eyes
　　　　and hear with their ears.
　　They might really understand in their minds.
　　　　If they did this, they would come back to me and be forgiven."

¹¹Then I asked, "Lord, how long should I do this?"
He answered,
　　"Do this until the cities are destroyed
　　　　and the people are gone.
　　Do this until there are no people left living in the houses.
　　　　Do this until the land is destroyed and left empty.
¹²　I will send the people far away.
　　　　And the land will be left empty.
¹³　One-tenth of the people will be left in the land.
　　　　But the land will be destroyed again.
　　These people will be like an oak tree.
　　　　When the tree is chopped down, a stump is left.

The people who remain will be like a stump
that will sprout again."

Prayer Starter: You are holy, O Lord, and the whole earth is filled with your glory!

Memory Verse: The Lord says, "Come, we will talk these things over. Your sins are red like deep red cloth. But they can be as white as snow. . . ."

—*Isaiah 1:18*

A Child Will Be Born

But suddenly there will be no more gloom for the land that suffered. In the past God made the lands of Zebulun and Naphtali hang their heads in shame. But in the future that land will be made great. That land stretches from the way along the Mediterranean Sea to the land along the Jordan River. And it goes north to Galilee where the people who are not Israelites live.

2 Now those people live in darkness.
    But they will see a great light.
They live in a place that is very dark.
    But a light will shine on them.
3 God, you will cause the nation to grow.
    You will make the people happy.
And they will show their happiness to you.
    It will be like the joy during harvest time.
It will be like the joy of people
    taking what they have won in war.
4 Like the time you defeated Midian,
    you will take away their heavy load.
You will take away the heavy pole from their backs.
    You will take away the rod the enemy uses to punish your people.
5 Every boot that marched in battle will be destroyed.
    Every uniform stained with blood will be destroyed.
    They will be thrown into the fire.
6 A child will be born to us.
    God will give a son to us.
    He will be responsible for leading the people.
His name will be Wonderful Counselor, Powerful God,
    Father Who Lives Forever, Prince of Peace.
7 Power and peace will be in his kingdom.
    It will continue to grow.
He will rule as king on David's throne
    and over David's kingdom.
He will make it strong,
    by ruling with goodness and fair judgment.
    He will rule it forever and ever.
The Lord of heaven's armies will do this
    because of his strong love for his people.

Prayer Starter: Dear heavenly Father, thank you for sending us your Son, Jesus.

Memory Verse: The Lord says, "Come, we will talk these things over. Your sins are red like deep red cloth. But they can be as white as snow. Your sins are bright red. . . ."
    —*Isaiah 1:18*

A New King from Jesse's Family

A branch will grow
   from a stump of a tree that was cut down.

So a new king will come
   from the family of Jesse.[n]

2 The Spirit of the Lord will rest upon that king.
   The Spirit gives him wisdom, understanding,
     guidance and power.
And the Spirit teaches him to know and respect the Lord.

3 This king will be glad to obey the Lord.
He will not judge by the way things look.
   He will not judge by what people say.

4 He will judge the poor honestly.
   He will be fair in his decisions for the poor people of the land.
At his command evil people will be punished.
   By his words the wicked will be put to death.

5 Goodness and fairness will give him strength.
   They will be like a belt around his waist.

6 Then wolves will live in peace with lambs.
   And leopards will lie down to rest with goats.
Calves, lions and young bulls will eat together.
   And a little child will lead them.

7 Cows and bears will eat together in peace.
   Their young will lie down together.
   Lions will eat hay as oxen do.

8 A baby will be able to play near a cobra's hole.
   A child will be able to put his hand into the nest
     of a poisonous snake.

9 They will not hurt or destroy each other
   on all my holy mountain.
The earth will be full of the knowledge of the Lord,
   as the sea is full of water.

10 At that time the new king from the family of Jesse will stand as a banner for the people. The nations will come together around him. And the place where he lives will be filled with glory.

[n]**Jesse** King David's father.

Prayer Starter: Thank you, Lord, for giving us wisdom, understanding, guidance, and power. Keep me reading your Word.

Memory Verse: The Lord says, "Come, we will talk these things over. Your sins are red like deep red cloth. But they can be as white as snow. Your sins are bright red. But you can be white like wool." —*Isaiah 1:18*

The Fallen Star

Ｋing of Babylon, morning star, you have fallen
from heaven
even though you were as bright
as the rising sun!
In the past all the nations on earth bowed down
before you.
But now you have been cut down.

¹³ You told yourself,
"I will go up to heaven.
I will put my throne
above God's stars.
I will sit on the mountain of the gods.
I will sit on the slopes of the sacred mountain.
¹⁴ I will go up above the tops of the clouds.
I will be like God Most High."
¹⁵ But you were brought down to the grave.
You were brought down to the deep places where the dead are.

¹⁶ Those who see you stare at you.
They think about what has happened to you.
They say, "Is this the same man who caused great fear on earth?
Is he the one who shook the kingdoms?
¹⁷ Is this the man who turned the land into a desert?
Is he the one who destroyed its cities?
Is he the one who captured people in war
and would not let them go home?"

¹⁸ Every king of the earth has been buried with honor.
Every king has his own grave.
¹⁹ But you are thrown out of your grave,
like an unwanted branch is cut from a tree and thrown away.
You are covered by bodies that died in battle.
You have been thrown into a rocky pit.
And other soldiers walk on you.
²⁰ You will not be buried like other people.
This is because you ruined your own country.
And you killed your own people.
So your children will never
be mentioned again.

Prayer Starter: O Lord our God, you have planned the future, and we are trusting you to keep your promises.

Memory Verse: The Lord of heaven's armies has made this promise . . .
—*Isaiah 14:24*

Egypt Punished

The message about Egypt:
Look, the Lord is coming on a fast cloud.
He will enter Egypt.
And the idols of Egypt will tremble before him.
Egypt's courage will melt away.

2 The Lord says, "I will cause the Egyptians
to fight against themselves.
Men will fight with their brothers.
Neighbors will fight neighbors.
Cities will fight cities.
Kingdoms will fight kingdoms.
3 The Egyptians will be afraid.
I will ruin their plans.
They will ask their idols and spirits of the dead
what they should do.
They will ask their mediums and fortune-tellers."
4 The Master, the Lord of heaven's armies, says,
"I will give Egypt to a hard
master.
A powerful king will rule
over them."

5 The sea will become dry.
The water will disappear
from the Nile River.
6 The canals will stink.
The streams of Egypt will decrease and dry up.
All the water plants will rot.
7 All the plants along the banks of the Nile will die.
Even the planted fields by the Nile
will dry up, blow away and disappear.
8 The fishermen, all those who catch fish from the Nile,
will groan and cry.
Those who depend on the Nile for food will be sad.
9 All the people who make cloth from flax will be sad.
Those who weave linen will lose hope.
10 Those who weave cloth will be broken.
All those who work for money will be sad.

Prayer Starter: Lord, all your plans for me are perfect. Help me to trust you.

Memory Verse: The Lord of heaven's armies has made this promise:
"These things will happen . . ."   —*Isaiah 14:24*

> The King
> in His
> Beauty

A person might do what is right.
> He might speak what is right.
He might refuse to take money unfairly.
> He might refuse to take money to hurt others.
He might not listen to plans of murder.
> He might refuse to think about evil.
¹⁶ This is the kind of person who will be safe.
> He will be protected as he would be in a high,
> walled city.

He will always have bread,
> and he will not run out of water.
¹⁷ Your eyes will see the king in his beauty.
> You will see the land that stretches far away.
¹⁸ You will think about the terror of the past.
> You will think, "Where is that officer?
> Where is the one who collected the taxes?
> Where is the officer in charge of our defense towers?"
¹⁹ You will not see those proud people from other countries anymore.
> No more will you hear their strange language
> that you couldn't understand.

²⁰ Look at Jerusalem, the city of our festivals.
> Look at Jerusalem, that beautiful place of
> rest.
It is like a tent that will never be moved.
> The pegs that hold her in place
> will never be moved.
Her ropes will never be broken.
²¹ There the Lord will be our Mighty One.
> That land is a place with streams
> and wide rivers.
But there will be no enemy boats on those rivers.
No powerful ship will sail on those rivers.
²² This is because the Lord is our judge.
> The Lord makes our laws.
The Lord is our king.
> He will save us.
²³ You sailors from other lands, hear:

Prayer Starter: Thank you, Lord, for the wonderful future you've promised those who love you.

Memory Verse: The Lord of heaven's armies has made this promise: "These things will happen exactly as I planned them. . . ." —*Isaiah 14:24*

The ropes on your boats hang loose.
The mast is not held firm.
The sails are not spread open.
The Lord will give us your wealth.
There will be so much wealth even the crippled people
will carry off a share.
²⁴ No one living in Jerusalem will say, "I am sick."
The people who live there will have their sins forgiven.

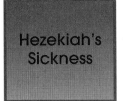

Hezekiah's Sickness

At that time Hezekiah became very sick. He was almost dead. The prophet Isaiah son of Amoz went to see him. Isaiah told him, "This is what the Lord says: You are going to die. So you should give your last orders to everyone. You will not get well."

2Hezekiah turned toward the wall and prayed to the Lord. 3He said, "Lord, please remember that I have always obeyed you. I have given myself completely to you. I have done what you said was right." And Hezekiah cried loudly.

4Then the Lord spoke his word to Isaiah: 5"Go to Hezekiah and tell him: 'This is what the Lord, the God of your ancestor David, says: I have heard your prayer. And I have seen your tears. I will add 15 years to your life. 6I will save you and this city from the king Assyria. I will defend this city.' "

21nThen Isaiah said, "Make a paste from figs. Put it on Hezekiah's boil. Then he will get well."

22Hezekiah asked Isaiah, "What will be the sign? What will show that I will go up to the Temple of the Lord?"

7Isaiah said, "The Lord will do what he says. This is the sign from the Lord to show you: 8The sun has made a shadow go down the stairway of Ahaz. I will make it go back ten steps." So the shadow made by the sun went back up the ten steps it had gone down.

9After Hezekiah king of Judah got well, he wrote this song:

10 I said, "I am in the middle of my life.
       Do I have to go through the gates where the dead are now?
       Will I have the rest of my life taken away from me?"

11 I said, "I will not see the Lord
       in the land of the living again.
    I will not again see the people
       who live on the earth.

12 Like a shepherd's tent,
       my home has been pulled down and taken from me.

I am finished like the cloth
   a weaver rolls up and cuts from the loom.
   In one day you brought me to this end.
¹³ All night I cried loudly.
   Like a lion, he crushed all my bones.
   In one day you brought me to this end.
¹⁴ I cried like a bird.
   I moaned like a dove.
My eyes became tired as I looked to the heavens.
   Lord, I have troubles. Please help me."

¹⁵ What can I say?
   The Lord told me what would happen and then made it happen.
I have had these troubles in my soul.
   So now I will be humble all my life.
¹⁶ Lord, because of you, men live.
   Because of you, my spirit also lives.
You made me well and let me live.
¹⁷ It was for my own good
   that I had such troubles.
Because you love me very much,
   you did not let me die.
You threw my sins
   far away.
¹⁸ People in the place where the dead are cannot praise you.
   Those who have died cannot sing praises to you.
Those who die don't trust you to help them.
¹⁹ The people who are alive are the ones who praise you.
   They praise you as I praise you today.
A father should tell his children
   that you provide help.

²⁰ The Lord saved me.
   So we will sing and play songs.
We will make music in the Temple of the Lord
   all the days of our lives.

"**Verses 21-22** These verses are generally found at the end of chapter 38. But the same story in
2 Kings 20:6-9 shows the events happened in this order.

Prayer Starter: May I praise you, heavenly Father, every day that I live.

Memory Verse: The Lord of heaven's armies has made this promise:
"These things will happen exactly as I planned them. These things will
happen . . ."
                                                        —*Isaiah 14:24*

False Gods

Some people make idols, but they
        are worth nothing
    People love them, but they are useless.
Those people are witnesses for the statues. But
        those people cannot see.
    They know nothing. They don't know enough
        to be ashamed.

10 Who made these false gods?
        Who made these useless idols?
11 The workmen who made those gods will be ashamed!
        Those workmen are only human.
    If they all would come together,
        they would all be ashamed and afraid.

14 A man cuts down cedar
        or gets cypress or oak trees.
    Those trees grew by their own power in the forest.
        Or he plants a pine tree, and the rain makes it grow.
15 Then he burns the tree.
        He uses some of the wood for a fire to keep himself warm.
        He also starts a fire to bake his bread.
    But he uses part of the wood to make a god. Then he worships it!
        He makes the idol and bows down to it!
16 The man burns half of the wood in the fire.
        He uses the fire to cook his meat.
        And he eats the meat until he is full.
    He burns the wood to keep himself warm. He says,
        "Good! Now I am warm. I can see because of the fire's light."
17 But the man makes a statue from the wood that is left. He calls it
            his god.
        He bows down to it and worships it.
    He prays to it and says,
        "You are my god. Save me!"
18 Those people don't know what they are doing.
            They don't understand!
        It is as if their eyes are covered so they can't see.
        Their minds don't understand.

Prayer Starter: You are the Lord my God. May nothing in my life be more important to me than you are.

Memory Verse: The Lord of heaven's armies has made this promise: "These things will happen exactly as I planned them. These things will happen exactly as I set them up."   —*Isaiah 14:24*

God Chooses Jeremiah

These are the words of Jeremiah son of Hilkiah. He belonged to the family of priests who lived in the town of Anathoth. That town is in the land that belongs to the tribe of Benjamin. ²The Lord spoke his word to Jeremiah. This happened during the thirteenth year that Josiah son of Amon was king of Judah. ³The Lord also spoke to Jeremiah while Jehoiakim son of Josiah was king of Judah. And the Lord spoke to Jeremiah during the 11 years and 5 months Zedekiah son of Josiah was king of Judah. After that, the people who lived in Jerusalem were taken away as captives out of their country.

⁴　The Lord spoke these words to me:
⁵　"Before I made you in your mother's womb, I chose you.
　　Before you were born, I set you apart for a special work.
　　I appointed you as a prophet to the nations."

⁶Then I said, "But Lord God, I don't know how to speak. I am only a boy."
⁷But the Lord said to me, "Don't say, 'I am only a boy.' You must go everywhere that I send you. You must say everything I tell you to say. ⁸Don't be afraid of anyone, because I am with you. I will protect you," says the Lord.
⁹Then the Lord reached out with his hand and touched my mouth. He said to me, "See, I am putting my words in your mouth. ¹⁰Today I have put you in charge of nations and kingdoms. You will pull up and tear down, destroy and overthrow. You will build up and plant."
¹¹The Lord spoke this word to me: "Jeremiah, what do you see?"
I answered the Lord and said, "I see a stick of almond wood."
¹²The Lord said to me, "You have seen correctly! And I am watching to make sure my words come true."
¹³The Lord spoke his word to me again: "Jeremiah, what do you see?"
I answered the Lord and said, "I see a pot of boiling water. It is tipping over from the north!"
¹⁴The Lord said to me, "Disaster will come from the north. It will happen to all the people who live in this country. ¹⁵In a short time I will call all of the people in the northern kingdoms," said the Lord.
　　"Those kings will come and set up their thrones
　　　　near the entrance of the gates of Jerusalem.
　　They will attack the city walls around Jerusalem.
　　　　They will attack all the cities in Judah."

Prayer Starter: You always watch to make sure your words come true, Lord. Help me to trust every one of them.

Memory Verse: God made the earth by his power. . . . —*Jeremiah 10:12*

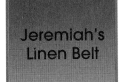

Jeremiah's Linen Belt

This is what the Lord said to me: "Go and buy a linen belt. Then put it around your waist. Don't let the belt get wet."

²So I bought a linen belt, just as the Lord told me. And I put it around my waist. ³Then the Lord spoke his word to me a second time: ⁴"Take the belt you bought and are wearing. Go to Perath. Hide the belt there in a crack in the rocks." ⁵So I went to Perath and hid the belt there, just as the Lord told me.

⁶Many days later the Lord said to me, "Now go to Perath. Get the belt that I told you to hide there." ⁷So I went to Perath and dug up the belt. I took it from where I had hidden it. But now it was ruined. It was good for nothing.

⁸Then the Lord spoke his word to me. ⁹This is what the Lord said: "In the same way I will ruin the pride of the people of Judah and the great pride of Jerusalem. ¹⁰These evil people refuse to listen to my warnings. They stubbornly do only what they want to do. They follow other gods to serve and worship them. So they will become like this linen belt. They will be good for nothing. ¹¹A belt is wrapped tightly around a man's waist. In the same way I wrapped the families of Israel and Judah around me," says the Lord. "I did that so they would be my people. Then they would bring fame, praise and honor to me. But my people would not listen to me."

15 Listen and pay attention.
    Don't be too proud.
    The Lord has spoken to you.
16 Honor the Lord your God.
    Give him glory before he brings darkness.
Praise him before you fall
    on the dark hills.
You hope for light.
    But the Lord will turn it into thick darkness.
    He will change it into deep gloom.

Prayer Starter: Lord, may I honor you in all I do—in my school work, in my chores, and in my play.

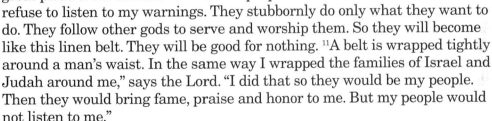

Memory Verse: God made the earth by his power. He used his wisdom . . .
    —*Jeremiah 10:12*

The Prophet's Scroll

The Lord spoke his word to Jeremiah. This was during the fourth year that Jehoiakim son of Josiah was king of Judah. This was his message: ²"Jeremiah, get a scroll. Write on it all the words I have spoken to you about Israel and Judah and all the nations. Write everything I have spoken to you since Josiah was king until now. ³Maybe the family of Judah will hear what disasters I am planning to bring on them. And maybe they will stop doing wicked things. Then I would forgive them for the sins and the evil things they have done."

⁴So Jeremiah called for Baruch son of Neriah. Jeremiah spoke the messages the Lord had given him. And Baruch wrote those messages on the scroll. ⁵Then Jeremiah said to Baruch, "I cannot go to the Temple of the Lord. I must stay here. ⁶So I want you to go to the Temple of the Lord. Go there on a day when the people are giving up eating. Read to all the people of Judah from the scroll. These people come into Jerusalem from the towns where they live. Read the messages from the Lord. Read the words that you wrote on the scroll as I spoke them to you. ⁷Perhaps they will ask the Lord to help them. Perhaps each one will stop doing wicked things. The Lord has announced that he is very angry with them." ⁸So Baruch son of Neriah did everything Jeremiah the prophet told him to do. He read aloud the scroll that had the Lord's messages written on it. He read it in the Lord's Temple.

⁹It was the ninth month of the fifth year that Jehoiakim son of Josiah was king. A special time to give up eating was announced. All the people of Jerusalem were supposed to give up eating to honor the Lord. And everyone who had come into Jerusalem from the towns of Judah was supposed to give up eating. ¹⁰At that time Baruch read the scroll that contained Jeremiah's words. Baruch read the scroll in the Temple of the Lord to all the people there. He was in the room of Gemariah son of Shaphan. Gemariah was a royal assistant. That room was in the upper courtyard at the entrance of the New Gate of the Temple.

¹⁴Then the officers sent a man named Jehudi son of Nethaniah to Baruch. (Nethaniah was the son of Shelemiah, who was the son of Cushi.) Jehudi said to Baruch, "Bring the scroll that you read to the people and come with me."

So Baruch son of Neriah took the scroll and went with Jehudi to the officers. ¹⁵Then the officers said to Baruch, "Sit down and read the scroll to us."

So Baruch read the scroll to them. ¹⁶When the officers heard all the words, they became afraid. And they looked at one another. They said to Baruch, "We must certainly tell the king about these words." ¹⁷Then the officers asked Baruch, "Tell us, Baruch, where did you get these words you wrote on the scroll? Did you write down what Jeremiah said to you?"

¹⁸"Yes," Baruch answered. "Jeremiah spoke, and I wrote down all the words with ink on this scroll."

¹⁹Then the officers said to Baruch, "You and Jeremiah must go and hide. Don't tell anyone where you are hiding."

²⁰Then the officers put the scroll in the room of Elishama the royal assistant. Then they went to the king in the courtyard and told him all about the scroll. ²¹So King Jehoiakim sent Jehudi to get the scroll. Jehudi brought the scroll from the room of Elishama the royal assistant. Then Jehudi read the scroll to the king. And he read it to all the officers who stood around the king. ²²This happened in the ninth month of the year. So King Jehoiakim was sitting in the winter apartment. There was a fire burning in a small firepot in front of him. ²³Jehudi began to read from the scroll. But after he had read three or four columns, the king cut those columns off of the scroll with a pen knife. And he threw them into the firepot. Finally, the whole scroll was burned in the fire. ²⁴King Jehoiakim and his servants heard the message from the scroll. But they were not frightened! They did not tear their clothes to show their sorrow. ²⁵Elnathan, Delaiah and Gemariah tried to talk King Jehoiakim into not burning the scroll. But the king would not listen to them.

Prayer Starter: Help me to always respect your Word, dear Lord. May I read it each day and obey it.

Memory Verse: God made the earth by his power. He used his wisdom to build the world. . . .
                                                              —Jeremiah 10:12

Jeremiah Rescued

Some of the officers heard what Jeremiah was prophesying. They were Shephaiah son of Mattan, Gedaliah son of Pashhur, Jehucal son of Shelemiah and Pashhur son of Malkijah. Jeremiah was telling all the people this message: ²"This is what the Lord says: 'Everyone who stays in Jerusalem will die in war. Or he will die of hunger or terrible diseases. But everyone who surrenders to the Babylonian army will live. They will escape with their lives and live.' ³And this is what the Lord says: 'This city of Jerusalem will surely be handed over to the army of the king of Babylon. He will capture this city!' "

⁴Then the officers said to the king, "Jeremiah must be put to death! He is making the soldiers who are still in the city become discouraged. He is discouraging everyone by the things he is saying. He does not want good to happen to us. He wants to ruin the people of Jerusalem."

⁵King Zedekiah said to them, "Jeremiah is in your control. I cannot do anything to stop you!"

⁶So the officers took Jeremiah and put him into the well of Malkijah, the king's son. That well was in the courtyard of the guards. The officers used ropes to lower Jeremiah into the well. It did not have any water in it, only mud. And Jeremiah sank down into the mud.

⁷But Ebed-Melech heard that the officers had put Jeremiah into the well. Ebed-Melech was a Cushite, and he was a eunuch in the palace. King Zedekiah was sitting at the Benjamin Gate. ⁸So Ebed-Melech left the palace and went to the king. Ebed-Melech said, ⁹"My master and king, the rulers have acted in an evil way. They have treated Jeremiah the prophet badly! They have thrown him into a well! They have left him there to die! When there is no more bread in the city, he will starve."

¹⁰Then King Zedekiah commanded Ebed-Melech the Cushite: "Ebed-Melech, take 30 men from the palace with you. Go and lift Jeremiah the prophet out of the well before he dies."

¹¹So Ebed-Melech took the men with him. And he went to a room under the storeroom in the palace. He took some old rags and worn-out clothes from that room. Then he let those rags down with some ropes to Jeremiah in the well. ¹²Ebed-Melech the Cushite said to Jeremiah, "Put these old rags and worn-out clothes under your arms. They will be pads for the ropes." So Jeremiah did as Ebed-Melech said. ¹³The men pulled Jeremiah up with the ropes and lifted him out of the well. And Jeremiah stayed under guard in the courtyard.

Prayer Starter: Protect your people all over the world, dear Lord. Keep us safe from those who would like to hurt us because of our faith in you.

Memory Verse: God made the earth by his power. He used his wisdom to build the world. He used his understanding . . .   —*Jeremiah 10:12*

Jerusalem Captured

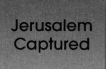

Zedekiah was 21 years old when he became king. And he was king in Jerusalem for 11 years. His mother's name was Hamutal daughter of Jeremiah." She was from Libnah. ²Zedekiah did what the Lord said was wrong, just as Jehoiakim had done. ³All this happened in Jerusalem and Judah because the Lord was angry with them. Finally, he threw them out of his presence. Zedekiah turned against the king of Babylon.

⁴Then Nebuchadnezzar king of Babylon marched against Jerusalem with his whole army. They made a camp around the city. Then they built devices all around the city walls to attack it. This happened during Zedekiah's ninth year, tenth month and tenth day as king. ⁵The city was under attack until Zedekiah's eleventh year as king.

⁶By the ninth day of the fourth month, the hunger was terrible in the city. There was no food for the people to eat. ⁷Then the city wall was broken through. And the whole army ran away at night. They went through the gate between the two walls for the king's garden. The Babylonians were still surrounding the city. Zedekiah and his men ran toward the Jordan Valley.

⁸But the Babylonian army chased King Zedekiah. They caught up with him in the plains of Jericho. All of his army was scattered from him. ⁹So they captured Zedekiah and took him to the king of Babylon at Riblah. Riblah is in the land of Hamath. There he passed sentence on Zedekiah. ¹⁰There at Riblah the king of Babylon killed Zedekiah's sons as he watched. The king also killed all the officers of Judah. ¹¹Then he put out Zedekiah's eyes. He put bronze chains on him and took him to Babylon. And the king kept Zedekiah in prison there until the day he died.

¹²Nebuzaradan was the commander of the king's special guards. This servant of the king of Babylon came to Jerusalem. This was on the tenth day of the fifth month. This was in Nebuchadnezzar's nineteenth year as king of Babylon. ¹³Nebuzaradan set fire to the Temple of the Lord and the

palace. He also set fire to all the houses of Jerusalem. Every important building was burned. [14]The whole Babylonian army broke down the walls around Jerusalem. That army was led by the commander of the king's special guards. [15]Nebuzaradan, the commander of the guards, took captive some of the poorest people. And he took those who were left in Jerusalem. He took captive those who had surrendered to the king of Babylon. And he took away the skilled craftsmen who were left in Jerusalem. [16]But Nebuzaradan left behind the rest of the poorest people of the land. They were to take care of the vineyards and fields.

[n]**Jeremiah** This is not the prophet Jeremiah but a different man with the same name.

Prayer Starter: It is so important to obey your commands, dear Lord. Help me and my friends to serve you.

Memory Verse: God made the earth by his power. He used his wisdom to build the world. He used his understanding to stretch out the skies.
—*Jeremiah 10:12*

Ezekiel Eats a Scroll

The Lord said to me [Ezekiel], "Human being, eat what you find. Eat this scroll. Then go and speak to the people of Israel." [2]So I opened my mouth, and the Lord gave me the scroll.

[3]The Lord said to me, "Human being, eat this scroll which I am giving you. Fill your stomach with it." Then I ate it. And it was sweet like honey in my mouth.

[4]Then the Lord said to me, "Human being, go to the people of Israel. Speak my words to them. [5]You are not being sent to people whose speech you can't understand. Their language is not difficult. You are being sent to Israel. [6]You are not being sent to many nations whose speech you can't understand. The language of Israel is not difficult. You are not being sent to people whose words you cannot understand. If I had sent you to them, they would have listened to you. [7]But the people of Israel are not willing to listen to you. This is because they are not willing to listen to me. Yes, all the people of Israel are stubborn and will not obey. [8]See, I have made you as stubborn as they are. You will be as hard as they are. [9]I have made you as hard as a diamond, harder than stone. Don't be afraid of them. Don't be frightened by them. They are a people who turn against me."

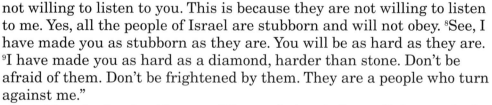

[10]Also, the Lord said to me, "Human being, believe all the words that I will speak to you. And listen carefully. [11]Go to the captives, your people. And speak to them, whether they listen or not. Tell them, 'The Lord God says this.' "

[12]Then the Spirit lifted me up. And I heard a loud rumbling sound behind me. A voice said, "Praise God in heaven." [13]I heard the wings of the living creatures touching each other. And I heard the sound of the wheels by them. It was a loud rumbling sound. [14]So the spirit lifted me up and took me away. I was unhappy and angry. I felt the great power of the Lord.

Prayer Starter: Help me to tell others about you, dear Lord. May I never be ashamed of Jesus.

Memory Verse: Daniel said . . .   *—Daniel 2:20*

Dry Bones

I felt the power of the Lord was on me. He brought me out by the Spirit of the Lord. And he put me down in the middle of a valley. It was full of bones. ²The Lord led me around among the bones. There were many bones on the bottom of the valley. I saw the bones were very dry. ³Then he asked me, "Human being, can these bones live?"

I answered, "Lord God, only you know."

⁴The Lord said to me, "Prophesy to these bones. Say to them, 'Dry bones, hear the word of the Lord. ⁵This is what the Lord God says to the bones: I will cause breath to enter you. Then you will live. ⁶I will put muscles on you. I will put flesh on you. I will cover you with skin. Then I will put breath in you, and you will live. Then you will know that I am the Lord.'"

⁷So I prophesied as I was commanded. While I prophesied, there was a noise and a rattling. The bones came together, bone to bone. ⁸I looked and saw muscles come on the bones. Flesh grew, and skin covered the bones. But there was no breath in them.

⁹Then the Lord said to me, "Prophesy to the wind." Prophesy, human being, and say to the wind: 'This is what the Lord God says: Wind, come from the four winds. Breathe on these people who were killed so they can live again.'" ¹⁰So I prophesied as the Lord commanded me. And the breath came into them, and they came to life. They stood on their feet. They were a very large army.

¹¹Then the Lord said to me: "Human being, these bones are like all the people of Israel. They say, 'Our bones are dried up, and our hope has gone. We are destroyed.' ¹²So, prophesy, and say to them: 'This is what the Lord God says: My people, I will open your graves. And I will cause you to come up out of your graves. Then I will bring you into the land of Israel. ¹³This is how you, my people, will know that I am the Lord. I will open your graves and cause you to come up from them. ¹⁴And I will put my Spirit inside you. You will come to life. Then I will put you in your own land. And you will know that I, the Lord, have spoken and done it, says the Lord.'"

¹⁵The Lord spoke his word to me. He said, ¹⁶"Human being, take a stick of wood. Write on it, 'For Judah and all the Israelites with him.' Then take another stick of wood. Write on it, 'The stick of Ephraim, for Joseph and all the Israelites with him.' ¹⁷Then join them together into one stick. Then they will be one in your hand.

¹⁸"Your people will say to you, 'Explain to us what you mean by this.' ¹⁹Tell them, 'This is what the Lord God says: I will take the stick which is for Joseph and the tribes of Israel with him. This stick is in the hand of Ephraim. Then I will put it with the stick of Judah. And I will make them into one stick. And they will be one in my hand.' ²⁰Hold the sticks of wood on

which you wrote these names. Hold them in your hands so the people can see them. ²¹Say to the people: 'This is what the Lord God says: I will take the people of Israel from among the nations where they have gone. I will gather them from all around. I will bring them into their own land. ²²I will make them one nation in the land, on the mountains of Israel. One king will rule all of them. They will never again be two nations. They will not be divided into two kingdoms anymore.' "

ⁿ**wind** This Hebrew word could also mean "breath" or "spirit."

Prayer Starter: Lord, you are so powerful. You can do anything you want— even make bones come to life.

Memory Verse: Daniel said: "Praise God . . ."   *—Daniel 2:20*

The Blazing Furnace

Nebuchadnezzar became very angry. He called for Shadrach, Meshach and Abednego. So those men were brought to the king. ¹⁴And Nebuchadnezzar said, "Shadrach, Meshach and Abednego, is it true that you do not serve my gods? And is it true that you did not worship the gold statue I have set up? ¹⁵Now, you will hear the sound of the horns, flutes, lyres, zithers, harps, pipes and all the other musical instruments. And you must be ready to bow down and worship the statue I made. That will be good. But if you do not worship it, you will be thrown quickly into the blazing furnace. Then no god will be able to save you from my power!"

¹⁶Shadrach, Meshach and Abednego answered the king. They said, "Nebuchadnezzar, we do not need to defend ourselves to you. ¹⁷You can throw us into the blazing furnace. The God we serve is able to save us from the furnace and your power. If he does this, it is good. ¹⁸But even if God does not save us, we want you, our king, to know this: We will not serve your gods. We will not worship the gold statue you have set up."

¹⁹Then Nebuchadnezzar was furious with Shadrach, Meshach and Abednego. He ordered the furnace to be heated seven times hotter than usual. ²⁰Then he commanded some of the strongest soldiers in his army to tie up Shadrach, Meshach and Abednego. The king told the soldiers to throw them into the blazing furnace.

²¹So Shadrach, Meshach and Abednego were tied up and thrown into the blazing furnace. They were still wearing their robes, trousers, turbans and other clothes. ²²The king was very angry when he gave the command. And the furnace was made very hot. The fire was so hot that the flames killed the strong soldiers who took Shadrach, Meshach and Abednego there. ²³Firmly tied, Shadrach, Meshach and Abednego fell into the blazing furnace.

²⁴Then King Nebuchadnezzar was very surprised and jumped to his feet. He asked the men who advised him, "Didn't we tie up only three men? Didn't we throw them into the fire?"

They answered, "Yes, our king."

²⁵The king said, "Look! I see four men. They are walking around in the fire. They are not tied up, and they are not burned. The fourth man looks like a son of the gods."

Prayer Starter: Our God, your name will be praised forever and ever. You are all-powerful, and you know everything.

Memory Verse: Daniel said: "Praise God forever and ever. . . .
—*Daniel 2:20*

Nebuchad-nezzar Eats Grass

King Nebuchadnezzar was walking on the roof[h] of his palace in Babylon. [30]And he said, "Look at Babylon. I built this great city. It is my palace. I built this great place by my power to show how great I am."

[31]The words were still in his mouth when a voice came from heaven. The voice said, "King Nebuchadnezzar, these things will happen to you: Your royal power has been taken away from you. [32]You will be forced away from people. You will live with the wild animals. You will be fed grass like an ox. Seven years will pass before you learn this lesson: The Most High God rules over the kingdoms of men. And the Most High God gives those kingdoms to anyone he wants."

[33]Those things happened quickly. Nebuchadnezzar was forced to go away from people. He began eating grass like an ox. He became wet from dew. His hair grew long like the feathers of an eagle. And his nails grew long like the claws of a bird.

[34]Then at the end of that time, I, Nebuchadnezzar, looked up toward heaven. And I could think correctly again. Then I gave praise to the Most High God. I gave honor and glory to him who lives forever.

God's rule is forever.
His kingdom continues for all time.

[h]**roof** In Bible times houses were built with flat roofs. The roof was used for drying things such as flax and fruit. And it was used as an extra room, as a place for worship and as a place to sleep in the summer.

Prayer Starter: Thank you for ruling over the nations, dear Lord. You are King of kings and Lord of lords. And I love you.

Memory Verse: Daniel said: "Praise God forever and ever. He has wisdom . . ."   *—Daniel 2:20*

Writing on the Wall

King Belshazzar gave a big banquet for 1,000 royal guests. And he drank wine with them. ²As Belshazzar was drinking his wine, he gave an order to his servants. He told them to bring the gold and silver cups that his ancestor Nebuchadnezzar had taken from the Temple in Jerusalem. King Belshazzar wanted his royal guests to drink from those cups. He also wanted his wives and his slave women to drink from them. ³So they brought the gold cups. They had been taken from the Temple of God in Jerusalem. And the king and his royal guests, his wives and his slave women drank from them. ⁴As they were drinking, they praised their gods. These gods were made from gold, silver, bronze, iron, wood and stone.

⁵Then suddenly a person's hand appeared. The fingers wrote words on the plaster on the wall. This was near the lampstand in the royal palace. The king watched the hand as it wrote.

⁶King Belshazzar was very frightened. His face turned white, and his knees knocked together. He could not stand up because his legs were too weak.

⁸So all the king's wise men came in. But they could not read the writing. And they could not tell the king what it meant.

¹³So they brought Daniel to the king. The king said to him, "Is your name Daniel? Are you one of the captives my father the king brought from Judah?

¹⁶"I have heard that you are able to explain what things mean. And you can find the answers to hard problems. Read this writing on the wall and explain it to me. If you can, I will give you purple clothes fit for a king. And I will put a gold chain around your neck. And you will become the third highest ruler in the kingdom."

¹⁷Then Daniel answered the king, "You may keep your gifts for yourself. Or you may give those rewards to someone else. I will read the writing on the wall for you. And I will explain to you what it means.

²⁵"These are the words that were written on the wall: 'Mene, mene, tekel, parsin.'

²⁶"This is what these words mean: Mene: God has counted the days until your kingdom will end. ²⁷Tekel: You have been weighed on the scales and found not good enough. ²⁸Parsin: Your kingdom is being divided. It will be given to the Medes and the Persians."

Prayer Starter: Lord, you are the one who raises up kings and brings down kings. May your will be done on earth.

Memory Verse: Daniel said: "Praise God forever and ever. He has wisdom and power."
                                                                    —Daniel 2:20

The Lions' Den

The supervisors and the governors went as a group to the king. They said: "King Darius, live forever!"

¹²So they went to the king. They talked to him about the law he had made. They said, "Didn't you write a law that says no one may pray to any god or man except you, our king? Doesn't it say that anyone who disobeys during the next 30 days will be thrown into the lions' den?"

The king answered, "Yes, I wrote that law. And the laws of the Medes and Persians cannot be canceled."

¹³Then those men spoke to the king. They said, "Daniel is one of the captives from Judah. And he is not paying attention to the law you wrote. Daniel still prays to his God three times every day." ¹⁴The king became very upset when he heard this. He decided he had to save Daniel. He worked until sunset trying to think of a way to save him.

¹⁵Then those men went as a group to the king. They said, "Remember, our king, the law of the Medes and Persians. It says that no law or command given by the king can be changed."

¹⁶So King Darius gave the order. They brought Daniel and threw him into the lions' den. The king said to Daniel, "May the God you serve all the time save you!" ¹⁷A big stone was brought. It was put over the opening of the lions' den. Then the king used his signet ring to put his special seal on the rock. And he used the rings of his royal officers to put their seals on the rock also. This showed that no one could move that rock and bring Daniel out. ¹⁸Then King Darius went back to his palace. He did not eat that night. He did not have any entertainment brought to entertain him. And he could not sleep.

¹⁹The next morning King Darius got up at dawn. He hurried to the lions' den. ²⁰As he came near the den, he was worried. He called out to Daniel. He said, "Daniel, servant of the living God! Has your God that you always worship been able to save you from the lions?"

²¹Daniel answered, "My king, live forever! ²²My God sent his angel to close the lions' mouths. They have not hurt me, because my God knows I am innocent. I never did anything wrong to you, my king."

²³King Darius was very happy. He told his servants to lift Daniel out of the lions' den. So they lifted him out and did not find any injury on him. This was because Daniel had trusted in his God.

Prayer Starter: May I be as faithful in praying each day as Daniel was, dear Lord.

Memory Verse: I am making a new law. . . .   —*Daniel 6:26a*

203

The Male Sheep and the Goat

During the third year Belshazzar was king, I saw this vision. This was after the other one. ²In this vision I saw myself in the capital city of Susa. Susa is in the area of Elam. I was standing by the Ulai River. ³I looked up, and I saw a male sheep standing beside the river. It had two long horns. But one horn was longer than the other. The long horn was newer than the other horn. ⁴I watched the male sheep charge to the west. He also charged to the north and the south. No animal could stand before him. And none could save another animal from his power. He did whatever he wanted. And he became very powerful.

⁵While I was thinking about this, I saw a male goat come from the west. This goat had one large horn that was easy to see. It was between his eyes. He crossed over the whole earth. But his feet did not touch the ground.

⁶That goat charged the male sheep with the two horns. This was the male sheep I had seen standing by the river. The goat was very angry. ⁷I watched the goat attack the male sheep. It broke the sheep's two horns. The sheep could not stop it. The goat knocked the sheep to the ground. Then the goat walked all over him. No one was able to save the sheep from the goat. ⁸So the male goat became very great. But when he was strong, his big horn broke off. Then four horns grew in place of the one big horn. Those four horns were easy to see. They pointed in four different directions.

²⁷I, Daniel, became very weak. I was sick for several days after that vision. Then I got up and went back to work for the king. But I was very upset about the vision. I didn't understand what it meant.

Prayer Starter: Thank you for being in control of everything, Lord—even the future.

Memory Verse: I am making a new law. This law is for people . . .
—Daniel 6:26a

During Cyrus' third year as king of Persia, Daniel learned about these things. (Daniel's other name is Belteshazzar.) The message was true. It was about a great war. But Daniel understood it, because it was explained to him in a vision.

²At that time I, Daniel, was very sad for three weeks. ³I did not eat any fancy food. I did not eat any meat or drink any wine. I did not use any perfumed oil. I did not do any of these things for three weeks.

⁴On the twenty-fourth day of the first month, I was standing beside the great Tigris River. ⁵While standing there, I looked up. And I saw a man dressed in linen clothes. A belt made of fine gold was wrapped around his waist. ⁶His body was like shiny yellow quartz. His face was bright like lightning, and his eyes were like fire. His arms and legs were shiny like polished bronze. His voice sounded like the roar of a crowd.

⁷I, Daniel, was the only person who saw the vision. The men with me did not see it. But they were badly frightened. They were so afraid they ran away and hid. ⁸So I was left alone, watching this great vision. I lost

my strength. My face turned white like a dead person, and I was helpless. ⁹Then I heard the man in the vision speaking. As I listened, I fell into a deep sleep. My face was on the ground.

¹⁰Then a hand touched me and set me on my hands and knees. I was so afraid that I was shaking. ¹¹The man in the vision said to me, "Daniel, God loves you very much. Think very carefully about the words I will speak to you. Stand up because I have been sent to you." And when he said this, I stood up. I was still shaking.

¹²Then the man said to me, "Daniel, do not be afraid. Some time ago you decided to try to get understanding. You wanted to be humble before God. Since that time God has listened to you. And I came to you because you have been praying. ¹³But the prince of Persia has been fighting against me for 21 days. Then Michael, one of the most important angels, came to help me. He came because I had been left there with the king of Persia. ¹⁴Now I have come to you, Daniel. I will explain to you what will happen to your people. The vision is about a time in the future."

¹⁵While he was speaking to me, I bowed facedown. I could not speak. ¹⁶Then one who looked like a man touched my lips. I opened my mouth and started to speak. I said to the one standing in front of me, "Master, I am upset and afraid. It is because of what I saw in the vision. I feel helpless. ¹⁷Master, I am Daniel your servant. How can I talk with you! My strength is gone, and it is hard for me to breathe."

¹⁸The one who looked like a man touched me again. And he gave me strength. ¹⁹He said, "Daniel, don't be afraid. God loves you very much. Peace be with you. Be strong now, be strong."

When he spoke to me, I became stronger. Then I said, "Master, speak, since you have given me strength."

²⁰So then he said, "Daniel, do you know why I have come to you? Soon I must go back to fight against the prince of Persia. When I go, the prince of Greece will come. ²¹But before I go, I must first tell you what is written in the Book of Truth. No one stands with me against them except Michael. He is the angel ruling over your people."

Prayer Starter: I believe you control human events, Lord. You give rulers their power and take it away. No one is like you.

Memory Verse: I am making a new law. This law is for people in every part of my kingdom. . . .
—*Daniel 6:26a*

Hosea and Gomer

The Lord spoke his word to Hosea son of Beeri. This was during the time that Uzziah, Jotham, Ahaz and Hezekiah were kings of Judah. During part of this time Jeroboam son of Jehoash was king of Israel.

²The Lord said to him, "Go, and marry a woman who will be unfaithful to you. She will give you children whose fathers are other men. Do this because people in this country have acted like an unfaithful wife toward the Lord." ³So Hosea married Gomer daughter of Diblaim. Gomer became pregnant and gave birth to Hosea's son.

⁴The Lord said to Hosea, "Name him Jezreel. This is because soon I will punish the family of Jehu for the people they killed at Jezreel. Then I will put an end to the kingdom of Israel. ⁵And I will also break the power of Israel's army in the Valley of Jezreel."

⁶Gomer became pregnant again and gave birth to a daughter. The Lord said to Hosea, "Name her Lo-Ruhamah.ⁿ This is because I will not pity Israel anymore. I will no longer forgive them. ⁷But I will show pity to the people of Judah. I will save them. I will not use bows or swords, horses or horsemen, or weapons of war to save them. I, the Lord their God, will save them."

⁸After Gomer had finished nursing Lo-Ruhamah, she became pregnant again. And she gave birth to another son. ⁹The Lord said, "Name him Lo-Ammiⁿ because you are not my people. And I am not your God.

¹⁰"But the people of Israel will become like the grains of sand of the sea. You cannot measure or count them. Now it is said to Israel, 'You are not my people.' But later they will be called 'children of the living God.' ¹¹Then the people of Judah and Israel will be joined together again. They will choose one leader for themselves. And again they will grow in their land. The day of Jezreel, when God plants, will be truly great."

ⁿ**Lo-Ruhamah** This name in Hebrew means "not pitied."
ⁿ**Lo-Ammi** This name in Hebrew means "not my people."

Prayer Starter: Lord, help me to obey you and be faithful to you in all I do.

Memory Verse: I am making a new law. This law is for people in every part of my kingdom. All of you must fear and respect . . . —*Daniel 6:26a*

Swarms of Locusts

The Lord spoke his word to Joel son of Pethuel:
2 Older leaders, listen to this message.
Listen to me, all you people who live
in the land.
Nothing like this has ever happened during
your lifetime.
Nothing like this has ever happened
during your fathers' lifetimes.

3 Tell your children about these things.
And let your children tell their children.
And let your grandchildren tell their children.
4 What the cutting locusts have not eaten,
the swarming locusts have eaten.
And what the swarming locusts have left,
the hopping locusts have eaten.
And what the hopping locusts have left,
the destroying locusts" have eaten.

5 Drunks, wake up and cry!
All of you people who drink wine, cry!
Cry because your sweet wine
has been taken away from you.
6 A powerful nation has come into my land.
It has too many soldiers to count.
It has teeth like a lion.
And it has fangs like a female lion.
7 That army has eaten my grapevines.
It has destroyed my fig trees.
It has eaten the bark off my trees
and left the branches white.

8 Cry as a young woman cries
when the man she was going to marry is killed.
9 There will be no more grain or drink offerings
to offer in the Temple of the Lord.
Because of this, the priests,
the servants of the Lord, cry.

"**cutting . . . locusts** These are different names for an insect like a large grasshopper. The locust can quickly destroy trees, plants and crops. In this destruction by locusts, Joel sees a warning. God will cause this type of destruction when he punishes his people.

Prayer Starter: Thank you for insects, Lord. Especially for lightning bugs, lady bugs, and caterpillars.

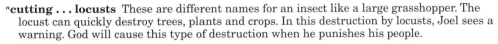

Memory Verse: I am making a new law. This law is for people in every part of my kingdom. All of you must fear and respect the God of Daniel.
—Daniel 6:26a

**Women
of Samaria**

L isten to this message, you rich women
　　on the Mountain of Samaria.
　You take things from the poor
　　and crush people who are in need.
　You tell your husbands,
　　"Bring us money so we can drink!"
² The Lord God has promised this:
"It is certain that I am a holy God.
So it is certain that the time will come
　when some of you will be taken away by hooks.
　The rest of you will be taken away with fishhooks.
³ You will go straight out of the city
　　through holes in the walls.
　And you will be thrown on the garbage dump," says the Lord.

⁴ "Go to the city of Bethel and sin.
　　Go to Gilgal and sin even more.
　Offer your sacrifices every morning.
　　Bring one-tenth of your crops on the third day.

⁵   Offer bread made with yeast as a sacrifice to show your thanks.
        And brag about the offerings you bring
            to show thanks to the Lord.
    Brag about these things, Israelites.
        This is what you love to do," says the Lord God.

⁶   "I did not give you any food to eat.
        There was not enough food in any of your towns.
        But you did not come back to me," says the Lord.
⁷   "I held back the rain from you
        three months before harvest time.
    Then I let it rain on one city
        but not on another.
    Rain fell on one field,
        but another field got none and dried up.
⁸   People weak from thirst went from town to town for water.
        But they could not get enough water to drink.
        But you still did not come back to me," says the Lord.
⁹   "I made your crops die from disease and mildew.
        I destroyed your gardens and your vineyards.
    Locusts ate your fig trees and olive trees.
        But you still did not come back to me," says the Lord.

Prayer Starter: Lord, help me to always be concerned for the poor and needy.

Memory Verse: All other nations follow . . .   *—Micah 4:5*

A Basket of Ripe Fruit

This is what the Lord showed me: a basket of ripe fruit. ²The Lord said to me, "Amos, what do you see?"

I said, "A basket of fruit from the end of the harvest."

Then the Lord said to me, "An end has come for my people, the Israelites. I will not overlook their sins anymore.

³"On that day the palace songs will become funeral songs," says the Lord God. "There will be dead bodies thrown everywhere! Silence!"

⁴ Listen to me you who walk on helpless people.
    You are trying to destroy the poor people of this country.
⁵ Your businessmen say,
    "When will the New Moon Festival be over
      so we can sell grain?
    When will the Sabbath be over
      so we can bring out wheat to sell?
    We can charge them more
      and give them less.
    We can change the scales to cheat the people.
⁶ We will buy poor people for silver.
    And we will buy needy people for the price of a pair of sandals.
    We will even sell the wheat that was swept up from the floor."

⁷The Lord used his name, the Pride of Jacob, to make a promise. He said, "I will never forget what these people did.
⁸ The whole land will shake because of it.
    Everyone who lives in the land will cry for those who died.
    The whole land will rise like the Nile.
    It will be shaken, and then it will fall
    like the Nile River in Egypt."

⁹The Lord God says:
    "At that time I will cause the sun to go down at noon.
    I will make the earth dark on a clear day."

Prayer Starter: Father, bless those who work in homeless shelters and among the poor around the world.

Memory Verse: All other nations follow their own gods. . . . —*Micah 4:5*

Jonah and the Fish

The Lord spoke his word to Jonah son of Amittai: ²"Get up, go to the great city of Nineveh and preach against it. I see the evil things they do."

³But Jonah got up to run away from the Lord. He went to the city of Joppa. There he found a ship that was going to the city of Tarshish. Jonah paid for the trip and went aboard. He wanted to go to Tarshish to run away from the Lord.

⁴But the Lord sent a great wind on the sea. This wind made the sea very rough. So the ship was in danger of breaking apart. ⁵The sailors were afraid. Each man cried to his own god. The men began throwing the cargo into the sea. This would make the ship lighter so it would not sink.

But Jonah had gone down into the ship to lie down. He fell fast asleep. ⁶The captain of the ship came and said, "Why are you sleeping? Get up! Pray to your god! Maybe your god will pay attention to us. Maybe he will save us!"

⁷Then the men said to each other, "Let's throw lots to see who caused these troubles to happen to us."

So the men threw lots. The lot showed that the trouble had happened because of Jonah.

¹²Jonah said to them, "Pick me up, and throw me into the sea. Then it will calm down. I know it is my fault that this great storm has come on you."

¹⁴So the men cried to the Lord, "Lord, please don't let us die because of taking this man's life. Please don't think we are guilty of killing an innocent man. Lord, you have caused all this to happen. You wanted it this way." ¹⁵Then the men picked up Jonah and threw him into the sea. So the sea became calm. ¹⁶Then they began to fear the Lord very much. They offered a sacrifice to the Lord. They also made promises to him.

¹⁷And the Lord caused a very big fish to swallow Jonah. Jonah was in the stomach of the fish three days and three nights.

Prayer Starter: I want to serve you with my whole heart, dear Lord, and with my whole life.

Memory Verse: All other nations follow their own gods. But we will follow . . .
—Micah 4:5

Angry Enough to Die

Then the Lord spoke his word to Jonah again. The Lord said, ²"Get up. Go to the great city Nineveh. Preach against it what I tell you."

³So Jonah obeyed the Lord. He got up and went to Nineveh. It was a very large city. It took a person three days just to walk across it. ⁴Jonah entered the city. When he had walked for one day, he preached to the people. He said, "After 40 days, Nineveh will be destroyed!"

⁵The people of Nineveh believed in God. They announced they would stop eating for a while. They put on rough cloth to show how sad they were. All the people in the city wore the cloth. People from the most important to the least important did this.

⁶When the king of Nineveh heard this news, he got up from his throne. He took off his robe. He covered himself with rough cloth and sat in ashes to show how upset he was.

¹⁰God saw what the people did. He saw that they stopped doing evil things. So God changed his mind and did not do what he had warned. He did not punish them.

4 But Jonah was very unhappy that God did not destroy the city. He was angry. ²He complained to the Lord and said, "I knew this would happen. I knew it when I was still in my own country. It is why I

quickly ran away to Tarshish. I knew that you are a God who is kind and shows mercy. You don't become angry quickly. You have great love. I knew that you would rather forgive than punish them. ³So now I ask you, Lord, please kill me. It is better for me to die than to live."

⁴Then the Lord said, "Do you think it is right for you to be angry?"

⁵Jonah went out and sat down east of the city. There he made a shelter for himself. And he sat there in the shade. He was waiting to see what would happen to the city. ⁶The Lord made a plant grow quickly up over Jonah. This made a cool place for him to sit. And it helped him to be more comfortable. Jonah was very pleased to have the plant for shade. ⁷The next day the sun rose. And God sent a worm to attack the plant. Then the plant died.

⁸When the sun was high in the sky, God sent a hot east wind to blow. The sun became very hot on Jonah's head. And he became very weak. He wished he were dead. Jonah said, "It is better for me to die than to live."

⁹But God said this to Jonah: "Do you think it is right for you to be angry because of the plant?"

Jonah answered, "It is right for me to be angry! I will stay angry until I die!"

¹⁰And the Lord said, "You showed concern for that plant. But you did not plant it or make it grow. It appeared in the night, and the next day it died. ¹¹Then surely I can show concern for the great city Nineveh. There are many animals in that city. And there are more than 120,000 people living there. Those people simply do not know right from wrong!"

Prayer Starter: Lord, help me be concerned about the needs of all the people and animals you have made.

Memory Verse: All other nations follow their own gods. But we will follow the Lord our God . . .
—*Micah 4:5*

Micah's Warning

Jotham, Ahaz and Hezekiah were kings of Judah. During the time they were kings, the word of the Lord came to Micah, who was from Moresheth. He saw these visions about Samaria and Jerusalem.

2 Hear this, all you nations.
    Listen, all you who live on the earth.
The Lord God will come from his Holy Temple.
He will come as a witness against you.
3 See, the Lord is coming out of his place in heaven.
    He is coming down to walk on the tops of the mountains.
4 The mountains will melt under him
        like wax in a fire.
The valleys will crack open
        as if split by water raging down a mountain.
5 This is because of Jacob's sin.
        It is because of the sins of the nation of Israel.
Who is responsible for Jacob's sin?
        Samaria!
Who is responsible for Judah's worshiping idols?
        Jerusalem!

6 "So I will make Samaria a pile of ruins in the open country.
        It will be like a place for planting vineyards.
I will pour Samaria's stones down into the valley.
        And I will destroy her down to her foundations.
7 All her idols will be broken into pieces.
        All the gifts to her idols will be burned with fire.
        I will destroy all her idols.
This is because Samaria earned her money
            by being unfaithful to me.
        So this money will be carried off by other people
            who are not faithful to me."

8 I will moan and cry because of this evil.
        I will go around barefoot and without clothes.
I will cry loudly like the wild dogs.
        I will cry like the ostriches.
9 I will do this because Samaria's wound cannot be healed.
        Her destruction will spread to Judah.
It will reach the city gate of my people.
        It will come all the way to Jerusalem.

Prayer Starter: Bless our nation, God. Turn it to you.

Memory Verse: All other nations follow their own gods. But we will follow the Lord our God forever and ever.   —*Micah 4:5*

In the Last Days

In the last days
the mountain on which the Lord's Temple stands
will become the most important of all mountains.
It will be raised above the hills.
People from other nations will come streaming
to it.
² Many nations will come and say,
"Come, let us go up to the mountain of the Lord.
Let us go to the Temple of the God of Jacob!
Then God will teach us his ways.
And we will obey his teachings."
The Lord's teachings will go out from Jerusalem.
The word of the Lord will go out from Jerusalem.
³ The Lord will settle arguments among many nations.
He will decide between strong nations that are far away.
Then the nations will make their swords into plows.
They will make their spears into hooks for trimming trees.
Nations will no longer fight other nations.
They will not even train for war anymore.
⁴ Everyone will sit under his own vine and fig tree.
No one will make them afraid.
This is because the Lord of heaven's armies has said it.
⁵ All other nations follow their own gods.
But we will follow the Lord our God forever and ever.

⁶ The Lord says, "At that time,
I will bring back to me the crippled.
I will bring back to Jerusalem those who were sent away.
I will bring back to me those who were hurt.
⁷ I will keep alive those who were crippled.
I will make a strong nation of those who were sent away.
The Lord will be their king in Mount Zion forever.
⁸ And you, watchtower of the flocks,ⁿ strong city of Jerusalem,
you will be a kingdom as in the past.
Jerusalem, the right to rule will come again to you."

ⁿ**watchtower . . . flocks** This probably means a part of Jerusalem. The leaders would be like shepherds in a tower watching their sheep.

Prayer Starter: Others may follow their gods, but we will always follow you, O Lord.

Memory Verse: The Lord is good. . . .   —*Nahum 1:7*

Micah 5:2–5a; 7:18–20

The Coming Ruler

"But you, Bethlehem Ephrathah,
are one of the smallest towns in Judah.
But from you will come one who will rule Israel
for me.
He comes from very old times,
from days long ago."

3   The Lord will leave his people in Babylon
until Jerusalem, who is in labor, gives birth to her children.
Then his brothers who are in captivity will return.
They will come back to the people of Israel living in Judah.
4   Then the ruler of Israel will stand
and take care of his people.
He will lead them with the Lord's power.
He will lead them in the wonderful name of the Lord his God.
They will live in safety.
And his greatness will be known all over the earth.
5   He will bring peace.

7 There is no God like you.
You forgive people who are
guilty of sin.
You don't look at the sins of
your people
who are left alive.
You, Lord, will not stay angry forever.
You enjoy being kind.
19   Lord, you will have mercy on us again.
You will conquer our sins.
You will throw away all our sins
into the deepest sea.
20   You will be true to the people of Jacob!
You will be kind to the people of Abraham.
You will do what you promised
to our ancesters long ago.

Prayer Starter: Thank you for being God. No one is like you!

Memory Verse: The Lord is good. He gives protection . . . .—*Nahum 1:7*

The Prophet Nahum

This is the message for the city of Nineveh.[n] This is the vision of Nahum, who was from the town of Elkosh.

2 The Lord is a jealous God who gives punishment.
  The Lord punishes wicked people and is filled
    with anger.
The Lord punishes those who are against him.
  He stays angry with his enemies.
3 The Lord does not become angry quickly.
  His power is great.
  The Lord will not let the guilty go unpunished.
Where the Lord goes, whirlwinds and storms show his power.
  The clouds are the dust that his feet kick up.
4 The Lord speaks to the sea and makes it dry.
  He dries up all the rivers.
The areas of Bashan and Carmel dry up.
  And the flowers of Lebanon die.
5 He shakes the mountains
  and makes the hills melt away.
The earth trembles when he comes.
  The world and all who live in it shake with fear.
6 No one can stay alive when the Lord is angry with him.
  No one can survive his strong anger.
His anger is poured out like fire.
  He smashes rocks that are in his path.

7 The Lord is good.
  He gives protection in times of trouble.
  He knows who trusts in him.

[n]**Nineveh** The capital city of the country of Assyria. Nahum uses Nineveh to stand for all of Assyria.

Prayer Starter: You are so good, dear Lord. Protect me in times of trouble.

Memory Verse: The Lord is good. He gives protection in times of trouble. . . .
—*Nahum 1:7*

<h2>Prayer of Habakkuk</h2>

This is the prayer of Habakkuk the prophet, on shigionoth.

2 Lord, I have heard the news about you.
Lord, I am amazed at the powerful things
you have done.
Do great things once again in our time.
Make those things happen again
in our own days.
Even when you are angry,
remember to be gentle with us.

3 God is coming from Teman in
the south.
The Holy One comes from
Mount Paran.*
The Lord's greatness covers the
heavens.
His praise fills the earth.
4 He is like a bright light.
Rays of light shine from his
hand.
And there he hides his power.

17 Fig trees may not grow figs.
There may be no grapes on the vines.
There may be no olives growing on the trees.
There may be no food growing in the fields.
There may be no sheep in the pens.
There may be no cattle in the barns.
18 But I will still be glad in the Lord.
I will rejoice in God my Savior.
19 The Lord God gives me my strength.
He makes me like a deer, which does not stumble.
He leads me safely on the steep mountains.

*Teman . . . Paran** God is seen as again coming from the direction of Mount Sinai. He came from Sinai when he rescued his people from Egypt.

Prayer Starter: Lord, your greatness covers the heavens and your glory fills the earth.

Memory Verse: The Lord is good. He gives protection in times of trouble. He knows . . .
—*Nahum 1:7*

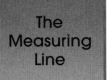

The Measuring Line

Then I [Zechariah] looked up. And I saw a man holding a line for measuring things. ²I asked him, "Where are you going?"

He said to me, "I am going to measure Jerusalem. I will see how wide and how long it is."

³Then the angel who was talking with me left. And another angel came out to meet him. ⁴The second angel said to him, "Run and tell that young man this: 'Jerusalem will become a city without walls because there will be so many people and cattle in it. ⁵I will be a wall of fire around it,' says the Lord. 'And I will be the glory within it.'

⁶"Hurry! Run away from Babylon. I have scattered you in all directions," says the Lord.

⁷"Hurry, people of Jerusalem! Escape from Babylon." ⁸This is what the Lord of heaven's armies says: "Whoever hurts you hurts what is precious to me."

So the Lord will honor me. And he will send me to speak against those nations who scattered you. ⁹"I will raise my hand against them. Their slaves will rob them."

Then you will know that the Lord of heaven's armies sent me.

¹⁰"Shout and be glad, Jerusalem. I am coming, and I will live among you," says the Lord. ¹¹"At that time people from many nations will come to the Lord. And they will become my people. I will live among you. And you will know that the Lord of heaven's armies has sent me to you. ¹²Judah will be the Lord's special part of the holy land. And Jerusalem will be his chosen city again. ¹³Be silent, everyone. The Lord is coming out of the holy place where he lives."

Prayer Starter: Thank you for making this day. I celebrate your goodness.

Memory Verse: The Lord is good. He gives protection in times of trouble. He knows who trusts in him.   *—Nahum 1:7*

Zechariah's Four Chariots

Ilooked up again. I saw four chariots coming from between two mountains. They were mountains of bronze. ²Red horses pulled the first chariot. Black horses pulled the second chariot. ³White horses pulled the third chariot. And strong, spotted horses pulled the fourth chariot. ⁴I spoke to the angel who was talking with me. I asked, "What are these, sir?"

⁵He said, "These are going to the four directions on earth. They have just come from the presence of the Lord of the whole world. ⁶The chariot

pulled by the black horses will go north. The white horses will go west. And the spotted horses will go south."

⁷The powerful horses were trying to go through all the earth. So he said, "Go through all the earth." And they did.

⁸Then he called to me, "Look. The horses that went north have calmed the Lord's anger that came from there to punish."

⁹The Lord spoke his word to me. He said: ¹⁰"Heldai, Tobijah and Jedaiah were captives in Babylon. Get silver and gold from them. Go that same day to the house of Josiah son of Zephaniah. ¹¹Make the silver and gold into a crown. And put it on the head of Joshua son of Jehozadak. Joshua is the high priest. ¹²Tell him this is what the Lord of heaven's armies says: 'There is a man whose name is the Branch. He will branch out from where he is. He will build the Temple of the Lord. ¹³One manⁿ will build the Temple of the Lord. And the otherⁿ will receive the honor of a king. One man will sit on his throne and rule. And the other will be a priest on his throne. And these two men will work together in peace.' ¹⁴The crown will be kept in the Temple of the Lord. It will remind Heldai, Tobijah, Jedaiah and Josiah son of Zephaniah of God's king. ¹⁵People living far away will come and build the Temple of the Lord. Then you will know the Lord of heaven's armies has sent me to you. This will happen if you completely obey the Lord your God."

ⁿ**One man** This probably refers to Zerubbabel.
ⁿ**other** This probably refers to Joshua.

Prayer Starter: You watch over all the earth, Lord. Help the world to be at peace.

Memory Verse: She will give birth to a son. . . . —*Matthew 1:21*

The Unending Day

The Lord's day of judging is coming. The wealth you have taken will be divided among you. ²I will bring all the nations together to fight Jerusalem. They will capture the city and rob the houses. The women will be attacked. Half the people will be taken away as captives. But the rest won't be taken from the city.

³Then the Lord will go to war against those nations. He will fight as in a day of battle. ⁴On that day he will stand on the Mount of Olives, east of Jerusalem. The Mount of Olives will split in two. A deep valley will run east and west. Half the mountain will move north. And half will move south. ⁵You will run through this mountain valley to the other side. You will run as you ran from the earthquake. That was when Uzziah was king of Judah. Then the Lord my God will come. And all the holy ones will be with him.

⁶On that day there will be no light, cold or frost. ⁷There will be no other day like it. The Lord knows when it will come. There will be no day or night. Even at evening it will still be light.

⁸At that time fresh water will flow from Jerusalem. Half of it will flow east to the Dead Sea. And half of it will flow west to the Mediterranean Sea. It will flow summer and winter.

⁹Then the Lord will be king over the whole world. At that time there will be only one Lord. And his name will be the only name.

¹⁰All the land south of Jerusalem from Geba to Rimmon will be turned into a plain. Jerusalem will be raised up. But it will stay in the same place. The city will reach from the Benjamin Gate to the First Gate to the Corner Gate. It will go from the Tower of Hananel to the king's winepresses. ¹¹People will live there. It will never be destroyed again. Jerusalem will be safe.

Prayer Starter: Father, thank you for Jesus, who is coming back to earth.

Memory Verse: She will give birth to a son. You will name the son Jesus. . . .
                                                              —*Matthew 1:21*

Bring a Tenth

"I am the Lord. I do not change. So you descendants of Jacob have not been destroyed. ⁷Like your ancestors before you, you have disobeyed my rules. You have not kept them. Return to me. Then I will return to you," says the Lord of heaven's armies.

"But you ask, 'How can we return?'

⁸"Should a man rob God? But you rob me.

"You ask, 'How have we robbed you?'

"You have robbed me in your offerings and the tenth of your crops. ⁹So a curse is on you because the whole nation has robbed me. ¹⁰Bring to the storehouse a tenth of what you gain. Then there will be food in my house. Test me in this," says the Lord of heaven's armies. "I will open the windows of heaven for you. I will pour out more blessings than you have room for. ¹¹I will stop the insects so they won't eat your crops. The grapes won't fall from your vines before they are ready to pick," says the Lord of heaven's armies. ¹²"All the nations will call you blessed. You will have a pleasant country," says the Lord of heaven's armies.

¹⁶Then those who honored the Lord spoke with each other. The Lord listened and heard them. The names of those who honored the Lord and respected him were written in a book. The Lord will remember them.

¹⁷The Lord of heaven's armies says, "They belong to me. On that day they will be my very own. A father shows mercy to his son who serves him. In the same way I will show mercy to my people. ¹⁸You will again see the difference between good and evil people. You will see the difference between those who serve God and those who don't."

Prayer Starter: Make me generous, Lord, in giving my money to your work.

Memory Verse: She will give birth to a son. You will name the son Jesus. Give him that name . . . —*Matthew 1:21*

Wise Men from the East

Jesus was born in the town of Bethlehem in Judea during the time when Herod was king. After Jesus was born, some wise men from the east came to Jerusalem. ²They asked, "Where is the baby who was born to be the king of the Jews? We saw his star in the east. We came to worship him."

³When King Herod heard about this new king of the Jews, he was troubled. And all the people in Jerusalem were worried too. ⁴Herod called a meeting of all the leading priests and teachers of the law. He asked them where the Christ would be born. ⁵They answered, "In the town of Bethlehem in Judea. The prophet wrote about this in the Scriptures."

⁹The wise men heard the king and then left. They saw the same star they had seen in the east. It went before them until it stopped above the place where the child was. ¹⁰When the wise men saw the star, they were filled with joy. ¹¹They went to the house where the child was and saw him with his mother, Mary. They bowed down and worshiped the child. They opened the gifts they brought for him. They gave him treasures of gold, frankincense, and myrrh. ¹²But God warned the wise men in a dream not to go back to Herod. So they went home to their own country by a different way.

Prayer Starter: Thank you, dear God, for Jesus, who was born on Christmas Day.

Memory Verse: She will give birth to a son. You will name the son Jesus. Give him that name because he will save his people . . .—*Matthew 1:21*

Hiding in Egypt

After they left, an angel of the Lord came to Joseph in a dream. The angel said, "Get up! Take the child and his mother and escape to Egypt. Herod will start looking for the child to kill him. Stay in Egypt until I tell you to return."

[14]So Joseph got up and left for Egypt during the night with the child and his mother. [15]Joseph stayed in Egypt until Herod died. This was to make clear the full meaning of what the Lord had said through the prophet. The Lord said, "I called my son out of Egypt."[n]

[16]When Herod saw that the wise men had tricked him, he was very angry. So he gave an order to kill all the baby boys in Bethlehem and in all the area around Bethlehem. He said to kill all the boys who were two years old or younger. This was in keeping with the time he learned from the wise men. [17]So what God had said through the prophet Jeremiah came true:

[18] "A sound was heard in Ramah.
>   It was painful crying and much sadness.
> Rachel cries for her children,
>   and she cannot be comforted,
>   because her children are dead."

[19]After Herod died, an angel of the Lord came to Joseph in a dream. This happened while Joseph was in Egypt. [20]The angel said, "Get up! Take the child and his mother and go to Israel. The people who were trying to kill the child are now dead."

[21]So Joseph took the child and his mother and went to Israel. [22]But he heard that Archelaus was now king in Judea. Archelaus became king when his father Herod died. So Joseph was afraid to go there. After being warned in a dream, he went to the area of Galilee. [23]He went to a town called Nazareth and lived there. And so what God had said through the prophets came true: "He will be called a Nazarene."[n]

[a]**"I called . . . Egypt."** Quotation from Hosea 11:1.
[n]**Nazarene** A person from the city of Nazareth, a name probably meaning "branch" (see Isaiah 11:1).

Prayer Starter: Lord, help the people of Israel and Egypt and all the other nations to know and love Jesus Christ.

Memory Verse: She will give birth to a son. You will name the son Jesus. Give him that name because he will save his people from their sins.
                                              —*Matthew 1:21*

Jesus Is Tempted by Satan

Then the Spirit led Jesus into the desert to be tempted by the devil. [2]Jesus ate nothing for 40 days and nights. After this, he was very hungry. [3]The devil came to Jesus to tempt him. The devil said, "If you are the Son of God, tell these rocks to become bread."

[4]Jesus answered, "It is written in the Scriptures, 'A person does not live only by eating bread. But a person lives by everything the Lord says.' "[n]

[5]Then the devil led Jesus to the holy city of Jerusalem. He put Jesus on a very high place of the Temple. [6]The devil said, "If you are the Son of God, jump off. It is written in the Scriptures,

'He has put his angels in charge of you.
They will catch you with their hands.
And you will not hit your foot on a rock.' "

[7]Jesus answered him, "It also says in the Scriptures, 'Do not test the Lord your God.' "[n]

[8]Then the devil led Jesus to the top of a very high mountain. He

showed Jesus all the kingdoms of the world and all the great things that are in those kingdoms. [9]The devil said, "If you will bow down and worship me, I will give you all these things."

[10]Jesus said to the devil, "Go away from me, Satan! It is written in the Scriptures, 'You must worship the Lord your God. Serve only him!' "[n]

[11]So the devil left Jesus. And then some angels came to Jesus and helped him.

[n]**A person . . . says.'** Quotation from Deuteronomy 8:3.
[n]**Do . . . God.'** Quotation from Deuteronomy 6:16.
[n]**You . . . him!'** Quotation from Deuteronomy 6:13.

Prayer Starter: Keep us safe from the devil's traps, Lord. Deliver us from evil.

Memory Verse: The thing you should want most . . . *—Matthew 6:33*

The Sermon on the Mount

Jesus went everywhere in Galilee. He taught in the synagogues and preached the Good News about the kingdom of heaven. And he healed all the people's diseases and sicknesses. 25Many people followed him. They came from Galilee, the Ten Towns,[n] Jerusalem, Judea, and the land across the Jordan River.

5 Jesus saw the crowds who were there. He went up on a hill and sat down. His followers came to him. 2Jesus taught the people and said:

3 "Those people who know they have great spiritual needs
    are happy.
The kingdom of heaven belongs to them.

4 Those who are sad now are happy.
    God will comfort them.

5 Those who are humble are happy.
    The earth will belong to them.

6 Those who want to do right more than anything else are happy.
    God will fully satisfy them.

7 Those who give mercy to others are happy.
    Mercy will be given to them.

8 Those who are pure in their thinking are happy.
    They will be with God.

9 Those who work to bring peace are happy.
    God will call them his sons.

10 Those who are treated badly for doing good are happy.
    The kingdom of heaven belongs to them.

11"People will say bad things about you and hurt you. They will lie and say all kinds of evil things about you because you follow me. But when they do these things to you, you are happy. 12Rejoice and be glad. You have a great reward waiting for you in heaven. People did the same evil things to the prophets who lived before you."

[n]**Ten Towns** In Greek, called "Decapolis." It was an area east of Lake Galilee that once had ten main towns.

Prayer Starter: Lord, bless us. May we depend only on you.

Memory Verse: The thing you should want most is God's kingdom . . .
—*Matthew 6:33*

When You Pray

"When you pray, don't be like the hypocrites. They love to stand in the synagogues and on the street corners and pray loudly. They want people to see them pray. I tell you the truth. They already have their full reward. ⁶When you pray, you should go into your room and close the door. Then pray to your Father who cannot be seen. Your Father can see what is done in secret, and he will reward you.

⁷"And when you pray, don't be like those people who don't know God. They continue saying things that mean nothing. They think that God will hear them because of the many things they say. ⁸Don't be like them. Your Father knows the things you need before you ask him. ⁹So when you pray, you should pray like this:

> 'Our Father in heaven,
> we pray that your name will always
>   be kept holy.
> ¹⁰ We pray that your kingdom will come.
> We pray that what you want will be
>   done,
>   here on earth as it is in heaven.
> ¹¹ Give us the food we need for each day.
> ¹² Forgive the sins we have done,
>   just as we have forgiven those who did wrong to us.
> ¹³ Do not cause us to be tested;
>   but save us from the Evil One.'

¹⁴Yes, if you forgive others for the things they do wrong, then your Father in heaven will also forgive you for the things you do wrong. ¹⁵But if you don't forgive the wrongs of others, then your Father in heaven will not forgive the wrong things you do.

¹⁶"When you give up eating,ⁿ don't put on a sad face like the hypocrites. They make their faces look strange to show people that they are giving up eating. I tell you the truth, those hypocrites already have their full reward. ¹⁷So when you give up eating, comb your hair and wash your face. ¹⁸Then people will not know that you are giving up eating. But your Father, whom you cannot see, will see you. Your Father sees what is done in secret, and he will reward you."

ⁿ**give up eating** This is called "fasting." The people would give up eating for a special time of prayer and worship to God. It was also done to show sadness.

Prayer Starter: Our Father in heaven, help us to honor your name.

Memory Verse: The thing you should want most is God's kingdom and doing what God wants. . . .   *—Matthew 6:33*

Don't Worry

"So I tell you, don't worry about the food you need to live. And don't worry about the clothes you need for your body. Life is more important than food. And the body is more important than clothes. [26]Look at the birds in the air. They don't plant or harvest or store food in barns. But your heavenly Father feeds the birds. And you know that you are worth much more than the birds. [27]You cannot add any time to your life by worrying about it.

[28]"And why do you worry about clothes? Look at the flowers in the field. See how they grow. They don't work or make clothes for themselves. [29]But I tell you that even Solomon with his riches was not dressed as beautifully as one of these flowers. [30]God clothes the grass in the field like that. The grass is living today, but tomorrow it is thrown into the fire to be burned. So you can be even more sure that God will clothe you. Don't have so little faith! [31]Don't worry and say, 'What will we eat?' or 'What will we drink?' or 'What will we wear?' [32]All the people who don't know God keep trying to get these things. And your Father in heaven knows that you need them. [33]The thing you should want most is God's kingdom and doing what God wants. Then all these other things you need will be given to you. [34]So don't worry about tomorrow. Each day has enough trouble of its own. Tomorrow will have its own worries."

Prayer Starter: Keep me from worry, dear Lord, for I know you love and care for me.

Memory Verse: The thing you should want most is God's kingdom and doing what God wants. Then all these other things you need . . .

—*Matthew 6:33*

Jesus Walks on Water

Then Jesus made his followers get into the boat. He told them to go ahead of him to the other side of the lake. Jesus stayed there to tell the people they could go home. ²³After he said good-bye to them, he went alone up into the hills to pray. It was late, and Jesus was there alone. ²⁴By this time, the boat was already far away on the lake. The boat was having trouble because of the waves, and the wind was blowing against it.

²⁵Between three and six o'clock in the morning, Jesus' followers were still in the boat. Jesus came to them. He was walking on the water. ²⁶When the followers saw him walking on the water, they were afraid. They said, "It's a ghost!" and cried out in fear.

²⁷But Jesus quickly spoke to them. He said, "Have courage! It is I! Don't be afraid."

²⁸Peter said, "Lord, if that is really you, then tell me to come to you on the water."

²⁹Jesus said, "Come." And Peter left the boat and walked on the water to Jesus. ³⁰But when Peter saw the wind and the waves, he became afraid and began to sink. He shouted, "Lord, save me!"

³¹Then Jesus reached out his hand and caught Peter. Jesus said, "Your faith is small. Why did you doubt?"

³²After Peter and Jesus were in the boat, the wind became calm. ³³Then those who were in the boat worshiped Jesus and said, "Truly you are the Son of God!"

³⁴After they crossed the lake, they came to the shore at Gennesaret. ³⁵The people there saw Jesus and knew who he was. So they told people all around there that Jesus had come. They brought all their sick to him. ³⁶They begged Jesus to let them just touch the edge of his coat to be healed. And all the sick people who touched it were healed.

Prayer Starter: Give me a stronger faith, dear Lord.

Memory Verse: The thing you should want most is God's kingdom and doing what God wants. Then all these other things you need will be given to you.
—*Matthew 6:33*

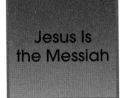

Jesus Is the Messiah

Jesus went to the area of Caesarea Philippi. He said to his followers, "I am the Son of Man. Who do the people say I am?"

[14]They answered, "Some people say you are John the Baptist. Others say you are Elijah. And others say that you are Jeremiah or one of the prophets."

[15]Then Jesus asked them, "And who do you say I am?"

[16]Simon Peter answered, "You are the Christ, the Son of the living God."

[17]Jesus answered, "You are blessed, Simon son of Jonah. No person taught you that. My Father in heaven showed you who I am. [18]So I tell you, you are Peter.[n] And I will build my church on this rock. The power of death will not be able to defeat my church. [19]I will give you the keys of the kingdom of heaven. The things you don't allow on earth will be the things that God does not allow. The things you allow on earth will be the things that God allows." [20]Then Jesus warned his followers not to tell anyone that he was the Christ.

[21]From that time on Jesus began telling his followers that he must go to Jerusalem. He explained that the older Jewish leaders, the leading priests, and the teachers of the law would make him suffer many things. And he told them that he must be killed. Then, on the third day, he would be raised from death.

[24]Then Jesus said to his followers, "If anyone wants to follow me, he must say 'no' to the things he wants. He must be willing even to die on a cross, and he must follow me."

[n]**Peter** The Greek name "Peter," like the Aramaic name "Cephas," means "rock."

Prayer Starter: Dear God, I praise you for Jesus, the Messiah, Son of the living God.

Memory Verse: "Praise to the Son of David! . . .   —*Matthew 21:9b*

Jesus, Moses, and Elijah

Six days later, Jesus took Peter, James, and John the brother of James up on a high mountain. They were all alone there. ²While they watched, Jesus was changed. His face became bright like the sun. And his clothes became white as light. ³Then two men were there, talking with him. The men were Moses and Elijah.ⁿ

⁴Peter said to Jesus, "Lord, it is good that we are here. If you want, I will put three tents here—one for you, one for Moses, and one for Elijah."

⁵While Peter was talking, a bright cloud covered them. A voice came from the cloud. The voice said, "This is my Son and I love him. I am very pleased with him. Obey him!"

⁶The followers with Jesus heard the voice. They were so frightened that they fell to the ground. ⁷But Jesus went to them and touched them. He said, "Stand up. Don't be afraid." ⁸When the followers looked up, they saw Jesus was now alone.

⁹When Jesus and the followers were coming down the mountain, Jesus commanded them, "Don't tell anyone about the things you saw on the mountain. Wait until the Son of Man has been raised from death. Then you may tell."

¹⁰The followers asked Jesus, "Why do the teachers of the law say that Elijah must come first, before the Christ comes?"

¹¹Jesus answered, "They are right to say that Elijah is coming. And it is true that Elijah will make everything the way it should be. ¹²But I tell you, Elijah has already come. People did not know who he was. They did to him everything they wanted to do. It will be the same with the Son of Man. Those same people will make the Son of Man suffer." ¹³Then the followers understood that Jesus was talking about John the Baptist.

ⁿ**Moses and Elijah** Two of the most important Jewish leaders in the past.

Prayer Starter: I love your Word, Lord. Thank you for every verse in the Bible.

Memory Verse: "Praise to the Son of David! God bless the One . . ."
—*Matthew 21:9b*

Jesus Enters Jerusalem

Jesus and his followers were coming closer to Jerusalem. But first they stopped at Bethphage at the hill called the Mount of Olives. From there Jesus sent two of his followers into the town. ²He said to them, "Go to the town you can see there. When you enter it, you will find a donkey tied there with its colt. Untie them and bring them to me. ³If anyone asks you why you are taking the donkeys, tell him, 'The Master needs them. He will send them back soon.' "

⁴This was to make clear the full meaning of what the prophet said:

5   "Tell the people of Jerusalem,
        'Your king is coming to you.
    He is gentle and riding on a donkey.
        He is on the colt of a donkey.' "
⁶The followers went and did what Jesus told them to do. ⁷They brought the donkey and the colt to Jesus. They laid their coats on the donkeys, and Jesus sat on them. ⁸Many people spread their coats on the road before Jesus. Others cut branches from the trees and spread them on the road. ⁹Some of the people were walking ahead of Jesus. Others were walking behind him. All the people were shouting,

"Praise[n] to the Son of David!
God bless the One who comes in the name of the Lord!
Praise to God in heaven!"

¹⁰Then Jesus went into Jerusalem. The city was filled with excitement. The people asked, "Who is this man?"
¹¹The crowd answered, "This man is Jesus. He is the prophet from the town of Nazareth in Galilee."
¹²Jesus went into the Temple. He threw out all the people who were buying and selling there. He turned over the tables that belonged to the men who were exchanging different kinds of money. And he upset the benches of those who were selling doves. ¹³Jesus said to all the people there, "It is written in the Scriptures, 'My Temple will be a house where people will pray.'[n] But you are changing God's house into a 'hideout for robbers.' "[n]

[n]**Praise** Literally, "Hosanna," a Hebrew word used at first in praying to God for help. At this
   time it was probably a shout of joy used in praising God or his Messiah.
[n]**My Temple . . . pray.'** Quotation from Isaiah 56:7.
[n]**hideout for robbers.'** Quotation from Jeremiah 7:11.

Prayer Starter: Praise to the Son of David! Praise to Jesus!

Memory Verse: "Praise to the Son of David! God bless the One who comes . . ."
                                                          —*Matthew 21:9b*

Peter Denies Christ

T hose men who arrested Jesus led him to the house of Caiaphas, the high priest. The teachers of the law and the older Jewish leaders were gathered there. ⁵⁸Peter followed Jesus but did not go near him. He followed Jesus to the courtyard of the high priest's house. He sat down with the guards to see what would happen to Jesus.

⁵⁹The leading priests and the Jewish council tried to find something false against Jesus so that they could kill him.

⁶⁹At that time, Peter was sitting in the courtyard. A servant girl came to him and said, "You were with Jesus, that man from Galilee."

⁷⁰But Peter said that he was never with Jesus. He said this to all the people there. Peter said, "I don't know what you are talking about."

⁷¹Then he left the courtyard. At the gate, another girl saw him. She said to the people there, "This man was with Jesus of Nazareth."

⁷²Again, Peter said that he was never with Jesus. Peter said, "I swear that I don't know this man Jesus!"

⁷³A short time later, some people standing there went to Peter. They said, "We know you are one of those men who followed Jesus. We know this because of the way you talk."

⁷⁴Then Peter began to curse. He said, "May a curse fall on me if I'm not telling the truth. I don't know the man." After Peter said this, a rooster crowed. ⁷⁵Then he remembered what Jesus had told him: "Before the rooster crows, you will say three times that you don't know me." Then Peter went outside and cried painfully.

Prayer Starter: Lord, keep me from ever being ashamed of being a Christian.

Memory Verse: "Praise to the Son of David! God bless the One who comes in the name of the Lord! . . ."
—*Matthew 21:9b*

Pilate the Governor

Every year at the time of Passover the governor would free one person from prison. This was always a person the people wanted to be set free. [16]At that time there was a man in prison who was known to be very bad. His name was Barabbas. [17]All the people gathered at Pilate's house. Pilate said, "Which man do you want to free: Barabbas, or Jesus who is called the Christ?" [18]Pilate knew that the people gave Jesus to him because they were jealous.

[19]Pilate said these things while he was sitting on the judge's seat. While he was sitting there, his wife sent a message to him. The message said, "Don't do anything to that man. He is not guilty. Today I had a dream about him, and it troubled me very much."

[20]But the leading priests and older leaders told the crowd to ask for Barabbas to be freed and for Jesus to be killed.

[21]Pilate said, "I have Barabbas and Jesus. Which do you want me to set free for you?"

The people answered, "Barabbas!"

[22]Pilate asked, "What should I do with Jesus, the one called the Christ?" They all answered, "Kill him on a cross!"

[23]Pilate asked, "Why do you want me to kill him? What wrong has he done?"

But they shouted louder, "Kill him on a cross!"

[24]Pilate saw that he could do nothing about this, and a riot was starting. So he took some water and washed his hands[n] in front of the crowd. Then he said, "I am not guilty of this man's death. You are the ones who are causing it!"

[25]All the people answered, "We will be responsible. We accept for ourselves and for our children any punishment for his death."

[26]Then Pilate freed Barabbas. Pilate told some of the soldiers to beat Jesus with whips. Then he gave Jesus to the soldiers to be killed on a cross.

[n]**washed his hands** He did this as a sign to show that he wanted no part in what the people did.

Prayer Starter: Heavenly Father, I thank you for the Lord Jesus Christ, who was willing to die on the cross for my sins.

Memory Verse: "Praise to the Son of David! God bless the One who comes in the name of the Lord! Praise to God in heaven!"   —*Matthew 21:9b*

Jesus Heals the Sick

Jesus and his followers went to Capernaum. On the Sabbath day Jesus went to the synagogue and began to teach. [22]The people there were amazed at his teaching. He did not teach like their teachers of the law. He taught like a person who had authority. [23]While he was in the synagogue, a man was there who had an evil spirit in him. The man shouted, [24]"Jesus of Nazareth! What do you want with us? Did you come to destroy us? I know who you are—God's Holy One!"

[25]Jesus said strongly, "Be quiet! Come out of the man!" [26]The evil spirit made the man shake violently. Then the spirit gave a loud cry and came out of him.

[27]The people were amazed. They asked each other, "What is happening here? This man is teaching something new. And he teaches with authority. He even gives commands to evil spirits, and they obey him." [28]And the news about Jesus spread quickly everywhere in the area of Galilee.

[29]Jesus and his followers left the synagogue. They all went at once with James and John to the home of Simon[n] and Andrew. [30]Simon's mother-in-law was sick in bed with a fever. The people there told Jesus about her. [31]So Jesus went to her bed, took her hand, and helped her up. Immediately the fever left her, and she was healed. Then she began serving them.

[32]That night, after the sun went down, the people brought to Jesus all who were sick. They also brought those who had demons in them. [33]The whole town gathered at the door of the house. [34]Jesus healed many who had different kinds of sicknesses. He also forced many demons to leave people. But he would not allow the demons to speak, because they knew who he was.

[n]**Simon** Simon's other name was Peter.

Prayer Starter: Dear God, help me to tell the good news about Jesus to someone today.

Memory Verse: He said to them, "Let the little children . . ."
—*Mark 10:14b*

Many Evil Spirits

Jesus and his followers went across the lake to the region of the Gerasene people. ²When Jesus got out of the boat, a man came to him from the caves where dead people were buried. This man, who lived in the caves, had an evil spirit living in him. ³No one could tie him up, not even with a chain. ⁴Many times people had used chains to tie the man's hands and feet. But he always broke the chains off. No one was strong enough to control him. ⁵Day and night he would wander around the burial caves and on the hills, screaming and cutting himself with stones. ⁶While Jesus was still far away, the man saw him. He ran to Jesus and knelt down before him.

⁷⁻⁸Jesus said to the man, "You evil spirit, come out of that man."

But the man shouted in a loud voice, "What do you want with me, Jesus, Son of the Most High God? I beg you, promise God that you will not punish me!" ⁹Then Jesus asked the man, "What is your name?"

The man answered, "My name is Legion,ⁿ because I have many spirits in me."

¹⁰The man begged Jesus again and again not to send the spirits out of that area.

¹¹A large herd of pigs was eating on a hill near there. ¹²The evil spirits begged Jesus, "Send us to the pigs. Let us go into them." ¹³So Jesus allowed them to do this. The evil spirits left the man and went into the pigs. Then the herd of pigs rushed down the hill into the lake and were drowned. There were about 2,000 pigs in that herd.

¹⁴The men who took care of the pigs ran away. They went to the town and to the countryside, telling everyone about this. So people went out to see what had happened. ¹⁵They came to Jesus and saw the man who had had the many evil spirits. The man was sitting there, clothed and in his right mind. The people were frightened. ¹⁶Some people were there who saw what Jesus had done. They told the others what had happened to the man who had the demons living in him. And they also told about the pigs.

ⁿ**Legion** Means very many. A legion was about 5,000 men in the Roman army.

Prayer Starter: You are stonger than the devil and all the demons, God. You are Lord over all the earth.

Memory Verse: He said to them, "Let the little children come to me . . ."
—Mark 10:14b

Jesus Gives Life

Jesus went in the boat back to the other side of the lake. There, a large crowd gathered around him. ²²A ruler from the synagogue, named Jairus, came to that place. Jairus saw Jesus and bowed before him. ²³The ruler begged Jesus again and again. He said, "My little daughter is dying. Please come and put your hands on her. Then she will be healed and will live." ²⁴So Jesus went with the ruler, and many people followed Jesus. They were pushing very close around him.

³⁵Some men came from the house of Jairus, the synagogue ruler. The men said, "Your daughter is dead. There is now no need to bother the teacher."

³⁶But Jesus paid no attention to what the men said. He said to the synagogue ruler, "Don't be afraid; only believe."

³⁷Jesus let only Peter, James, and John the brother of James go with him to Jairus's house. ³⁸They came to the house of the synagogue ruler, and Jesus found many people there crying loudly. There was much confusion. ³⁹Jesus entered the house and said to the people, "Why are you crying and making so much noise? This child is not dead. She is only asleep." ⁴⁰But they only laughed at Jesus. He told all the people to leave. Then he went into the room where the child was. He took the child's father and mother and his three followers into the room with him. ⁴¹Then he took hold of the girl's hand and said to her, "Talitha, koum!" (This means, "Little girl, I tell you to stand up!") ⁴²The girl stood right up and began walking. (She was 12 years old.) The father and mother and the followers were amazed.

Prayer Starter: O Lord, give me faith in you when I am afraid. May I learn to trust you more each day.

Memory Verse: He said to them, "Let the little children come to me. Don't stop them. . . ."   —*Mark 10:14b*

Jesus Feeds 5,000

The apostles that Jesus had sent out to preach returned. They gathered around him and told him about all the things they had done and taught. ³¹Crowds of people were coming and going. Jesus and his followers did not even have time to eat. He said to them, "Come with me. We will go to a quiet place to be alone. There we will get some rest."

³²So they went in a boat alone to a place where there were no people. ³³But many people saw them leave and recognized them. So people from all the towns ran to the place where Jesus was going. They got there before Jesus arrived. ³⁴When he landed, he saw a great crowd waiting. Jesus felt sorry for them, because they were like sheep without a shepherd. So he taught them many things.

³⁵It was now late in the day. Jesus' followers came to him and said, "No one lives in this place. And it is already very late. ³⁶Send the people away. They need to go to the farms and towns around here to buy some food to eat."

³⁷But Jesus answered, "You give them food to eat."

They said to him, "We can't buy enough bread to feed all these people! We would all have to work a month to earn enough money to buy that much bread!"

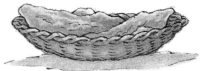

³⁸Jesus asked them, "How many loaves of bread do you have now? Go and see."

When they found out, they came to him and said, "We have five loaves and two fish."

³⁹Then Jesus said to the followers, "Tell all the people to sit in groups on the green grass." ⁴⁰So all the people sat in groups. They sat in groups of 50 or groups of 100. ⁴¹Jesus took the five loaves and two fish. He looked up to heaven and thanked God for the bread. He divided the bread and gave it to his followers for them to give to the people. Then he divided the two fish among them all. ⁴²All the people ate and were satisfied. ⁴³The followers filled 12 baskets with the pieces of bread and fish that were not eaten. ⁴⁴There were about 5,000 men there who ate.

Prayer Starter: Thank you, Lord, for fish and bread and pizzas and cherry pies, and for all good things to eat.

Memory Verse: He said to them, "Let the little children come to me. Don't stop them. The kingdom of God belongs to people . . ." —*Mark 10:14b*

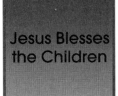

Jesus Blesses the Children

Some Pharisees came to Jesus and tried to trick him. They asked, "Is it right for a man to divorce his wife?"

³Jesus answered, "What did Moses command you to do?"

⁴They said, "Moses allowed a man to write out divorce papers and send her away."[n]

⁵Jesus said, "Moses wrote that command for you because you refused to accept God's teaching. ⁶But when God made the world, 'he made them male and female.'[n] ⁷'So a man will leave his father and mother and be united with his wife. ⁸And the two people will become one body.'[n] So the people are not two, but one. ⁹God has joined the two people together. So no one should separate them."

¹⁰Later, the followers and Jesus were in the house. They asked Jesus again about the question of divorce. ¹¹He answered, "Anyone who divorces his wife and marries another woman is guilty of adultery against her. ¹²And the woman who divorces her husband and marries another man is also guilty of adultery."

¹³Some people brought their small children to Jesus so he could touch them. But his followers told the people to stop bringing their children to him. ¹⁴When Jesus saw this, he was displeased. He said to them, "Let the little children come to me. Don't stop them. The kingdom of God belongs to people who are like these little children. ¹⁵I tell you the truth. You must accept the kingdom of God as a little child accepts things, or you will never enter it." ¹⁶Then Jesus took the children in his arms. He put his hands on them and blessed them.

[n]**"Moses . . . away."** Quotation from Deuteronomy 24:1.
[n]**'he made . . . female.'** Quotation from Genesis 1:27.
[n]**'So . . . body.'** Quotation from Genesis 2:24.

Prayer Starter: Thank you, Lord, for loving me. Thank you for blessing me.

Memory Verse: He said to them, "Let the little children come to me. Don't stop them. The kingdom of God belongs to people who are like these little children." —*Mark 10:14b*

The Lord's Supper

It was now the first day of the Feast of Unleavened Bread. This was a time when the Jews always sacrificed the Passover lambs. Jesus' followers came to him. They said, "We will go and prepare everything for the Passover Feast. Where do you want to eat the feast?"

13Jesus sent two of his followers and said to them, "Go into the city. A man carrying a jar of water will meet you. Follow him. 14He will go into a house. Tell the owner of the house, 'The Teacher asks that you show us the room where he and his followers can eat the Passover Feast.' 15The owner will show you a large room upstairs. This room is ready. Prepare the food for us there."

16So the followers left and went into the city. Everything happened as Jesus had said. So they prepared the Passover Feast.

17In the evening, Jesus went to that house with the 12. 18While they were all eating, Jesus said, "I tell you the truth. One of you will give me to my enemies—one of you eating with me now."

19The followers were very sad to hear this. Each one said to Jesus, "I am not the one, am I?"

20Jesus answered, "The man who is against me is 1 of you 12. He is the 1 who dips his bread into the bowl with me. 21The Son of Man must go and die. The Scriptures say this will happen. But how terrible it will be for the person who gives the Son of Man to be killed. It would be better for that person if he had never been born."

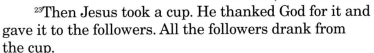

22While they were eating, Jesus took some bread. He thanked God for it and broke it. Then he gave it to his followers and said, "Take it. This bread is my body."

23Then Jesus took a cup. He thanked God for it and gave it to the followers. All the followers drank from the cup.

24Then Jesus said, "This is my blood which begins the new agreement that God makes with his people. This blood is poured out for many. 25I tell you the truth. I will not drink of this fruit of the vine[n] again until that day when I drink it new in the kingdom of God."

26They sang a hymn and went out to the Mount of Olives.

[n]**fruit of the vine** Product of the grapevine; this may also be translated "wine."

Prayer Starter: O God, how precious is the body and blood of my Lord Jesus.

Memory Verse: "My soul . . ." —*Luke 1:46b–47*

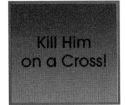

Kill Him
on a Cross!

Very early in the morning, the leading priests, the older Jewish leaders, the teachers of the law, and all the Jewish council decided what to do with Jesus. They tied him, led him away, and turned him over to Pilate, the governor.

²Pilate asked Jesus, "Are you the king of the Jews?" Jesus answered, "Yes, I am."

³The leading priests accused Jesus of many things. ⁴So Pilate asked Jesus another question. He said, "You can see that these people are accusing you of many things. Why don't you answer?"

⁵But Jesus still said nothing. Pilate was very surprised at this.

⁶Every year at the Passover time the governor would free one person from prison. He would free any person the people wanted him to free. ⁷At that time, there was a man named Barabbas in prison. He was a rebel

and had committed murder during a riot. [8]The crowd came to Pilate and asked him to free a prisoner as he always did.

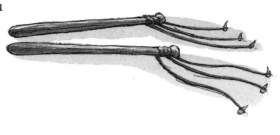

[9]Pilate asked them, "Do you want me to free the king of the Jews?" [10]Pilate knew that the leading priests had given Jesus to him because they were jealous of Jesus. [11]And the leading priests had persuaded the people to ask Pilate to free Barabbas, not Jesus.

[12]Pilate asked the crowd again, "So what should I do with this man you call the king of the Jews?"

[13]They shouted, "Kill him on a cross!"

[14]Pilated asked, "Why? What wrong has he done?"

But they shouted louder and louder, "Kill him on a cross!"

[15]Pilate wanted to please the crowd. So he freed Barabbas for them. And Pilate told the soldiers to beat Jesus with whips. Then he gave Jesus to the soldiers to be killed on a cross.

Prayer Starter: I love you, dear Lord, for being the one who suffered for me on the cross.

Memory Verse: "My soul praises the Lord . . ."   —*Luke 1:46b–47*

Soldiers Make Fun of Jesus

Pilate's soldiers took Jesus into the governor's palace (called the Praetorium). They called all the other soldiers together. ¹⁷They put a purple robe on Jesus. Then they used thorny branches to make a crown. They put it on his head. ¹⁸Then they called out to him, "Hail, King of the Jews!" ¹⁹The soldiers beat Jesus on the head many times with a stick. They also spit on him. Then they made fun of him by bowing on their knees and worshiping him. ²⁰After they finished making fun of him, the soldiers took off the purple robe and put his own clothes on him again. Then they led Jesus out of the palace to be killed on a cross.

²¹There was a man from Cyrene coming from the fields to the city. The man was Simon, the father of Alexander and Rufus. The soldiers forced Simon to carry the cross for Jesus. ²²They led Jesus to the place called Golgotha. (Golgotha means the Place of the Skull.) ²³At Golgotha the soldiers tried to give Jesus wine to drink. This wine was mixed with myrrh. But he refused to drink it. ²⁴The soldiers nailed Jesus to a cross. Then they divided his clothes among themselves. They threw lots to decide which clothes each soldier would get.

²⁵It was nine o'clock in the morning when they nailed Jesus to the cross. ²⁶There was a sign with the charge against Jesus written on it. The sign read: "THE KING OF THE JEWS." ²⁷They also put two robbers on crosses beside Jesus, one on the right, and the other on the left.

Prayer Starter: Thank you, Lord; thank you for Christ Jesus.

Memory Verse: "My soul praises the Lord; my heart is happy . . ."
—*Luke 1:46b–47*

An Angel Visits Mary

During Elizabeth's sixth month of pregnancy, God sent the angel Gabriel to a virgin who lived in Nazareth, a town in Galilee. She was engaged to marry a man named Joseph from the family of David. Her name was Mary. [28]The angel came to her and said, "Greetings! The Lord has blessed you and is with you."

[29]But Mary was very confused by what the angel said. Mary wondered, "What does this mean?"

[30]The angel said to her, "Don't be afraid, Mary, because God is pleased with you. [31]Listen! You will become pregnant. You will give birth to a son, and you will name him Jesus. [32]He will be great, and people will call him the Son of the Most High.

The Lord God will give him the throne of King David, his ancestor. [33]He will rule over the people of Jacob forever. His kingdom will never end."

[34]Mary said to the angel, "How will this happen? I am a virgin!"

[35]The angel said to Mary, "The Holy Spirit will come upon you, and the power of the Most High will cover you. The baby will be holy. He will be called the Son of God. [36]Now listen! Elizabeth, your relative, is very old. But she is also pregnant with a son. Everyone thought she could not have a baby, but she has been pregnant for six months. [37]God can do everything!"

[38]Mary said, "I am the servant girl of the Lord. Let this happen to me as you say!" Then the angel went away.

Prayer Starter: I am your servant, Lord. Use me.

Memory Verse: "My soul praises the Lord; my heart is happy because God . . ."
—*Luke 1:46b–47*

Mary and Elizabeth

Mary got up and went quickly to a town in the mountains of Judea. ⁴⁰She went to Zechariah's house and greeted Elizabeth. ⁴¹When Elizabeth heard Mary's greeting, the unborn baby inside Elizabeth jumped. Then Elizabeth was filled with the Holy Spirit.

⁴²She cried out in a loud voice, "God has blessed you more than any other woman. And God has blessed the baby which you will give birth to. ⁴³You are the mother of my Lord, and you have come to me! Why has something so good happened to me? ⁴⁴When I heard your voice, the baby inside me jumped with joy. ⁴⁵You are blessed because you believed what the Lord said to you would really happen."

⁴⁶ Then Mary said,
"My soul praises the Lord;
⁴⁷   my heart is happy because God is my Savior.
⁴⁸ I am not important, but God has shown his care for me,
          his servant girl.
     From now on, all people will say that I am blessed,
⁴⁹   because the Powerful One has done great things for me.
          His name is holy.
⁵⁰ God will always give mercy
          to those who worship him.
⁵¹ God's arm is strong.
          He scatters the people who are proud
          and think great things about themselves.
⁵² God brings down rulers from their thrones,
          and he raises up the humble.
⁵³ God fills the hungry with good things,
          but he sends the rich away with nothing.
⁵⁴ God has helped his people Israel who serve him.
          He gave them his mercy.
⁵⁵ God has done what he promised to our ancestors,
          to Abraham and to his children forever."

⁵⁶Mary stayed with Elizabeth for about three months and then returned home.

Prayer Starter: With all my heart I praise you, Lord.

Memory Verse: "My soul praises the Lord; my heart is happy because God is my Savior."   *—Luke 1:46b–47*

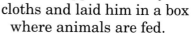

**Jesus
Is Born**

At that time, Augustus Caesar sent an order to all people in the countries that were under Roman rule. The order said that they must list their names in a register. ²This was the first registration[n] taken while Quirinius was governor of Syria. ³And everyone went to their own towns to be registered.

⁴So Joseph left Nazareth, a town in Galilee. He went to the town of Bethlehem in Judea. This town was known as the town of David. Joseph went there because he was from the family of David. ⁵Joseph registered with Mary because she was engaged to marry him. (Mary was now pregnant.) ⁶While Joseph and Mary were in Bethlehem, the time came for her to have the baby. ⁷She gave birth to her first son. There were no rooms left in the inn. So she wrapped the baby with

cloths and laid him in a box where animals are fed.

⁸That night, some shepherds were in the fields nearby watching their sheep. ⁹An angel of the Lord stood before them. The glory of the Lord was shining around them, and suddenly they became very frightened. ¹⁰The angel said to them, "Don't be afraid, because I am bringing you some good news. It will be a joy to all the people. ¹¹Today your Savior was born in David's town. He is Christ, the Lord. ¹²This is how you will know him: You will find a baby wrapped in cloths and lying in a feeding box."

¹³Then a very large group of angels from heaven joined the first angel. All the angels were praising God, saying:

¹⁴ "Give glory to God in heaven,
     and on earth let there be peace to the people who please God."

¹⁵Then the angels left the shepherds and went back to heaven. The shepherds said to each other, "Let us go to Bethlehem and see this thing that has happened. We will see this thing the Lord told us about."

¹⁶So the shepherds went quickly and found Mary and Joseph. ¹⁷And the shepherds saw the baby lying in a feeding box. Then they told what the angels had said about this child. ¹⁸Everyone was amazed when they heard what the shepherds said to them. ¹⁹Mary hid these things in her heart; she continued to think about them. ²⁰Then the shepherds went back to their sheep, praising God and thanking him for everything that they had seen and heard. It was just as the angel had told them.

[n]**registration** Census. A counting of all the people and the things they own.

Prayer Starter: Thank you, dear God, for sending Jesus. Help me to think about him just as Mary did.

Memory Verse: Jesus continued to learn . . .   —*Luke 2:52*

Simeon and Anna

The time came for Mary and Joseph to do what the law of Moses taught about being made pure.*ⁿ* They took Jesus to Jerusalem to present him to the Lord. ²³It is written in the law of the Lord: "Give every firstborn male to the Lord."*ⁿ* ²⁴Mary and Joseph also went to offer a sacrifice, as the law of the Lord says: "You must sacrifice two doves or two young pigeons."*ⁿ*

²⁵A man named Simeon lived in Jerusalem. He was a good man and very religious. He was waiting for the time when God would help Israel. The Holy Spirit was in him. ²⁶The Holy Spirit told Simeon that he would not die before he saw the Christ promised by the Lord. ²⁷The Spirit led Simeon to the Temple. Mary and Joseph brought the baby Jesus to the Temple to do what the law said they must do. ²⁸Then Simeon took the baby in his arms and thanked God:

29 "Now, Lord, you can let me, your servant,
　　 die in peace as you said.
30 I have seen your Salvation*ⁿ* with my own eyes.
31 　　 You prepared him before all people.
32 He is a light for the non-Jewish people to see.
　　 He will bring honor to your people, the Israelites."

³³Jesus' father and mother were amazed at what Simeon had said about him. ³⁴Then Simeon blessed them and said to Mary, "Many in Israel will fall and many will rise because of this child. He will be a sign from God that many people will not accept. ³⁵The things they think in secret will be made known. And the things that will happen will make your heart sad, too."

³⁶Anna, a prophetess, was there at the Temple. She was from the family of Phanuel in the tribe of Asher. Anna was very old. She had once been married for seven years. ³⁷Then her husband died and she lived alone. She was now 84

years old. Anna never left the Temple. She worshiped God by going without food and praying day and night. ³⁸She was standing there at that
time, thanking God. She talked about Jesus to all who were waiting for
God to free Jerusalem.

ⁿ**pure** The law of Moses said that 40 days after a Jewish woman gave birth to a baby, she must
    be cleansed by a ceremony at the Temple.
ⁿ**"Give . . . Lord"** Quotation from Exodus 13:2.
ⁿ**"You . . . pigeons."** Quotation from Leviticus 12:8.
ⁿ**Salvation** Simeon was talking about Jesus. The name Jesus means "salvation."

Prayer Starter: Lord, your mighty power is a light for all the nations.

Memory Verse: Jesus continued to learn more and more . . .
                                                        —*Luke 2:52*

The Child Jesus

Joseph and Mary finished doing everything that the law of the Lord commanded. Then they went home to Nazareth, their own town in Galilee. ⁴⁰The little child began to grow up. He became stronger and wiser, and God's blessings were with him.

⁴¹Every year Jesus' parents went to Jerusalem for the Passover Feast. ⁴²When Jesus was 12 years old, they went to the feast as they always did. ⁴³When the feast days were over, they went home. The boy Jesus stayed behind in Jerusalem, but his parents did not know it. ⁴⁴Joseph and Mary traveled for a whole day. They thought that Jesus was with them in the group. Then they began to look for him among their family and friends, ⁴⁵but they did not find him. So

they went back to Jerusalem to look for him there. ⁴⁶After three days they found him. Jesus was sitting in the Temple with the religious teachers, listening to them and asking them questions. ⁴⁷All who heard him were amazed at his understanding and wise answers. ⁴⁸When Jesus' parents saw him, they were amazed. His mother said to him, "Son, why did you do this to us? Your father and I were very worried about you. We have been looking for you."

⁴⁹Jesus asked, "Why did you have to look for me? You should have known that I must be where my Father's work is!" ⁵⁰But they did not understand the meaning of what he said.

⁵¹Jesus went with them to Nazareth and obeyed them. His mother was still thinking about all that had happened. ⁵²Jesus continued to learn more and more and to grow physically. People liked him, and he pleased God.

Prayer Starter: May I be like Jesus, dear Father. Make me wise and strong.

Memory Verse: Jesus continued to learn more and more and to grow physically. . . .   —*Luke 2:52*

John the Baptist

It was the fifteenth year of the rule of Tiberius Caesar. These men were under Caesar: Pontius Pilate was the ruler of Judea. Herod was the ruler of Galilee. Philip, Herod's brother, was the ruler of Iturea and Trachonitis. And Lysanias was the ruler of Abilene. [2]Annas and Caiaphas were the high priests. At this time, a command from God came to John son of Zechariah. John was living in the desert. [3]He went all over the area around the Jordan River and preached to the people. He preached a baptism of changed hearts and lives for the forgiveness of their sins. [4]As it is written in the book of Isaiah the prophet:

> "This is a voice of a man
> > who calls out in the desert:
> 'Prepare the way for the Lord.
> > Make the road straight for him.
> [5] Every valley should be filled in.
> > Every mountain and hill should be made flat.
> Roads with turns should be made straight,
> > and rough roads should be made smooth.
> [6] And all people will know about the salvation of God!' "

[15]All the people were hoping for the Christ to come, and they wondered about John. They thought, "Maybe he is the Christ."

[16]John answered everyone, "I baptize you with water, but there is one coming later who can do more than I can. I am not good enough to untie his sandals. He will baptize you with the Holy Spirit and with fire. [17]He will come ready to clean the grain. He will separate the good grain from the chaff. He will put the good part of the grain into his barn. Then he will burn the chaff with a fire that cannot be put out."[n] [18]And John continued to preach the Good News, saying many other things to encourage the people.

[21]When all the people were being baptized by John, Jesus was also baptized. While Jesus was praying, heaven opened and [22]the Holy Spirit came down on him. The Spirit was in the form of a dove. Then a voice came from heaven and said, "You are my Son and I love you. I am very pleased with you."

[n]**He will . . . out.** This means that Jesus will come to separate the good people from the bad people, saving the good and punishing the bad.

Prayer Starter: Lord, you are well pleased with your son Jesus. Be pleased with me, too.

Memory Verse: Jesus continued to learn more and more and to grow physically. People liked him . . .
—*Luke 2:52*

Young Man, Get Up

The next day Jesus went to a town called Nain. His followers and a large crowd were traveling with him. [12]When he came near the town gate, he saw a funeral. A mother, who was a widow, had lost her only son. A large crowd from the town was with the mother while her son was being carried out. [13]When the Lord saw her, he felt very sorry for her. Jesus said to her, "Don't cry." [14]He went up to the coffin and touched it. The men who were carrying it stopped. Jesus said, "Young man, I tell you, get up!" [15]And the son sat up and began to talk. Then Jesus gave him back to his mother.

[16]All the people were amazed. They began praising God. They said, "A great prophet has come to us! God is taking care of his people."

[17]This news about Jesus spread through all Judea and into all the places around there.

[18]John's followers told him about all these things. He called for two of his followers. [19]He sent them to the Lord to ask, "Are you the One who is coming, or should we wait for another?"

[20]So the men came to Jesus. They said, "John the Baptist sent us to you with this question: 'Are you the One who is coming, or should we wait for another?'"

[21]At that time, Jesus healed many people of their sicknesses, diseases, and evil spirits. He healed many blind people so that they could see again. [22]Then Jesus said to John's followers, "Go tell John the things that you saw and heard here. The blind can see. The crippled can walk. People with a harmful skin disease are healed. The deaf can hear, and the dead are given life. And the Good News is told to the poor. [23]The person who does not lose faith is blessed!"

Prayer Starter: Thank you, Lord, for helping those with problems.

Memory Verse: Jesus continued to learn more and more and to grow physically. People liked him, and he pleased God. —*Luke 2:52*

A Woman Washes Jesus' Feet

One of the Pharisees asked Jesus to eat with him. Jesus went into the Pharisee's house and sat at the table. [37]A sinful woman in the town learned that Jesus was eating at the Pharisee's house. So she brought an alabaster jar of perfume. [38]She stood at Jesus' feet, crying, and began to wash his feet with her tears. She dried his feet with her hair, kissed them many times and rubbed them with the perfume. [39]The Pharisee who asked Jesus to come to his house saw this. He thought to himself, "If Jesus were a prophet, he would know that the woman who is touching him is a sinner!"

[40]Jesus said to the Pharisee, "Simon, I have something to say to you."

Simon said, "Teacher, tell me."

[41]Jesus said, "There were two men. Both men owed money to the same banker. One man owed the banker 500 silver coins.[n] The other man owed the banker 50 silver coins. [42]The men had no money; so they could not pay what they owed. But the banker told the men that they did not have to pay him. Which one of the two men will love the banker more?"

[43]Simon, the Pharisee, answered, "I think it would be the one who owed him the most money."

Jesus said to Simon, "You are right." [44]Then Jesus turned toward the woman and said to Simon, "Do you see this woman? When I came into your house, you gave me no water for my feet. But she washed my feet with her tears and dried my feet with her hair. [45]You did not kiss me, but she has been kissing my feet since I came in! [46]You did not rub my head with oil, but she rubbed my feet with perfume. [47]I tell you that her many

sins are forgiven. This is clear because she showed great love. But the person who has only a little to be forgiven will feel only a little love."

⁴⁸Then Jesus said to her, "Your sins are forgiven."

⁴⁹The people sitting at the table began to think to themselves, "Who is this man? How can he forgive sins?"

⁵⁰Jesus said to the woman, "Because you believed, you are saved from your sins. Go in peace."

ⁿ**silver coins** A Roman denarius. One coin was the average pay for one day's work.

Prayer Starter: Thank you, Lord, for forgiveness of sins—no matter how big or small.

Memory Verse: Look at the birds. . . .   —*Luke 12:24*

The Good Samaritan

Then a teacher of the law stood up. He was trying to test Jesus. He said, "Teacher, what must I do to get life forever?"

²⁶Jesus said to him, "What is written in the law? What do you read there?"

²⁷The man answered, "Love the Lord your God. Love him with all your heart, all your soul, all your strength, and all your mind."ⁿ Also, "You must love your neighbor as you love yourself."ⁿ

²⁸Jesus said to him, "Your answer is right. Do this and you will have life forever."

²⁹But the man wanted to show that the way he was living was right. So he said to Jesus, "And who is my neighbor?"

³⁰To answer this question, Jesus said, "A man was going down the road from Jerusalem to Jericho. Some robbers attacked him. They tore off his clothes and beat him. Then they left him lying there, almost dead. ³¹It happened that a Jewish priest was going down that road. When the priest saw the man, he walked by on the other side of the road. ³²Next, a Leviteⁿ came there. He went over and looked at the man. Then he walked by on the other side of the road. ³³Then a Samaritanⁿ traveling down the road came to where the hurt man was lying. He saw the man and felt very sorry for him. ³⁴The Samaritan went to him and poured olive oil and wineⁿ on his wounds and bandaged them. He put the hurt man on his own donkey and took him to an inn. At the inn, the Samaritan took care of him. ³⁵The next day, the Samaritan brought out two silver coinsⁿ and gave them to the innkeeper. The Samaritan said, 'Take care of this man. If you spend more money on him, I will pay it back to you when I come again.'"

³⁶Then Jesus said, "Which one of these three men do you think was a neighbor to the man who was attacked by the robbers?"

³⁷The teacher of the law answered, "The one who helped him."

Jesus said to him, "Then go and do the same thing he did!"

ⁿ**"Love . . . mind."** Quotation from Deuteronomy 6:5.
ⁿ**"You . . . yourself."** Quotation from Leviticus 19:18.
ⁿ**Levite** Levites were men from the tribe of Levi who helped the Jewish priests with their work in the Temple.
ⁿ**Samaritan** Samaritans were people from Samaria. These people were part Jewish, but the Jews did not accept them as true Jews. Samaritans and Jews hated each other.
ⁿ**olive oil and wine** Oil and wine were used like medicine to soften and clean wounds.
ⁿ**silver coins** A Roman denarius. One coin was the average pay for one day's work.

Prayer Starter: Show me someone I can help this week, Lord.

Memory Verse: Look at the birds. They don't plant or harvest. . . .
—*Luke 12:24*

Foolish Rich Man

One of the men in the crowd said to Jesus, "Teacher, tell my brother to divide with me the property our father left us." [14]But Jesus said to him, "Who said that I should be your judge or decide how to divide the property between you two?" [15]Then Jesus said to them, "Be careful and guard against all kinds of greed. A man's life is not measured by the many things he owns."

[16]Then Jesus used this story: "There was a rich man who had some land, which grew a good crop of food. [17]The rich man thought to himself, 'What will I do? I have no place to keep all my crops.' [18]Then he said, 'I know what I will do. I will tear down my barns and build bigger ones! I will put all my grain and other goods together in my new barns. [19]Then I can say to myself, I have enough good things stored to last for many years. Rest, eat, drink, and enjoy life!'

[20]"But God said to that man, 'Foolish man! Tonight you will die. So who will get those things you have prepared for yourself?'

[21]"This is how it will be for anyone who stores things up only for himself and is not rich toward God."

Prayer Starter: Thank you for taking care of all the birds, Lord, and for taking care of me.

Memory Verse: Look at the birds. They don't plant or harvest. They don't save food in houses or barns. . . .   —*Luke 12:24*

Healing on the Sabbath

Jesus was teaching in one of the synagogues on the Sabbath day. ¹¹In the synagogue there was a woman who had an evil spirit in her. This spirit had made the woman a cripple for 18 years. Her back was always bent; she could not stand up straight. ¹²When Jesus saw her, he called her over and said, "Woman, your sickness has left you!" ¹³Jesus put his hands on her. Immediately she was able to stand up straight and began praising God.

¹⁴The synagogue leader was angry because Jesus healed on the Sabbath day. He said to the people, "There are six days for work. So come to be healed on one of those days. Don't come for healing on the Sabbath day."

¹⁵The Lord answered, "You people are hypocrites! All of you untie your work animals and lead them to drink water every day—even on the Sabbath day! ¹⁶This woman that I healed is our Jewish sister. But Satan has held her for 18 years. Surely it is not wrong for her to be freed from her sickness on a Sabbath day!" ¹⁷When Jesus said this, all the men who were criticizing him were ashamed. And all the people were happy for the wonderful things Jesus was doing.

[18]Then Jesus said, "What is God's kingdom like? What can I compare it with? [19]God's kingdom is like the seed of the mustard plant.[n] A man plants this seed in his garden. The seed grows and becomes a tree. The wild birds build nests on its branches."

[20]Jesus said again, "What can I compare God's kingdom with? [21]It is like yeast that a woman mixes into a big bowl of flour. The yeast makes all the dough rise."

14 On a Sabbath day, Jesus went to the home of a leading Pharisee to eat with him. The people there were all watching Jesus very closely. [2]A man with dropsy[n] was brought before Jesus. [3]Jesus said to the Pharisees and teachers of the law, "Is it right or wrong to heal on the Sabbath day?" [4]But they would not answer his question. So Jesus took the man, healed him, and sent him away. [5]Jesus said to the Pharisees and teachers of the law, "If your son or ox falls into a well on the Sabbath day, will you not pull him out quickly?" [6]And they could not answer him.

[n]**mustard plant** The seed is very small, but the plant grows taller than a man.
[n]**dropsy** A sickness that causes the body to swell larger and larger.

Prayer Starter: Lord, please help those who are sick today.

Memory Verse: Look at the birds. They don't plant or harvest. They don't save food in houses or barns. But God takes care of them . . .
—*Luke 12:24*

Jesus Tells Stories

Many tax collectors and "sinners" came to listen to Jesus. [2]The Pharisees and the teachers of the law began to complain: "Look! This man welcomes sinners and even eats with them!"

[3]Then Jesus told them this story: [4]"Suppose one of you has 100 sheep, but he loses 1 of them. Then he will leave the other 99 sheep alone and go out and look for the lost sheep. The man will keep on searching for the lost sheep until he finds it. [5]And when he finds it, the man is very happy. He puts it on his shoulders [6]and goes home. He calls to his friends and neighbors and says, 'Be happy with me because I found my lost sheep!' [7]In the same way, I tell you there is much joy in heaven when 1 sinner changes his heart. There is more joy for that 1 sinner than there is for 99 good people who don't need to change.

[8]"Suppose a woman has ten silver coins,[n] but she loses one of them. She will light a lamp and clean the house. She will look carefully for the coin until she finds it. [9]And when she finds it, she will call her friends and neighbors and say, 'Be happy with me because I have found the coin that I lost!' [10]In the same way, there is joy before the angels of God when 1 sinner changes his heart."

[n]**silver coins** A Roman denarius. One coin was the average pay for one day's work.

Prayer Starter: May more and more people turn to you, O Lord.

Memory Verse: Look at the birds! They don't plant or harvest. They don't save food in houses or barns. But God takes care of them. And you are worth much more than birds.　　　　　　　　　*—Luke 12.24*

A Son
Comes
Home

Then Jesus said, "A man had two sons. [12]The younger son said to the father, 'Give me my share of the property.' So the father divided the property between his two sons. [13]Then the younger son gathered up all that was his and left. He traveled far away to another country. There he wasted his money in foolish living. [14]He spent everything that he had. Soon after that, the land become very dry, and there was no rain. There was not enough food to eat anywhere in the country. The son was hungry and needed money. [15]So he got a job with one of the citizens there. The man sent the son into the fields to feed pigs. [16]The son was so hungry that he was willing to eat the food the pigs were eating. But no one gave him anything. [17]The

son realized that he had been very foolish. He thought, 'All of my father's servants have plenty of food. But I am here, almost dying with hunger. [18]I will leave and return to my father. I'll say to him: Father, I have sinned against God and have done wrong to you. [19]I am not good enough to be called your son. But let me be like one of your servants.' [20]So the son left and went to his father.

"While the son was still a long way off, his father saw him coming. He felt sorry for his son. So the father ran to him, and hugged and kissed him. [21]The son said, 'Father, I have sinned against God and have done wrong to you. I am not good enough to be called your son.' [22]But the father said to his servants, 'Hurry! Bring the best clothes and put them on him. Also, put a ring on his finger and sandals on his feet. [23]And get our fat calf and kill it. Then we can have a feast and celebrate! [24]My son was dead, but now he is alive again! He was lost, but now he is found!' So they began to celebrate.

[25]"The older son was in the field. As he came closer to the house, he heard the sound of music and dancing. [26]So he called to one of the servants and asked, 'What does all this mean?' [27]The servant said, 'Your brother has come back. Your father killed the fat calf to eat because your brother came home safely!' [28]The older son was angry and would not go in to the feast. So his father went out and begged him to come in. [29]The son said to his father, 'I have served you like a slave for many years! I have always obeyed your commands. But you never even killed a young goat for me to have a feast with my friends. [30]But your other son has wasted all your money on prostitutes. Then he comes home, and you kill the fat calf for him!' [31]The father said to him, 'Son, you are

always with me. All that I have is yours. [32]We had to celebrate and be happy because your brother was dead, but now he is alive. He was lost, but now he is found.' "

Prayer Starter: Give us love in our family for each other, Lord.

Memory Verse: He said to them . . .　　　　　　　　*—Luke 24:46*

Zacchaeus Sees Jesus

Jesus was going through the city of Jericho. ²In Jericho there was a man named Zacchaeus. He was a wealthy, very important tax collector. ³He wanted to see who Jesus was, but he was too short to see above the crowd. ⁴He ran ahead to a place where he knew Jesus would come. He climbed a sycamore tree so he could see Jesus. ⁵When Jesus came to that place, he looked up and saw Zacchaeus in the tree. He said to him, "Zacchaeus, hurry and come down! I must stay at your house today."

⁶Zacchaeus came down quickly. He was pleased to have Jesus in his house. ⁷All the people saw this and began to complain, "Look at the kind of man Jesus stays with. Zacchaeus is a sinner!"

⁸But Zacchaeus said to the Lord, "I will give half of my money to the poor. If I have cheated anyone, I will pay that person back four times more!"

⁹Jesus said, "Salvation has come to this house today. This man truly belongs to the family of Abraham. ¹⁰The Son of Man came to find lost people and save them."

Prayer Starter: Thank you, Lord, for coming to save lost people from their sins.

Memory Verse: He said to them: "It is written . . ."   —*Luke 24:46*

**Not What
I Want**

Jesus left the city and went to the Mount of Olives. His followers went with him. (Jesus went there often.) He said to his followers, "Pray for strength against temptation."

[41]Then Jesus went about a stone's throw away from them. He kneeled down and prayed, [42]"Father, if it is what you want, then let me not have this cup[n] of suffering. But do what you want, not what I want." [43]Then an angel from heaven appeared to him to help him. [44]Jesus was full of pain; he prayed even more. Sweat dripped from his face as if he were bleeding. [45]When he finished praying, he went to his followers. They were asleep. (Their sadness had made them very tired.) [46]Jesus said to them, "Why are you sleeping? Get up and pray for strength against temptation."

[47]While Jesus was speaking, a crowd came up. One of the 12 apostles was leading them. He was Judas. He came close to Jesus so that he could kiss him.

[48]But Jesus said to him, "Judas, are you using the kiss to give the Son of Man to his enemies?"

[49]The followers of Jesus were standing there too. They saw what was happening. They said to Jesus, "Lord, should we use our swords?" [50]And one of them did use his sword. He cut off the right ear of the servant of the high priest.

[51]Jesus said, "Stop!" Then he touched the servant's ear and healed him.

[52]Those who came to arrest Jesus were the leading priests, the soldiers who guarded the Temple, and the older Jewish leaders. Jesus said to them, "Why did you come out here with swords and sticks? Do you think I am a criminal? [53]I was with you every day in the Temple. Why didn't you try to arrest me there? But this is your time—the time when darkness rules."

[n]**cup** Jesus is talking about the bad things that will happen to him. Accepting these things will be hard, like drinking a cup of something that tastes very bitter.

Prayer Starter: Lord, teach me to pray as Jesus did.

Memory Verse: He said to them: "It is written that the Christ would be killed . . ."
                                                              —*Luke 24.46*

Travelers to Emmaus

That same day two of Jesus' followers were going to a town named Emmaus. It is about seven miles from Jerusalem. [14]They were talking about everything that had happened. [15]While they were discussing these things, Jesus himself came near and began walking with them. [16](They were not allowed to recognize Jesus.) [17]Then he said, "What are these things you are talking about while you walk?"

The two followers stopped. Their faces were very sad. [18]The one named Cleopas answered, "You must be the only one in Jerusalem who does not know what just happened there."

[19]Jesus said to them, "What are you talking about?"

The followers said, "It is about Jesus of Nazareth. He was a prophet from God to all the people. He said and did many powerful things. [20]Our leaders and the leading priests gave him up to be judged and killed. They nailed him to a cross. [21]But we were hoping that he would free the Jews. It is now the third day since this happened. [22]And today some women among us told us some amazing things. Early this morning they went to the tomb, [23]but they did not find his body there. They came and told us that they had seen a vision of angels. The angels said that Jesus was alive! [24]So some of our group went to the tomb, too. They found it just as the women said, but they did not see Jesus."

[25]Then Jesus said to them, "You are foolish and slow to realize what is true. You should believe everything the prophets said. [26]They said that the Christ must suffer these things before he enters his glory." [27]Then Jesus began to explain everything that had been written about himself in the Scriptures. He started with Moses, and then he talked about what all the prophets had said about him.

Prayer Starter: I'm so glad Jesus is alive, Lord! Hallelujah!

Memory Verse: He said to them: "It is written that the Christ would be killed and rise from death . . ."
—*Luke 24.46*

Jesus Returns to Heaven

While the two followers were telling this, Jesus himself stood among those gathered. He said to them, "Peace be with you."

³⁷They were fearful and terrified. They thought they were seeing a ghost. ³⁸But Jesus said, "Why are you troubled? Why do you doubt what you see? ³⁹Look at my hands and my feet. It is I myself! Touch me. You can see that I have a living body; a ghost does not have a body like this."

⁴⁰After Jesus said this, he showed them his hands and feet. ⁴¹The followers were amazed and very happy. They still could not believe it. Jesus said to them, "Do you have any food here?" ⁴²They gave him a piece of cooked fish. ⁴³While the followers watched, Jesus took the fish and ate it.

⁴⁴He said to them, "Remember when I was with you before? I said that everything written about me must happen—everything in the law of Moses, the books of the prophets, and the Psalms."

⁴⁵Then Jesus opened their minds so they could understand the Scriptures. ⁴⁶He said to them, "It is written that the Christ would be killed and rise from death on the third day. ⁴⁷⁻⁴⁸You saw these things happen—you are witnesses. You must tell people to change their hearts and lives. If they do this, their sins will be forgiven. You must start at Jerusalem and preach these things in my name to all nations. ⁴⁹Listen! My Father has promised you something; I will send it to you. But you must stay in Jerusalem until you have received that power from heaven."

⁵⁰Jesus led his followers out of Jerusalem almost to Bethany. He raised his hands and blessed them. ⁵¹While he was blessing them, he was separated from them and carried into heaven. ⁵²They worshiped him and then went back to the city very happy. ⁵³They stayed in the Temple all the time, praising God.

Prayer Starter: Dear God, help me to tell others about you and all that you have done.

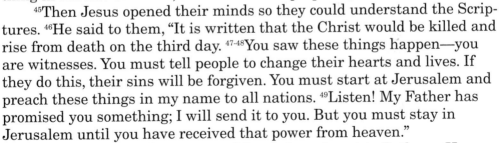

Memory Verse: He said to them: "It is written that the Christ would be killed and rise from death on the third day."   —*Luke 24.46*

281

A Wedding in Cana

Two days later there was a wedding in the town of Cana in Galilee. Jesus' mother was there. ²Jesus and his followers were also invited to the wedding. ³When all the wine was gone, Jesus' mother said to him, "They have no more wine."

⁴Jesus answered, "Dear woman, why come to me? My time has not yet come."

⁵His mother said to the servants, "Do whatever he tells you to do."

⁶In that place there were six stone water jars. The Jews used jars like these in their washing ceremony." Each jar held about 20 or 30 gallons.

⁷Jesus said to the servants, "Fill the jars with water." So they filled the jars to the top.

⁸Then he said to them, "Now take some out and give it to the master of the feast."

So the servants took the water to the master. ⁹When he tasted it, the water had become wine. He did not know where the wine came from. But the servants who brought the water knew. The master of the wedding called the bridegroom ¹⁰and said to him, "People always serve the best wine first. Later, after the guests have been drinking a lot, they serve the cheaper wine. But you have saved the best wine till now."

¹¹So in Cana of Galilee, Jesus did his first miracle. There he showed his glory, and his followers believed in him.

¹²Then Jesus went to the town of Capernaum with his mother, brothers and his followers. They all stayed in Capernaum for a few days.

"**washing ceremony** The Jews washed themselves in special ways before eating, before worshiping in the Temple, and at other special times.

Prayer Starter: Help me to do whatever Jesus tells me to, Lord.

Memory Verse: For God loved the world so much . . .   —*John 3:16*

Nicodemus Visits Jesus

There was a man named Nicodemus who was one of the Pharisees. He was an important Jewish leader. ²One night Nicodemus came to Jesus. He said, "Teacher, we know that you are a teacher sent from God. No one can do the miracles you do, unless God is with him."

³Jesus answered, "I tell you the truth. Unless one is born again, he cannot be in God's kingdom."

⁴Nicodemus said, "But if a man is already old, how can he be born again? He cannot enter his mother's body again. So how can he be born a second time?"

⁵But Jesus answered, "I tell you the truth. Unless one is born from water and the Spirit, he cannot enter God's kingdom. ⁶A person's body is born from his human parents. But a person's spiritual life is born from the Spirit. ⁷Don't be surprised when I tell you, 'You must all be born again.' ⁸The wind blows where it wants to go. You hear the wind blow. But you don't know where the wind comes from or where it is going. It is the same with every person who is born from the Spirit."

⁹Nicodemus asked, "How can all this be possible?"

¹⁰Jesus said, "You are an important teacher in Israel. But you still don't understand these things? ¹¹I tell you the truth. We talk about what we know. We tell about what we have seen. But you don't accept what we tell you. ¹²I have told you about things here on earth, but you do not believe me. So surely you will not believe me if I tell you about the things of heaven! ¹³The only one who has ever gone up to heaven is the One who came down from heaven—the Son of Man."

Prayer Starter: Thank you, God, for loving the people of this world enough to give your only Son to save them.

Memory Verse: For God loved the world so much that he gave his only Son. . . .
—*John 3.16*

285

The Woman at the Well

The Pharisees heard that Jesus was making and baptizing more followers than John. ²(But really Jesus himself did not baptize people. His followers did the baptizing.) Jesus knew that the Pharisees had heard about him. ³So he left Judea and went back to Galilee. ⁴On the way he had to go through the country of Samaria.

⁵In Samaria Jesus came to the town called Sychar. This town is near the field that Jacob gave to his son Joseph. ⁶Jacob's well was there. Jesus was tired from his long trip. So he sat down beside the well. It was about noon. ⁷A Samaritan woman came to the well to get some water. Jesus said to her, "Please give me a drink." ⁸(This happened while Jesus' followers were in town buying some food.)

⁹The woman said, "I am surprised that you ask me for a drink. You are a Jew and I am a Samaritan." (Jews are not friends with Samaritans.ⁿ)

¹⁰Jesus said, "You don't know what God gives. And you don't know who asked you for a drink. If you knew, you would have asked me, and I would have given you living water."

¹¹The woman said, "Sir, where will you get that living water? The well is very deep, and you have nothing to get water with. ¹²Are you greater than Jacob, our father? Jacob is the one who gave us this well. He drank from it himself. Also, his sons and flocks drank from this well."

¹³Jesus answered, "Every person who drinks this water will be thirsty again. ¹⁴But whoever drinks the water I give will never be thirsty again. The water I give will become a spring of water flowing inside him. It will give him eternal life."

ⁿ**Jews . . . Samaritans** This can also be translated "Jews don't use things that Samaritans have used."

Prayer Starter: You give me the water of life, Lord. Thank you.

Memory Verse: For God loved the world so much that he gave his only Son. God gave his Son . . .
　　　　　　　　　　　　　　　　　　　　　　　　—John 3.16

Jesus' Brothers

After this, Jesus traveled around Galilee. He did not want to travel in Judea, because the Jews there wanted to kill him. [2]It was time for the Jewish Feast of Shelters. [3]So Jesus' brothers said to him, "You should leave here and go to Judea. Then your followers there can see the miracles you do. [4]Anyone who wants to be well known does not hide what he does. If you are doing these things, show yourself to the world." [5](Even Jesus' brothers did not believe in him.)

[6]Jesus said to his brothers, "The right time for me has not yet come. But any time is right for you. [7]The world cannot hate you. But it hates me, because I tell about the evil things it does. [8]So you go to the feast. I will not go now. The right time for me has not yet come." [9]After saying this, Jesus stayed in Galilee.

[10]So Jesus' brothers left to go to the feast. When they had gone, Jesus went, too. But he did not let people see him. [11]At the feast the Jews were looking for him. They said, "Where is that man?"

[12]There was a large crowd of people there. Many of them were whispering to each other about Jesus. Some said, "He is a good man."

Others said, "No, he fools the people." [13]But no one was brave enough to talk about Jesus openly. They were afraid of the Jews.

[37]The last day of the feast came. It was the most important day. On that day Jesus stood up and said in a loud voice, "If anyone is thirsty, let him come to me and drink. [38]If a person believes in me, rivers of living water will flow out from his heart. This is what the Scripture says." [39]Jesus was talking about the Holy Spirit. The Spirit had not yet been given because Jesus had not yet been raised to glory. But later, those who believed in Jesus would receive the Spirit.

Prayer Starter: Father, help me to share the water of life with others.

Memory Verse: For God loved the world so much that he gave his only Son. God gave his Son so that whoever believes in him may not be lost . . .

—John 3.16

The Blind Man

As Jesus was walking along, he saw a man who had been born blind. [2]His followers asked him, "Teacher, whose sin caused this man to be born blind—his own sin or his parents' sin?"

[3]Jesus answered, "It is not this man's sin or his parents' sin that made him be blind. This man was born blind so that God's power could be shown in him. [4]While it is daytime, we must continue doing the work of the One who sent me. The night is coming. And no one can work at night. [5]While I am in the world, I am the light of the world."

[6]After Jesus said this, he spit on the ground and made some mud with it. He put the mud on the man's eyes. [7]Then he told the man, "Go and wash in the Pool of Siloam." (Siloam means Sent.) So the man went to the pool. He washed and came back. And he was able to see.

[8]Some people had seen this man begging before. They and the man's neighbors said, "Look! Is this the same man who always sits and begs?"

⁹Some said, "Yes! He is the one." But others said, "No, he's not the same man. He only looks like him."

So the man himself said, "I am the man."

¹⁰They asked, "What happened? How did you get your sight?"

¹¹He answered, "The man named Jesus made some mud and put it on my eyes. Then he told me to go to Siloam and wash. So I went and washed and came back seeing."

¹²They asked him, "Where is this man?"

The man answered, "I don't know."

¹³Then the people took to the Pharisees the man who had been blind. ¹⁴The day Jesus had made mud and healed his eyes was a Sabbath day. ¹⁵So now the Pharisees asked the man, "How did you get your sight?"

He answered, "He put mud on my eyes. I washed, and now I can see."

¹⁶Some of the Pharisees were saying, "This man does not keep the Sabbath day. He is not from God!"

Others said, "But a man who is a sinner can't do miracles like these." So they could not agree with each other.

¹⁷They asked the man again, "What do you say about him? It was your eyes he opened."

The man answered, "He is a prophet."

¹⁸The Jews did not believe that he had been blind and could now see again. So they sent for the man's parents ¹⁹and asked them, "Is this your son? You say that he was born blind. Then how does he see now?"

²⁰His parents answered, "We know that this is our son, and we know that he was born blind. ²¹But we don't know how he can see now. We don't know who opened his eyes. Ask him. He is old enough to answer for himself." ²²His parents said this because they were afraid of the Jews. The Jews had already decided that anyone who said that Jesus was the Christ would be put out of the synagogue. ²³That is why his parents said, "He is old enough. Ask him."

²⁴So for the second time, they called the man who had been blind. They said, "You should give God the glory by telling the truth. We know that this man is a sinner."

²⁵He answered, "I don't know if he is a sinner. But one thing I do know. I was blind, and now I can see."

Prayer Starter: I'm amazed at Jesus' power! I praise and worship him.

Memory Verse: For God loved the world so much that he gave his only Son. God gave his Son so that whoever believes in him may not be lost, but have eternal life.   *—John 3.16*

The Good Shepherd

So Jesus said again, "I tell you the truth. I am the door for the sheep. ⁸All the people who came before me were thieves and robbers. The sheep did not listen to them. ⁹I am the door. The person who enters through me will be saved. He will be able to come in and go out and find pasture. ¹⁰A thief comes to steal and kill and destroy. But I came to give life—life in all its fullness.

¹¹"I am the good shepherd. The good shepherd gives his life for the sheep. ¹²The worker who is paid to keep the sheep is different from the shepherd who owns them. So when the worker sees a wolf coming, he runs away and leaves the sheep alone. Then the wolf attacks the sheep and scatters them. ¹³The man runs away because he is only a paid worker. He does not really care for the sheep.

¹⁴⁻¹⁵"I am the good shepherd. I know my sheep, as the Father knows me. And my sheep know me, as I know the Father. I give my life for the sheep. ¹⁶I have other sheep that are not in this flock here. I must bring them also. They will listen to my voice, and there will be one flock and one shepherd."

Prayer Starter: Lord, give me life to the fullest!

Memory Verse: A thief comes to steal . . .   —*John 10:10*

Lazarus, Come Out!

Jesus arrived in Bethany. There he learned that Lazarus had already been dead and in the tomb for four days.

²⁰Martha heard that Jesus was coming, and she went out to meet him. But Mary stayed at home. ²¹Martha said to Jesus, "Lord, if you had been here, my brother would not have died. ²²But I know that even now God will give you anything you ask."

²⁵Jesus said to her, "I am the resurrection and the life. He who believes in me will have life even if he dies. ²⁶And he who lives and believes in me will never die. Martha, do you believe this?"

²⁷Martha answered, "Yes, Lord. I believe that you are the Christ, the Son of God. You are the One who was coming to the world."

³³Jesus saw that Mary was crying and that the Jews who came with her were crying, too. Jesus felt very sad in his heart and was deeply troubled. ³⁴He asked, "Where did you bury him?"

"Come and see, Lord," they said.

³⁵Jesus cried.

³⁶So the Jews said, "See how much he loved him."

³⁷But some of them said, "If Jesus healed the eyes of the blind man, why didn't he keep Lazarus from dying?"

³⁸Again Jesus felt very sad in his heart. He came to the tomb. The tomb was a cave with a large stone covering the entrance. ³⁹Jesus said, "Move the stone away."

Martha said, "But, Lord, it has been four days since he died. There will be a bad smell." Martha was the sister of the dead man.

⁴⁰Then Jesus said to her, "Didn't I tell you that if you believed, you would see the glory of God?"

⁴¹So they moved the stone away from the entrance. Then Jesus looked up and said, "Father, I thank you that you heard me. ⁴²I know that you always hear me. But I said these things because of the people here around me. I want them to believe that you sent me." ⁴³After Jesus said this, he cried out in a loud voice, "Lazarus, come out!" ⁴⁴The dead man came out. His hands and feet were wrapped with pieces of cloth, and he had a cloth around his face.

Jesus said to them, "Take the cloth off of him and let him go."

Prayer Starter: Father, I thank you for answering my prayers.

Memory Verse: A thief comes to steal and kill . . .   —*John 10:10*

Washing
Feet

It was almost time for the Jewish Passover Feast. Jesus knew that it was time for him to leave this world and go back to the Father. He had always loved those who were his own in the world, and he loved them all the way to the end.

²Jesus and his followers were at the evening meal. The devil had already persuaded Judas Iscariot to turn against Jesus. (Judas was the son of Simon.) ³Jesus knew that the Father had given him power over everything. He also knew that he had come from God and was going back to God. ⁴So during the meal Jesus stood up and took off his outer clothing. Taking a towel, he wrapped it around his waist. ⁵Then he poured water into a bowl and began to wash the followers' feet. He dried them with the towel that was wrapped around him.

⁶Jesus came to Simon Peter. But Peter said to Jesus, "Lord, are you going to wash my feet?"

⁷Jesus answered, "You don't understand what I am doing now. But you will understand later."

⁸Peter said, "No! You will never wash my feet."

Jesus answered, "If I don't wash your feet, then you are not one of my people."

⁹Simon Peter answered, "Lord, after you wash my feet, wash my hands and my head, too!"

¹⁰Jesus said, "After a person has had a bath, his whole body is clean. He needs only to wash his feet. And you men are clean, but not all of you." ¹¹Jesus knew who would turn against him. That is why Jesus said, "Not all of you are clean."

¹²When he had finished washing their feet, he put on his clothes and sat down again. Jesus asked, "Do you understand what I have just done for you? ¹³You call me 'Teacher' and 'Lord.' And this is right, because that is what I am. ¹⁴I, your Lord and Teacher, have washed your feet. So you also should wash each other's feet. ¹⁵I did this as an example for you. So you should do as I have done for you. ¹⁶I tell you the truth. A servant is not greater than his master. A messenger is not greater than the one who sent him. ¹⁷If you know these things, you will be happy if you do them.

¹⁸"I am not talking about all of you. I know those I have chosen. But what the Scripture said must happen: 'The man who ate at my table has now turned against me.'ⁿ ¹⁹I am telling you this now before it happens. Then when it happens you will believe that I am he. ²⁰I tell you the truth. Whoever accepts anyone I send also accepts me. And whoever accepts me also accepts the One who sent me."

ⁿ**The man . . . me.'** Quotation from Psalm 41:9.

Prayer Starter: Make me a humble servant, just like the Lord Jesus.

Memory Verse: A thief comes to steal and kill and destroy. . . .
                                                              —John 10:10

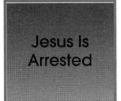

Jesus Is Arrested

When Jesus finished praying, he left with his followers. They went across the Kidron Valley. On the other side there was a garden of olive trees. Jesus and his followers went there.

²Judas knew where this place was, because Jesus met there often with his followers. Judas was the one who turned against Jesus. ³So Judas led a group of soldiers to the garden. Judas also brought some guards from the leading priests and the Pharisees. They were carrying torches, lanterns, and weapons.

⁴Jesus knew everything that would happen to him. Jesus went out and asked, "Who is it you are looking for?"

⁵The men answered, "Jesus from Nazareth."

Jesus said, "I am Jesus." (Judas, the one who turned against Jesus, was standing there with them.) ⁶When Jesus said, "I am Jesus," the men moved back and fell to the ground.

⁷Jesus asked them again, "Who is it you are looking for?"

They said, "Jesus of Nazareth."

⁸Jesus said, "I told you that I am he. So if you are looking for me, then let these other men go." ⁹This happened so that the words Jesus said before might come true: "I have not lost any of the men you gave me."

¹⁰Simon Peter had a sword. He took out the sword and struck the servant of the high priest, cutting off his right ear. (The servant's name was Malchus.) ¹¹Jesus said to Peter, "Put your sword back. Shall I not drink of the cup[n] the Father has given me?"

¹²Then the soldiers with their commander and the Jewish guards arrested Jesus. They tied him ¹³and led him first to Annas. Annas was the father-in-law of Caiaphas, the high priest that year. ¹⁴Caiaphas was the one who had told the Jews that it would be better if one man died for all the people.

[n]**cup** Jesus is talking about the bad things that will happen to him. Accepting these things will be very hard, like drinking a cup of something that tastes very bitter.

Prayer Starter: Help me to be patient, Lord, with people I don't like.

Memory Verse: A thief comes to steal and kill and destroy. But I came to give life . . .   —*John 10:10*

King of the Jews

The soldiers took charge of Jesus. [17]Carrying his own cross, Jesus went out to a place called The Place of the Skull. (In the Jewish language[n] this place is called Golgotha.) [18]There they nailed Jesus to the cross. They also put two other men on crosses, one on each side of Jesus with Jesus in the middle. [19]Pilate wrote a sign and put it on the cross. It read: "JESUS OF NAZARETH, THE KING OF THE JEWS." [20]The sign was written in the Jewish language, in Latin, and in Greek. Many of the Jews read the sign, because this place where Jesus was killed was near the city. [21]The leading Jewish priests said to Pilate, "Don't write, 'The King of Jews.' But write, 'This man said, I am the King of the Jews.' "

[22]Pilate answered, "What I have written, I have written!"

[23]After the soldiers nailed Jesus to the cross, they took his clothes. They divided them into four parts. Each soldier got one part. They also took his long shirt. It was all one piece of cloth, woven from top to bottom. [24]So the soldiers said to each other, "We should not tear this into parts. We should throw lots to see who will get it." This happened to give full meaning to the Scripture:

> "They divided my clothes among them.
> And they threw lots for my clothing."

So the soldiers did this.

[25]Jesus' mother stood near his cross. His mother's sister was also standing there, with Mary the wife of Clopas, and Mary Magdalene. [26]Jesus saw his mother. He also saw the follower he loved standing there. He said to his mother, "Dear woman, here is your son." [27]Then he said to the follower, "Here is your mother." From that time on, this follower took her to live in his home.

[28]After this, Jesus knew that everything had been done. To make the Scripture come true, he said, "I am thirsty."[n] [29]There was a jar full of vinegar there, so the soldiers soaked a sponge in it. Then they put the sponge on a branch of a hyssop plant and lifted it to Jesus' mouth. [30]Jesus tasted the vinegar. Then he said, "It is finished." He bowed his head and died.

[n]**Jewish language** Aramaic, the language of the Jews in the first century.
[n]**"I am thirsty."** Read Psalms 22:15; 69:21.

Prayer Starter: Thank you for the cross of Jesus, and for the empty tomb.

Memory Verse: A thief comes to steal and kill and destroy. But I came to give life—life in all its fullness.   —*John 10:10*

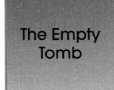

The Empty Tomb

Later, a man named Joseph from Arimathea asked Pilate if he could take the body of Jesus. (Joseph was a secret follower of Jesus, because he was afraid of the Jews.) Pilate gave his permission. So Joseph came and took Jesus' body away. ³⁹Nicodemus went with Joseph. Nicodemus was the man who earlier had come to Jesus at night. He brought about 75 pounds of spices. This was a mixture of myrrh and aloes. ⁴⁰These two men

took Jesus' body and wrapped it with the spices in pieces of linen cloth. (This is how the Jews bury people.) ⁴¹In the place where Jesus was killed, there was a garden. In the garden was a new tomb where no one had ever been buried. ⁴²The men laid Jesus in that tomb because it was near, and the Jews were preparing to start their Sabbath day.

20Early on the first day of the week, Mary Magdalene went to the tomb. It was still dark. Mary saw that the large stone had been moved away from the tomb. ²So Mary ran to Simon Peter and the other follower (the one Jesus loved). Mary said, "They have taken the Lord out of the tomb. We don't know where they have put him."

³So Peter and the other follower started for the tomb. ⁴They were

both running, but the other follower ran faster than Peter. So the other follower reached the tomb first. ⁵He bent down and looked in. He saw the strips of linen cloth lying there, but he did not go in. ⁶Then following him came Simon Peter. He went into the tomb and saw the strips of linen lying there. ⁷He also saw the cloth that had been around Jesus' head. The cloth was folded up and laid in a different place from the strips of linen. ⁸Then the other follower, who had reached the tomb first, also went in. He saw and believed. ⁹(These followers did not yet understand from the Scriptures that Jesus must rise from death.)

¹⁰Then the followers went back home.

Prayer Starter: Remind me each day, Lord, that Jesus is alive.

Memory Verse: But the Holy Spirit will come to you . . .   —*Acts 1:8*

Jesus Appears to Mary

But Mary stood outside the tomb, crying. While she was still crying, she bent down and looked inside the tomb. [12]She saw two angels dressed in white. They were sitting where Jesus' body had been, one at the head and one at the feet.

[13]They asked her, "Woman, why are you crying?"

She answered, "They have taken away my Lord. I don't know where they have put him." [14]When Mary said this, she turned around and saw Jesus standing there. But she did not know that it was Jesus.

[15]Jesus asked her, "Woman, why are you crying? Whom are you looking for?"

Mary thought he was the gardener. So she said to him, "Did you take him away, sir? Tell me where you put him, and I will get him."

[16]Jesus said to her, "Mary."

Mary turned toward Jesus and said in the Jewish language,[n] "Rabboni." (This means Teacher.)

[17]Jesus said to her, "Don't hold me. I have not yet gone up to the Father. But go to my brothers and tell them this: 'I am going back to my Father and your Father. I am going back to my God and your God.' "

[18]Mary Magdalene went and said to the followers, "I saw the Lord!" And she told them what Jesus had said to her.

[n]**Jewish language** Aramaic, the language of the Jews in the first century.

Prayer Starter: Help me to tell others the good news that Jesus rose from the dead.

Jesus and Thomas

It was the first day of the week. That evening the followers were together. The doors were locked, because they were afraid of the Jews. Then Jesus came and stood among them. He said, "Peace be with you!" ²⁰After he said this, he showed them his hands and his side. The followers were very happy when they saw the Lord.

²¹Then Jesus said again, "Peace be with you! As the Father sent me, I now send you." ²²After he said this, he breathed on them and said, "Receive the Holy Spirit. ²³If you forgive anyone his sins, they are forgiven. If you don't forgive them, they are not forgiven."

²⁴Thomas (called Didymus) was not with the followers when Jesus came. Thomas was 1 of the 12. ²⁵The other followers told Thomas, "We saw the Lord."

But Thomas said, "I will not believe it until I see the nail marks in his hands. And I will not believe until I put my finger where the nails were and put my hand into his side."

²⁶A week later the followers were in the house again. Thomas was with them. The doors were locked, but Jesus came in and stood among them. He said, "Peace be with you!" ²⁷Then he said to Thomas, "Put your finger here. Look at my hands. Put your hand here in my side. Stop doubting and believe."

²⁸Thomas said to him, "My Lord and my God!"

²⁹Then Jesus told him, "You believe because you see me. Those who believe without seeing me will be truly happy."

Prayer Starter: Thank you, heavenly Father, for Jesus who is my Lord and my God.

Memory Verse: But the Holy Spirit will come to you. Then you will receive power. You will be my witnesses . . .
　　　　　　　　　　　　　　　　　　　　　　　　　　—*Acts 1:8*

Two Men Dressed in White

I wrote about the whole life of Jesus, from the beginning until the day he was taken up into heaven. Before this, Jesus talked to the apostles he had chosen. With the help of the Holy Spirit, Jesus told them what they should do. ³After his death, he showed himself to them and proved in many ways that he was alive. The apostles saw Jesus during the 40 days after he was raised from death. He spoke to them about the kingdom of God. ⁴Once when he was eating with them, he told them not to leave Jerusalem. He said, "The Father has made you a promise which I told you about before. Wait here to receive this promise. ⁵John baptized people with water, but in a few days you will be baptized with the Holy Spirit."

⁶The apostles were all together. They asked Jesus, "Lord, are you at this time going to give the kingdom back to Israel?"

⁷Jesus said to them, "The Father is the only One who has the authority to decide dates and times. These things are not for you to know. ⁸But the Holy Spirit will come to you. Then you will receive power. You will be my witnesses—in Jerusalem, in all of Judea, in Samaria, and in every part of the world."

⁹After he said this, as they were watching, he was lifted up. A cloud hid him from their sight. ¹⁰As he was going, they were looking into the sky. Suddenly, two men wearing white clothes stood beside them. ¹¹They said, "Men of Galilee, why are you standing here looking into the sky? You saw Jesus taken away from you into heaven. He will come back in the same way you saw him go."

Prayer Starter: Please hurry and come back to earth, Lord. We love you.

Memory Verse: But the Holy Spirit will come to you. Then you will receive power. You will be my witnesses—in Jerusalem, in all of Judea, in Samaria . . .

—*Acts 1:8*

The Disciples Meet

When they entered the city, they went to the upstairs room where they were staying. Peter, John, James, Andrew, Philip, Thomas, Bartholomew, Matthew, James son of Alphaeus, Simon (known as the Zealot), and Judas son of James were there. [14]They all continued praying together. Some women, including Mary the mother of Jesus, and Jesus' brothers were also there with the apostles.

[15]During this time there was a meeting of the believers. (There were about 120 of them.) Peter stood up and said, [16-17]"Brothers, in the Scriptures the Holy Spirit said through David that something must happen. The Spirit was talking about Judas, one of our own group, who served together with us. The Spirit said that Judas would lead men to arrest Jesus."

[21-22]"So now a man must join us and become a witness of Jesus' being raised from death. He must be one of the men who were part of our group during all the time the Lord Jesus was with us. He must have been with us from the time John began to baptize people until the day when Jesus was taken up from us to heaven."

[23]They put the names of two men before the group. One was Joseph Barsabbas, who was also called Justus. The other was Matthias. [24-25]The apostles prayed, "Lord, you know the minds of everyone. Show us which one of these two you have chosen to do this work. Judas turned away from it and went where he belongs. Lord, show us which one should take his place as an apostle!" [26]Then they used lots to choose between them, and the lots showed that Matthias was the one. So he became an apostle with the other 11.

Prayer Starter: Show me your choices for me, each day, O Lord.

Memory Verse: But the Holy Spirit will come to you. Then you will receive power. You will be my witnesses—in Jerusalem, in all of Judea, in Samaria, and in every part of the world.
—*Acts 1:8*

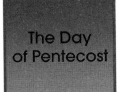

The Day of Pentecost

When the day of Pentecost came, they were all together in one place. [2]Suddenly a noise came from heaven. It sounded like a strong wind blowing. This noise filled the whole house where they were sitting. [3]They saw something that looked like flames of fire. The flames were separated and stood over each person there. [4]They were all filled with the Holy Spirit, and they began to speak different languages. The Holy Spirit was giving them the power to speak these languages.

[5]There were some religious Jews staying in Jerusalem who were from every country in the world. [6]When they heard this noise, a crowd came together. They were all surprised, because each one heard them speaking in his own language. [7]They were completely amazed at this. They said, "Look! Aren't all these men that we hear speaking from Galilee?[n] [8]But each of us hears them in his own language. How is this possible? We are from different places: [9]Parthia, Media, Elam, Mesopotamia, Judea, Cappadocia, Pontus, Asia, [10]Phrygia, Pamphylia, Egypt, the areas of Libya near Cyrene, Rome [11](both Jews and those who had become Jews), Crete and Arabia. But we hear these men telling in our own languages about the great things God has done!"

[n]**from Galilee** The people thought men from Galilee could speak only their own language.

Prayer Starter: Thank you for giving me a tongue for speaking. Help me to use it to share Christ with others.

Memory Verse: Jesus is the only One . . .   —*Acts 4:12*

Peter Heals a Crippled Man

One day Peter and John went to the Temple. It was three o'clock in the afternoon. This was the time for the daily prayer service. [2]There, at the Temple gate called Beautiful Gate, was a man who had been crippled all his life. Every day he was carried to this gate to beg. He would ask for money from the people going into the Temple. [3]The man saw Peter and John going into the Temple and asked them for money. [4]Peter and John looked straight at him and said, "Look at us!" [5]The man looked at them; he thought they were going to give him some money. [6]But Peter said, "I don't have any silver or gold, but I do have something else I can give you: By the power of Jesus Christ from Nazareth—stand up and walk!" [7]Then Peter took the man's right hand and lifted him up. Immediately the man's feet and ankles became strong. [8]He jumped up, stood on his feet, and began to walk. He went into the Temple with them, walking and jumping, and praising God. [9-10]All the people recognized him. They knew he was the crippled man who always sat by the Beautiful Gate begging for money. Now they saw this same man walking and praising God. The people were amazed. They could not understand how this could happen.

Prayer Starter: Thank you for my feet and legs. Thank you for giving me energy each day.

Memory Verse: Jesus is the only One who can save people . . .

—Acts 4:12

Peter and John Arrested

While Peter and John were speaking to the people, a group of men came up to them. There were Jewish priests, the captain of the soldiers that guarded the Temple, and some Sadducees. ²They were upset because the two apostles were teaching the people. Peter and John were preaching that people will rise from death through the power of Jesus. ³The Jewish leaders grabbed Peter and John and put them in jail. It was already night, so they kept them in jail until the next day. ⁴But many of those who heard Peter and John preach believed the things they said. There were now about 5,000 men in the group of believers.

⁵The next day the Jewish leaders, the older Jewish leaders, and the teachers of the law met in Jerusalem. ⁶Annas the high priest, Caiaphas, John, and Alexander were there. Everyone from the high priest's family was there. ⁷They made Peter and John stand before them. The Jewish leaders asked them: "By what power or authority did you do this?"

⁸Then Peter was filled with the Holy Spirit. He said to them, "Rulers of the people and you older leaders, ⁹are you questioning us about a good thing that was done to a crippled man? Are you asking us who made him well? ¹⁰We want all of you and all the Jewish people to know that this

man was made well by the power of Jesus Christ from Nazareth! You nailed him to a cross, but God raised him from death. This man was crippled, but he is now well and able to stand here before you because of the power of Jesus! [11]Jesus is

'the stone[n] that you builders did not want.

It has become the cornerstone.'

[12]Jesus is the only One who can save people. His name is the only power in the world that has been given to save people. And we must be saved through him!"

[13]The Jewish leaders saw that Peter and John were not afraid to speak. They understood that these men had no special training or education. So they were amazed. Then they realized that Peter and John had been with Jesus. [14]They saw the crippled man standing there beside the two apostles. They saw that the man was healed. So they could say nothing against them. [15]The Jewish leaders told them to leave the meeting. Then the leaders talked to each other about what they should do. [16]They said, "What shall we do with these men? Everyone in Jerusalem knows that they have done a great miracle! We cannot say it is not true. [17]But we must warn them not to talk to people anymore using that name. Then this thing will not spread among the people."

[18]So they called Peter and John in again. They told them not to speak or to teach at all in the name of Jesus. [19]But Peter and John answered them, "What do you think is right? What would God want? Should we obey you or God? [20]We cannot keep quiet. We must speak about what we have seen and heard." [21-22]The Jewish leaders could not find a way to punish them because all the people were praising God for what had been done. (This miracle was a proof from God. The man who was healed was more than 40 years old!) So the Jewish leaders warned the apostles again and let them go free.

[n]**stone** A symbol meaning Jesus.

Prayer Starter: Lord, your name is the only one in all the earth that can save anyone.

Memory Verse: Jesus is the only One who can save people. His name is the only power in the world . . .   —*Acts 4:12*

**Ananias
and
Sapphira**

The group of believers were joined in their hearts, and they had the same spirit. No person in the group said that the things he had were his own. Instead, they shared everything. [33]With great power the apostles were telling people that the Lord Jesus was truly raised from death. And God blessed all the believers very much. [34]They all received the things they needed. Everyone that owned fields or houses sold them. They brought the money [35]and gave it to the apostles. Then each person was given the things he needed.

[36]One of the believers was named Joseph. The apostles called him Barnabas. (This name means "one who encourages.") He was a Levite, born in Cyprus. [37]Joseph owned a field. He sold it, brought the money, and gave it to the apostles.

5 A man named Ananias and his wife Sapphira sold some land. [2]But he gave only part of the money to the apostles. He secretly kept some of it for himself. His wife knew about this, and she agreed to it. [3]Peter said, "Ananias, why did you let Satan rule your heart? You lied to the Holy Spirit. Why did you keep part of the money you received for the land for yourself? [4]Before you sold the land, it belonged to you. And even after you sold it, you could have used the money any way you wanted. Why did you think of doing this? You lied to God, not to men!"

[5-6]When Ananias heard this, he fell down and died. Some young men came in, wrapped up his body, carried it out, and buried it. And everyone who heard about this was filled with fear.

[7]About three hours later his wife came in. She did not know what

had happened. [8]Peter said to her, "Tell me how much money you got for your field. Was it this much?"

Sapphira answered, "Yes, that was the price."

[9]Peter said to her, "Why did you and your husband agree to test the Spirit of the Lord? Look! The men who buried your husband are at the door! They will carry you out." [10]At that moment Sapphira fell down by his feet and died. The young men came in and saw that she was dead. They carried her out and buried her beside her husband. [11]The whole church and all the others who heard about these things were filled with fear.

Prayer Starter: Help me to always be honest, Lord. Keep me from cheating and lying.

Memory Verse: Jesus is the only One who can save people. His name is the only power in the world that has been given to save people. . . .
—Acts 4:12

Many Miracles

The apostles did many signs and miracles among the people. And they would all meet together on Solomon's Porch. [13]None of the others dared to stand with them. All the people were saying good things about them. [14]More and more men and women believed in the Lord and were added to the group of believers. [15]As Peter was passing by, the people brought their sick into the streets. They put their sick on beds and mats so at

least Peter's shadow might fall on them. [16]Crowds came from all the towns around Jerusalem. They brought their sick and those who were bothered by evil spirits. All of them were healed.

[17]The high priest and all his friends (a group called the Sadducees) became very jealous. [18]They took the apostles and put them in jail. [19]But during the night, an angel of the Lord opened the doors of the jail. He led the apostles outside and said, [20]"Go and stand in the Temple. Tell the people everything about this new life." [21]When the apostles heard this, they obeyed and went into the Temple. It was early in the morning, and they began to teach.

The high priest and his friends arrived. They called a meeting of the Jewish leaders and all the important older men of the Jews. They sent some men to the jail to bring the apostles to them. [22]When the men went to the jail, they could not find the apostles. So they went back and told the Jewish leaders about this. ²³They said, "The jail was closed and locked. The guards were standing at the doors. But when we opened the doors, the jail was empty!" ²⁴Hearing this, the captain of the Temple guards and the leading priests were confused. They wondered, "What will happen because of this?"

²⁵Then someone came and told them, "Listen! The men you put in jail are standing in the Temple. They are teaching the people!" ²⁶Then the captain and his men went out and brought the apostles back. But the soldiers did not use force, because they were afraid that the people would kill them with stones.

Prayer Starter: Thank you, Lord, for the angels who watch over us.

Memory Verse: Jesus is the only One who can save people. His name is the only power in the world that has been given to save people. And we must be saved through him!   —*Acts 4:12*

Apostles Beaten

The soldiers brought the apostles to the meeting and made them stand before the Jewish leaders. The high priest questioned them. ²⁸He said, "We gave you strict orders not to go on teaching in that name. But look what you have done! You have filled Jerusalem with your teaching. You are trying to make us responsible for this man's death."

²⁹Peter and the other apostles answered, "We must obey God, not men! ³⁰You killed Jesus. You hung him on a cross. But God, the same God our ancestors had, raised Jesus up from death! ³¹Jesus is the One whom God raised to be on his right side. God made Jesus our Leader and Savior. God did this so that all Jews could change their hearts and lives and have their sins forgiven. ³²We saw all these things happen. The Holy Spirit also proves that these things are true. God has given the Spirit to all who obey him."

³³When the Jewish leaders heard this, they became very angry and wanted to kill them. ³⁴A Pharisee named Gamaliel stood up in the meeting. He was a teacher of the law, and all the people respected him. He ordered the apostles to leave the meeting for a little while. ³⁵Then he said to them, "Men of Israel, be careful of what you are planning to do to these men! ³⁶Remember when Theudas appeared? He said that he was a great man, and about 400 men joined him. But he was killed. And all his followers were scattered. They were able to do nothing. ³⁷Later, a man named Judas came from Galilee at the time of the registration.ⁿ He led a group of followers, too. He was also killed, and all his followers were scattered. ³⁸And so now I tell you: Stay away from these men. Leave them alone. If their plan comes from men, it will fail. ³⁹But if it is from God, you will not be able to stop them. You might even be fighting against God himself!"

The Jewish leaders agreed with what Gamaliel said. ⁴⁰They called the apostles in again. They beat the apostles and told them not to speak in the name of Jesus again. Then they let them go free. ⁴¹The apostles left the meeting full of joy because they were given the honor of suffering disgrace for Jesus. ⁴²The apostles did not stop teaching people. Every day in the Temple and in people's homes they continued to tell the Good News— that Jesus is the Christ.

ⁿ**registration** Census. A counting of all the people and the things they own.

Prayer Starter: Lord, give me the courage to be your follower, even when it's hard.

Memory Verse: And everywhere . . .   *—Acts 8:4*

Stephen

The 12 apostles called the whole group of followers together. They said, "It is not right for us to stop our work of teaching God's word in order to serve tables. [3]So, brothers, choose seven of your own men. They must be men who are good. They must be full of wisdom and full of the Spirit. We will put them in charge of this work. [4]Then we can use all our time to pray and to teach the word of God."

[5]The whole group liked the idea. So they chose these seven men: Stephen (a man with great faith and full of the Holy Spirit), Philip,[n] Procorus, Nicanor, Timon, Parmenas, and Nicolas (a man from Antioch who

had become a Jew).

[8]Stephen was richly blessed by God. God gave him the power to do great miracles and signs among the people. [9]But some Jews were against him. They belonged to a synagogue of Free Men[n] (as it was called). (This synagogue was also for Jews from Cyrene and from Alexandria.) Jews from Cilicia and Asia were also with them. They all came and argued with Stephen.

[10]But the Spirit was helping him to speak with wisdom. His words were so strong that they could not argue with him. [11]So they paid some men to say, "We heard him say things against Moses and against God!"

[12]This upset the people, the older Jewish leaders, and the teachers of the law. They came to Stephen, grabbed him and brought him to a meeting of the Jewish leaders. [13]They brought in some men to tell lies about Stephen. They said, "This man is always saying things against this holy place and the law of Moses. [14]We heard him say that Jesus from Nazareth will destroy this place. He also said that Jesus will change the things that Moses told us to do." [15]All the people in the meeting were watching Stephen closely. His face looked like the face of an angel.

[n]**Philip** Not the apostle named Philip.
[n]**Free Men** Jews who had been slaves or whose fathers had been slaves, but were now free.

Prayer Starter: Lord, give me faith and wisdom like Stephen's.

Memory Verse: And everywhere they were scattered . . . —*Acts 8:4*

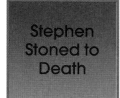

Stephen Stoned to Death

Stephen continued speaking: "You stubborn Jewish leaders! You have not given your hearts to God! You won't listen to him! You are always against what the Holy Spirit is trying to tell you. Your ancestors were like this, and you are just like them! ⁵²Your fathers tried to hurt every prophet who ever lived. Those prophets said long ago that the Righteous One would come. But your father killed them. And now you have turned against the Righteous One and killed him. ⁵³You received the law of Moses, which God gave you through his angels. But you don't obey it!"

⁵⁴When the leaders heard Stephen saying all these things, they became very angry. They were so mad that they were grinding their teeth at Stephen. ⁵⁵But Stephen was full of the Holy Spirit. He looked up to heaven and saw the glory of God. He saw Jesus standing at God's right side. ⁵⁶He said, "Look! I see heaven open. And I see the Son of Man standing at God's right side!"

⁵⁷Then they all shouted loudly. They covered their ears with their hands and all ran at Stephen. ⁵⁸They took him out of the city and threw stones at him until he was dead. The men who told lies against Stephen left their coats with a young man named Saul. ⁵⁹While they were throwing stones, Stephen prayed, "Lord Jesus, receive my spirit!" ⁶⁰He fell on

his knees and cried in a loud voice, "Lord, do not hold this sin against them!" After Stephen said this, he died.

8 Saul agreed that the killing of Stephen was a good thing. ²⁻³Some religious men buried Stephen. They cried very loudly for him. On that day people began trying to hurt the church in Jerusalem and make it suffer. Saul was also trying to destroy the church. He went from house to house. He dragged out men and women and put them in jail. All the believers, except the apostles, went to different places in Judea and Samaria. ⁴And everywhere they were scattered, they told people the Good News.

⁵Philip[n] went to the city of Samaria and preached about the Christ. ⁶The people there heard Philip and saw the miracles he was doing. They all listened carefully to the things he said. ⁷Many of these people had evil spirits in them. But Philip made the evil spirits leave them. The spirits made a loud noise when they came out. There were also many weak and crippled people there. Philip healed them, too. ⁸So the people in that city were very happy.

[n]**Philip** Not the apostle named Philip.

Prayer Starter: Lord, as I go from place to place, may I tell the good news.

Memory Verse: And everywhere they were scattered, they told . . .
　　　　　　　　　　　　　　　　　　　　　　—Acts 8:4

Simon

But there was a man named Simon in that city. Before Philip came there, Simon had practiced magic. He amazed all the people of Samaria with his magic. He bragged and called himself a great man. [10]All the people—the least important and the most important—paid attention to what Simon said. They said, "This man has the power of God, called 'the Great Power'!" [11]Simon had amazed them all with his magic tricks so long that the people became his followers. [12]But Philip told them the Good News about the kingdom of God and the power of Jesus Christ. Men and women believed Philip and were baptized. [13]Simon himself believed and was baptized. He stayed very close to Philip. When he saw the miracles and the very powerful things that Philip did, Simon was amazed.

[14]The apostles were still in Jerusalem. They heard that the people of Samaria had accepted the word of God. So they sent Peter and John to them. [15]When Peter and John arrived, they prayed that the Samaritan believers might receive the Holy Spirit. [16]These people had been baptized in the name of the Lord Jesus. But the Holy Spirit had not yet entered any of them. [17]Then, when the two apostles began laying their hands on[n] the people, they received the Holy Spirit.

[18]Simon saw that the Spirit was given to people when the apostles laid their hands on them. So he offered the apostles money. [19]He said, "Give me also this power so that when I lay my hands on a person, he will receive the Holy Spirit."

[20]Peter said to him, "You and your money should both be destroyed! You thought you could buy God's gift with money. [21]You cannot share with us in this work. Your heart is not right before God. [22]Change your heart! Turn away from this evil thing you have done. Pray to the Lord. Maybe he will forgive you for thinking this."

Prayer Starter: Lord, keep me from loving money too much.

Memory Verse: And everywhere they were scattered, they told people . . .
—Acts 8:4

Philip and the Ethiopian

An angel of the Lord spoke to Philip.[n] The angel said, "Get ready and go south. Go to the road that leads down to Gaza from Jerusalem—the desert road." [27]So Philip got ready and went. On the road he saw a man from Ethiopia, a eunuch. He was an important officer in the service of Candace, the queen of the Ethiopians. He was responsible for taking care of all her money. He had gone to Jerusalem to worship, and [28]now he was on his way home. He was sitting in his chariot and reading from the book of Isaiah, the prophet.

[29]The Spirit said to Philip, "Go to that chariot and stay near it."

[30]So Philip ran toward the chariot. He heard the man reading from Isaiah, the prophet. Philip asked, "Do you understand what you are reading?"

[31]He answered, "How can I understand? I need someone to explain it to me!" Then he invited Philip to climb in and sit with him.

[32]The verse of Scripture that he was reading was this:

"He was like a sheep being led to be killed.
　　He was quiet, as a sheep is quiet while its wool is being cut.
　　He said nothing.
[33]　　He was shamed and was treated unfairly.
　　He died without children to continue his family.
　　　His life on earth has ended."

[34]The officer said to Philip, "Please tell me, who is the prophet talking about? Is he talking about himself or about someone else?" [35]Philip began to speak. He started with this same Scripture and told the man the Good News about Jesus.

[n]**Philip**　Not the apostle named Philip.

Prayer Starter: Lord, bless all your preachers, teachers, and evangelists who are explaining the good news about Jesus.

Memory Verse: And everywhere they were scattered, they told people the Good News.
　　　　　　　　　　　　　　　　　　　　　　　　　　　　　　—*Acts 8:4*

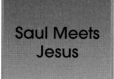

Saul Meets Jesus

In Jerusalem Saul was still trying to frighten the followers of the Lord by saying he would kill them. So he went to the high priest ²and asked him to write letters to the synagogues in the city of Damascus. Saul wanted the high priest to give him the authority to find people in Damascus who were followers of Christ's Way. If he found any there, men or women, he would arrest them and bring them back to Jerusalem.

³So Saul went to Damascus. As he came near the city, a bright light

from heaven suddenly flashed around him. [4]Saul fell to the ground. He heard a voice saying to him, "Saul, Saul! Why are you doing things against me?"

[5]Saul said, "Who are you, Lord?"

The voice answered, "I am Jesus. I am the One you are trying to hurt. [6]Get up now and go into the city. Someone there will tell you what you must do."

[7]The men traveling with Saul stood there, but they said nothing. They heard the voice, but they saw no one. [8]Saul got up from the ground. He opened his eyes, but he could not see. So the men with Saul took his hand and led him into Damascus. [9]For three days Saul could not see, and he did not eat or drink.

[10]There was a follower of Jesus in Damascus named Ananias. The Lord spoke to Ananias in a vision, "Ananias!"

Ananias answered, "Here I am, Lord."

[11]The Lord said to him, "Get up and go to the street called Straight Street. Find the house of Judas.[n] Ask for a man named Saul from the city of Tarsus. He is there now, praying. [12]Saul has seen a vision. In it a man named Ananias comes to him and lays his hands on him. Then he sees again."

[13]But Ananias answered, "Lord, many people have told me about this man and the terrible things he did to your people in Jerusalem. [14]Now he has come here to Damascus. The leading priests have given him the power to arrest everyone who worships you."

[15]But the Lord said to Ananias, "Go! I have chosen Saul for an important work. He must tell about me to non-Jews, to kings, and to the people of Israel. [16]I will show him how much he must suffer for my name."

[17]So Ananias went to the house of Judas. He laid his hands on Saul and said, "Brother Saul, the Lord Jesus sent me. He is the one you saw on the road on your way here. He sent me so that you can see again and be filled with the Holy Spirit." [18]Immediately, something that looked like fish scales fell from Saul's eyes. He was able to see again! Then Saul got up and was baptized.

[n]**Judas** This is not either of the apostles named Judas.

Prayer Starter: May my friends who don't know Christ come to love and trust him, just as Saul did.

Memory Verse: God accepts . . .   —*Acts 10:35*

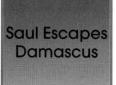

Saul Escapes Damascus

Saul stayed with the followers of Jesus in Damascus for a few days. ²⁰Soon he began to preach about Jesus in the synagogues, saying, "Jesus is the Son of God!"

²¹All the people who heard him were amazed. They said, "This is the man who was in Jerusalem. He was trying to destroy those who trust in this name! He came here to do the same thing. He came here to arrest the followers of Jesus and take them back to the leading priests."

²²But Saul became more and more powerful. His proofs that Jesus is the Christ were so strong that the Jews in Damascus could not argue with him.

²³After many days, the Jews made plans to kill Saul. ²⁴They were watching the city gates day and night. They wanted to kill him, but Saul learned about their plan. ²⁵One night some followers of Saul helped him leave the city. They lowered him in a basket through an opening in the city wall.

²⁶Then Saul went to Jerusalem. He tried to join the group of followers, but they were all afraid of him. They did not believe that he was really a follower. ²⁷But Barnabas accepted Saul and took him to the apostles. Barnabas told them that Saul had seen the Lord on the road. He explained how the Lord had spoken to Saul. Then he told them how boldly Saul had preached in the name of Jesus in Damascus.

²⁸And so Saul stayed with the followers. He went everywhere in Jerusalem, preaching boldly in the name of Jesus. ²⁹He would often talk and argue with the Jews who spoke Greek. But they were trying to kill him. ³⁰When the brothers learned about this, they took Saul to Caesarea. From there they sent him to Tarsus.

³¹The church everywhere in Judea, Galilee, and Samaria had a time of peace. With the help of the Holy Spirit, the group became stronger. The believers showed that they respected the Lord by the way they lived. Because of this, the group of believers grew larger and larger.

Prayer Starter: Help me to speak bravely in the name of the Lord.

Memory Verse: God accepts anyone who worships him . . .
—*Acts 10:35*

Tabitha

As Peter was traveling through all the area, he visited God's people who lived in Lydda. ³³There he met a paralyzed man named Aeneas. Aeneas had not been able to leave his bed for the past eight years. ³⁴Peter said to him, "Aeneas, Jesus Christ heals you. Stand up and make your bed!" Aeneas stood up immediately. ³⁵All the people living in Lydda and on the Plain of Sharon saw him. These people turned to the Lord.

³⁶In the city of Joppa there was a follower named Tabitha. (Her Greek name, Dorcas, means "a deer.") She was always doing good and helping the poor. ³⁷While Peter was in Lydda, Tabitha became sick and died. Her body was washed and put in a room upstairs. ³⁸The followers in Joppa heard that Peter was in Lydda. (Lydda is near Joppa.) So they sent two men to Peter. They begged him, "Hurry, please come to us!" ³⁹Peter got ready and went with them. When he arrived, they took him to the upstairs room. All the widows stood around Peter, crying. They showed him the shirts and coats that Tabitha had made when she was still alive. ⁴⁰Peter sent everyone out of the room. He kneeled and prayed. Then he turned to the body and said, "Tabitha, stand up!" She opened her eyes,

and when she saw Peter, she sat up. [41]He gave her his hand and helped her up. Then he called the saints and the widows into the room. He showed them Tabitha; she was alive! [42]People everywhere in Joppa learned about this, and many believed in the Lord. [43]Peter stayed in Joppa for many days with a man named Simon who was a leatherworker.

Prayer Starter: I love to read your Bible each day, Lord. Thank you for stories like this one.

Memory Verse: God accepts anyone who worships him and does what is right. . . .
—*Acts 10.35*

Peter's Chains Fall Off

During that same time King Herod began to do terrible things to some who belonged to the church. [2]He ordered James, the brother of John, to be killed by the sword. [3]Herod saw that the Jews liked this, so he decided to arrest Peter, too. (This happened during the time of the Feast of Unleavened Bread.)

[4]After Herod arrested Peter, he put him in jail and handed him over to be guarded by 16 soldiers. Herod planned to bring Peter before the people for trial after the Passover Feast. [5]So Peter was kept in jail. But the church kept on praying to God for him.

[6]The night before Herod was to bring him to trial, Peter was sleeping. He was between two soldiers, bound with two chains. Other soldiers were guarding the door of the jail. [7]Suddenly, an angel of the Lord stood there. A light shined in the room. The angel touched Peter on the side and woke him up. The angel said, "Hurry! Get up!" And the chains fell off Peter's hands. [8]The angel said to him, "Get dressed and put on your sandals." And so Peter did this. Then the angel said, "Put on your coat and follow me." [9]So the angel went out, and Peter followed him. Peter did not know if what the angel was doing was real. He thought he might be seeing a vision. [10]They went past the first and the second guard. They came to the iron gate that separated them from the city. The gate opened itself for them. They went through the gate and walked down a street. And the angel suddenly left him.

[11]Then Peter realized what had happened. He thought, "Now I know that the Lord really sent his angel to me. He rescued me from Herod and from all the things the Jewish people thought would happen."

[12]When he realized this, he went to the home of Mary. She was the mother of John. (John was also called Mark.) Many people were gathered there, praying. [13]Peter knocked on the outside door. A servant girl named Rhoda came to answer it. [14]She recognized Peter's voice, and she was very happy. She even forgot to open the door. She ran inside and told the group, "Peter is at the door!"

[15]They said to her, "You are crazy!" But she kept on saying that it was true. So they said, "It must be Peter's angel."

[16]Peter continued to knock. When they opened the door, they saw him and were amazed. [17]Peter made a sign with his hand to tell them to be quiet. He explained how the Lord led him out of the jail. And he said, "Tell James and the other believers what happened." Then he left to go to another place.

[18]The next day the soldiers were very upset. They wondered what

had happened to Peter. [19]Herod looked everywhere for Peter but could not find him. So he questioned the guards and ordered that they be killed.

Prayer Starter: Send your angels to watch over us, Lord, just as they cared for Peter.

Memory Verse: God accepts anyone who worships him and does what is right. It is not important . . .　　　　　　　—*Acts 10.35*

Elymas, Son of the Devil

In the church at Antioch there were these prophets and teachers: Barnabas, Simeon (also called Niger), Lucius (from the city of Cyrene), Manaen (who had grown up with Herod, the ruler) and Saul. [2]They were all worshiping the Lord and giving up eating.[n] The Holy Spirit said to them, "Give Barnabas and Saul to me to do a special work. I have chosen them for it."

[3]So they gave up eating and prayed. They laid their hands on[n] Barnabas and Saul and sent them out.

[4]Barnabas and Saul were sent out by the Holy Spirit. They went to the city of Seleucia. From there they sailed to the island of Cyprus. [5]When they came to Salamis, they preached the Good News of God in the Jewish synagogues. John Mark was with them to help.

[6]They went across the whole island to Paphos. In Paphos they met a Jew who was a magician. His name was Bar-Jesus. He was a false prophet, [7]who always stayed close to Sergius Paulus, the governor. Sergius Paulus was a smart man. He asked Barnabas and Saul to come to him, because he wanted to hear the message of God. [8]But Elymas, the magician, was against them. (Elymas is the name for Bar-Jesus in the Greek language.) He tried to stop the governor from believing in Jesus. [9]But Saul was filled with the Holy Spirit. (Saul's other name was Paul.) He looked straight at Elymas [10]and said, "You son of the devil! You are an enemy of everything that is right! You are full of evil tricks and lies. You are always trying to change the Lord's truth into lies! [11]Now the Lord will touch you, and you will be blind. For a time you will not be able to see anything—not even the light from the sun."

Then everything became dark for Elymas. He walked around, trying to find someone to lead him by the hand. [12]When the governor saw this, he believed. He was amazed at the teaching about the Lord.

[n]**giving up eating** This is called "fasting." The people would give up eating for a special time of prayer and worship to God. It was also done to show sadness.

[n]**laid their hands on** Here, this was a sign to show that these men were given a special work of God.

Prayer Starter: Lord, help me to stay close to you. Thank you for keeping me from evil.

Memory Verse: God accepts anyone who worships him and does what is right. It is not important what country a person comes from. —*Acts 10.35*

Paul and Barnabas Preach

"David did God's will during his lifetime. Then he died and was buried with his fathers. And his body did rot in the grave! ³⁷But the One God raised from death did not rot in the grave. ³⁸⁻³⁹Brothers, you must understand what we are telling you: You can have forgiveness of your sins through Jesus. The law of Moses could not free you from your sins. But everyone who believes is free from all sins through him. ⁴⁰Be careful! Don't let what the prophets said happen to you:

⁴¹ 'Listen, you people who doubt!
    You can wonder, and then die.
  I will do something in your lifetime that will amaze you.
    You won't believe it even when you are told about it!' "

⁴²While Paul and Barnabas were leaving the synagogue, the people asked them to tell them more about these things on the next Sabbath. ⁴³After the meeting, many Jews followed Paul and Barnabas from that place. With the Jews there were many who had changed to the Jewish religion and worshiped God. Paul and Barnabas were persuading them to continue trusting in God's kindness.

⁴⁴On the next Sabbath day, almost all the people in the city came to hear the word of the Lord. ⁴⁵Seeing the crowd, the Jews became very jealous. They said insulting things and argued against what Paul said. ⁴⁶But Paul and Barnabas spoke very boldly. They said, "We must speak the message of God to you first. But you refuse to listen. You are judging yourselves not worthy of having eternal life! So we will now go to the people of other nations! ⁴⁷This is what the Lord told us to do. The Lord said:

'I have made you a light for the non-Jewish nations.
    You will show people all over the world the way to be saved.' "

⁴⁸When the non-Jewish people heard Paul say this, they were happy. They gave honor to the message of the Lord. And many of the people believed the message. They were the ones chosen to have life forever.

⁴⁹And so the message of the Lord was spreading through the whole country.

Prayer Starter: I want to trust you, Lord, when things seem to be going badly.

Memory Verse: When you talk, do not say harmful things. . . .

—*Ephesians 4:29*

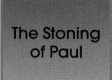

The Stoning of Paul

In Lystra there sat a man who had been born crippled; he had never walked. ⁹This man was listening to Paul speak. Paul looked straight at him and saw that the man believed God could heal him. ¹⁰So he cried out, "Stand up on your feet!" The man jumped up and began walking around. ¹¹When the crowds saw what Paul did, they shouted in their own Lycaonian language. They said, "The gods have become like men! They have come down to us!" ¹²And the people began to call Barnabas "Zeus."ⁿ They called Paul "Hermes,"ⁿ because he was the main speaker. ¹³The temple of Zeus was near the city. The priest of this temple brought some bulls and flowers to the city gates. The priest and the people wanted to offer a sacrifice to Paul and Barnabas. ¹⁴But when the apostles, Barnabas and Paul, understood what they were about to do, they tore their clothes in anger. Then they ran in among the people and shouted, ¹⁵"Men, why are you doing these things? We are only men, human beings like you! We are bringing you the Good News. We are telling you to turn away from these worthless things and turn to the true living God. He is the One who made the sky, the earth, the sea, and everything that is in them. ¹⁶In the past, God let all the nations do what they wanted. ¹⁷Yet he did things to prove he is real: He shows kindness to you. He gives you rain from heaven and crops at the right times. He gives you food and fills your hearts with joy." ¹⁸Even with these words, they were barely able to keep the crowd from offering sacrifices to them.

¹⁹Then some Jews came from Antioch and Iconium. They persuaded the people to turn against Paul. And so they threw stones at Paul and dragged him out of town. They thought that they had killed him. ²⁰But the followers gathered around him, and he got up and went back into the town. The next day, he and Barnabas left and went to the city of Derbe.

ⁿ**"Zeus"** The Greeks believed in many gods. Zeus was their most important god.
ⁿ**"Hermes"** The Greeks believed he was a messenger for the other gods.

Prayer Starter: Thank you for giving us food and filling our hearts with joy.

Memory Verse: When you talk, do not say harmful things. But say what people need . . .   —*Ephesians 4:29*

The Jerusalem Meeting

T hen some men came to Antioch from Judea. They began teaching the non-Jewish brothers: "You cannot be saved if you are not circumcised. Moses taught us to do this." ²Paul and Barnabas were against this teaching and argued with the men about it. So the group decided to send Paul, Barnabas, and some other men to Jerusalem. There they could talk more about this with the apostles and elders.

³The church helped the men leave on the trip. They went through the countries of Phoenicia and Samaria, telling all about how the non-Jewish people had turned to God. This made all the believers very happy. ⁴When they arrived in Jerusalem, the apostles, the elders, and the church welcomed them. Paul, Barnabas, and the others told about all the things

that God had done with them. ⁵But some of the believers who had belonged to the Pharisee group came forward. They said, "The non-Jewish believers must be circumcised. We must tell them to obey the law of Moses!"

⁶The apostles and the elders gathered to study this problem. ⁷There was a long debate. Then Peter stood up and said to them, "Brothers, you

know what happened in the early days. God chose me from among you to preach the Good News to the non-Jewish people. They heard the Good News from me, and they believed. ⁸God, who knows the thoughts of all men, accepted them. He showed this to us by giving them the Holy Spirit, just as he did to us. ⁹To God, those people are not different from us. When they believed, he made their hearts pure. ¹⁰So now why are you testing God? You are putting a heavy load around the necks of the non-Jewish brothers. It is a load that neither we nor our fathers were able to carry. ¹¹But we believe that we and they too will be saved by the grace of the Lord Jesus!"

¹²Then the whole group became quiet. They listened to Paul and Barnabas speak. Paul and Barnabas told about all the miracles and signs that God did through them among the non-Jewish people. ¹³After they finished speaking, James spoke. He said, "Brothers, listen to me. ¹⁴Simon has told us how God showed his love for the non-Jewish people. For the first time he has accepted them and made them his people. ¹⁵The words of the prophets agree with this too.

¹⁹"So I think we should not bother the non-Jewish brothers who have turned to God. ²⁰Instead, we should write a letter to them. We should tell them these things: Do not eat food that has been offered to idols. (This makes the food unclean.) Do not take part in any kind of sexual sin. Do not taste blood. Do not eat animals that have been strangled. ²¹They should not do these things, because there are still men in every city who teach the law of Moses. For a long time the words of Moses have been read in the synagogue every Sabbath day."

Prayer Starter: Thank you for your church, dear Lord.

Memory Verse: When you talk, do not say harmful things. But say what people need—words that will help others become stronger. . . .

—Ephesians 4:29

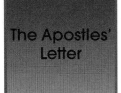

The Apostles' Letter

The apostles, the elders, and the whole church decided to send some of their men with Paul and Barnabas to Antioch. They chose Judas Barsabbas and Silas, who were respected by the believers. ²³They sent the following letter with them:

From the apostles and elders, your brothers.

To all the non-Jewish brothers in Antioch, Syria and Cilicia:

Dear Brothers,

²⁴We have heard that some of our men have come to you and said things that trouble and upset you. But we did not tell them to do this! ²⁵We have all agreed to choose some men and send them to you. They will be with our dear friends Barnabas and Paul—²⁶men who have given their lives to serve our Lord Jesus Christ. ²⁷So we have sent Judas and Silas with them. They will tell you the same things. ²⁸It has pleased the Holy Spirit that you should not have a heavy load to carry, and we agree. You need to do only these things: ²⁹Do not eat any food that has been offered to idols. Do not taste blood. Do not eat any animals that have been strangled. Do not take part in any kind of sexual sin. If you stay away from these things, you will do well.

Good-bye.

³⁰So the men left Jerusalem and went to Antioch. There they gathered the church and gave them the letter. ³¹When they read it, they were very happy because of the encouraging letter.

Prayer Starter: Bless those, O Lord, who have gone to other nations, taking the message of Jesus.

Memory Verse: When you talk, do not say harmful things. But say what people need—words that will help others become stronger. Then what you say will help . . .
—*Ephesians 4:29*

Paul's Travels

Paul came to Derbe and Lystra. A follower named Timothy was there. Timothy's mother was Jewish and a believer. His father was a Greek. ²The brothers in Lystra and Iconium respected Timothy and said good things about him. ³Paul wanted Timothy to travel with him. But all the Jews living in that area knew that Timothy's father was Greek. So Paul circumcised Timothy to please the Jews. ⁴Paul and the men with him traveled from town to town. They gave the decisions made by the apostles and elders in Jerusalem for the people to obey. ⁵So the churches became stronger in the faith and grew larger every day.

⁶Paul and the men with him went through the areas of Phrygia and Galatia. The Holy Spirit did not let them preach the Good News in the country of Asia. ⁷When they came near the country of Mysia, they tried to go into Bithynia. But the Spirit of Jesus did not let them. ⁸So they passed by Mysia and went to Troas. ⁹That night Paul had a vision. In the vision, a man from Macedonia came to him. The man stood there and begged, "Come over to Macedonia. Help us!" ¹⁰After Paul had seen the vision, we immediately prepared to leave for Macedonia. We understood that God had called us to tell the Good News to those people.

Prayer Starter: Lead me day by day, dear Lord, just as you led the apostle Paul.

Memory Verse: When you talk, do not say harmful things. But say what people need—words that will help others become stronger. Then what you say will help those who listen to you. *—Ephesians 4:29*

Followers in Philippi

We left Troas in a ship, and we sailed straight to the island of Samothrace. The next day we sailed to Neapolis.[n] [12]Then we went by land to Philippi, the leading city in that part of Macedonia. It is also a Roman colony.[n] We stayed there for several days.

[13]On the Sabbath day we went outside the city gate to the river. There we thought we would find a special place for prayer. Some women had gathered there, so we sat down and talked with them. [14]There was a woman named Lydia from the city of Thyatira. Her job was selling purple cloth. She worshiped the true God. The Lord opened her mind to pay attention to what Paul was saying. [15]She and all the people in her house were baptized. Then Lydia invited us to her home. She said, "If you think I am truly a believer in the Lord, then come stay in my house." And she persuaded us to stay with her.

[n]**Neapolis** City in Macedonia. It was the first city Paul visited on the continent of Europe.
[n]**Roman colony** A town begun by Romans with Roman laws, customs and privileges.

Prayer Starter: Teach me to pray each day, to talk to you friend-to-friend.

Memory Verse: They said to him . . .   —*Acts 16:31*

Paul and Silas in Jail

Once, while we were going to the place for prayer, a servant girl met us. She had a special spirit[n] in her. She earned a lot of money for her owners by telling fortunes. [17]This girl followed Paul and us. She said loudly, "These men are servants of the Most High God! They are telling you how you can be saved!"

[18]She kept this up for many days. This bothered Paul, so he turned and said to the spirit, "By the power of Jesus Christ, I command you to come out of her!" Immediately, the spirit came out.

[19]The owners of the servant girl saw this. These men knew that now they could not use her to make money. So they grabbed Paul and Silas and dragged them before the city rulers in the marketplace. [20]Here they brought Paul and Silas to the Roman rulers and said, "These men are Jews and are making trouble in our city. [21]They are teaching things that are not right for us as Romans to do."

[22]The crowd joined the attack against them. The Roman officers tore the clothes of Paul and Silas and had them beaten with rods again and again. [23]Then Paul and Silas were thrown into jail. The jailer was ordered to guard them carefully. [24]When he heard this order, he put them far inside the jail. He pinned down their feet between large blocks of wood.

[25]About midnight Paul and Silas were praying and singing songs to God. The other prisoners were listening to them. [26]Suddenly, there was a big earthquake. It was so strong that it shook the foundation of the jail. Then all the doors of the jail broke open. All the prisoners were freed from their chains. [27]The jailer woke up and saw that the jail doors were open. He thought that the prisoners had already escaped. So he got his sword and was about to kill himself.[n] [28]But Paul shouted, "Don't hurt yourself! We are all here!"

[29]The jailer told someone to bring a light. Then he ran inside. Shaking with fear, he fell down before Paul and Silas. [30]Then he brought them outside and said, "Men, what must I do to be saved?"

[31]They said to him, "Believe in the Lord Jesus and you will be saved— you and all the people in your house." [32]So Paul and Silas told the message of the Lord to the jailer and all the people in his house. [33]At that hour of the night the jailer took Paul and Silas and washed their wounds. Then he and all his people were baptized immediately. [34]After this the jailer took Paul and Silas home and gave them food. He and his family were very happy because they now believed in God.

[n]**spirit** This was a sign from the devil. It caused her to say she had special knowledge.
[n]**kill himself** He thought the leaders would kill him for letting the prisoners escape.

Prayer Starter: Be with those in the jails and prisons, Lord, and give them the hope of the Lord Jesus.

Memory Verse: They said to him, "Believe in the Lord Jesus . . ."
—Acts 16:31

Paul's Sermon in Athens

Paul was waiting for Silas and Timothy in Athens. He was troubled because he saw that the city was full of idols. [17]In the synagogue, he talked with the Jews and the Greeks who worshiped the true God. He also talked every day with people in the marketplace.

[18]Some of the Epicurean and Stoic philosophers[n] argued with him. Some of them said, "This man doesn't know what he is talking about. What is he trying to say?" Paul was telling them the Good News of Jesus' rising from death. They said, "He seems to be telling us about some other gods." [19]They got Paul and took him to a meeting of the Areopagus.[n] They said, "Please explain to us this new idea that you have been teaching. [20]The things you are saying are new to us. We want to know what this teaching means." [21](All the people of Athens and those from other countries always used their time talking about all the newest ideas.)

[22]Then Paul stood before the meeting of the Areopagus. He said, "Men of Athens, I can see that you are very religious in all things. [23]I was going through your city, and I saw the things you worship. I found an altar that had these words written on it: "TO A GOD WHO IS NOT KNOWN." You worship a god that you don't know. This is the God I am telling you about! [24]He is the God who made the whole world and everything in it. He is the Lord of the land and the sky. He does not live in temples that men build! [25]This God is the One who gives life, breath, and everything else to people. He does not need any help from them. He has everything he needs. [26]God began by making one man. From him came all the different people who live everywhere in the world. He decided exactly when and where they must live. [27]God wanted them to look for him and perhaps search all around for him and find him. But he is not far from any of us: [28]'We live in him. We walk in him. We are in him.' Some of your own poets have said: 'For we are his children.' [29]We are God's children. So, you must not think that God is like something that people imagine or make. He is not like gold, silver, or rock. [30]In the past, people did not understand God, but God ignored this. But now, God tells everyone in the world to change his heart and life. [31]God has decided on a day that he will judge all the world. He will be fair. He will use a man to do this. God chose that man long ago. And God has proved this to everyone by raising that man from death!"

[n]**Epicurean and Stoic philosophers** Philosophers were those who searched for truth. Epicureans believed that pleasure, especially pleasures of the mind, were the goal of life. Stoics believed that life should be without feelings of joy or grief.

[n]**Areopagus** A council or group of important leaders in Athens. They were like judges.

Prayer Starter: Dear God, help me not to worship anyone or anything but you.

Memory Verse: They said to him, "Believe in the Lord Jesus and you will be saved . . ."
—*Acts 16:31*

Making
Tents

L ater, Paul left Athens and went to Corinth.
[2]Here he met a Jew named Aquila. Aquila was born in the country of Pontus. But Aquila and his wife, Priscilla, had recently moved to Corinth from Italy. They left Italy because Claudius[n] commanded that all Jews must leave Rome. Paul went to visit Aquila and Priscilla. [3]They were tentmakers, just as he was. He stayed with them and worked with them. [4]Every Sabbath day he talked with the Jews and Greeks in the synagogue. Paul tried to persuade these people to believe in Jesus.

[5]Silas and Timothy came from Macedonia and joined Paul in Corinth. After this, Paul used all his time telling people the Good News. He showed the Jews that Jesus is the Christ. [6]But they would not accept Paul's teaching and said some evil things. So he shook off the dust from his clothes.[n] He said to them, "If you are not saved, it will be your own

fault! I have done all I can do! After this, I will go only to non-Jewish people!" [7]Paul left the synagogue and moved into the home of Titius Justus. It was next to the synagogue. This man worshiped the true God. [8]Crispus was the leader of that synagogue. He and all the people living in his house believed in the Lord. Many others in Corinth also listened to Paul. They too believed and were baptized.

Claudius The emperor (ruler) of Rome, A.D. 41-54.
shook . . . clothes This was a warning. It showed that Paul was finished talking to the Jews.

Prayer Starter: Give me good friends, Lord, who will help me be stronger.

Memory Verse: They said to him, "Believe in the Lord Jesus and you will be saved—you and all the people . . ."   —*Acts 16:31*

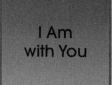

I Am with You

During the night, Paul had a vision. The Lord said to him, "Don't be afraid! Continue talking to people and don't be quiet! ¹⁰I am with you. No one will hurt you because many of my people are in this city." ¹¹Paul stayed there for a year and a half, teaching God's word to the people.

¹²Gallio became the governor of the country of Southern Greece. At that time, some of the Jews came together against Paul and took him to the court. ¹³They said to Gallio, "This man is teaching people to worship God in a way that is against our law!"

¹⁴Paul was about to say something, but Gallio spoke to the Jews. Gallio said, "I would listen to you Jews if you were complaining about a crime or some wrong. ¹⁵But the things you are saying are only questions about words and names—arguments about your own law. So you must solve this problem yourselves. I don't want to be a judge of these things!" ¹⁶Then Gallio made them leave the court.

¹⁷Then they all grabbed Sosthenes. (Sosthenes was now the leader of the synagogue.) They beat him there before the court. But this did not bother Gallio.

¹⁸Paul stayed with the believers for many more days. Then he left and sailed for Syria. Priscilla and Aquila went with him. At Cenchrea, Paul cut off his hair.ⁿ This showed that he had made a promise to God.

ⁿ**cut . . . hair** Jews did this to show that the time of a special promise to God was finished.

Prayer Starter: Give strength to Christians around the world who are being mistreated because of their faith in you, O Lord.

Memory Verse: They said to him, "Believe in the Lord Jesus and you will be saved—you and all the people in your house."   —*Acts 16:31*

Priscilla, Aquila, and Apollos

Then they went to Ephesus, where Paul left Priscilla and Aquila. While Paul was there, he went into the synagogue and talked with the Jews. ²⁰When they asked him to stay with them longer, he refused. ²¹He left them, but he said, "I will come back to you again if God wants me to." And so he sailed away from Ephesus.

²²Paul landed at Caesarea. Then he went and gave greetings to the church in Jerusalem. After that, Paul went to Antioch. ²³He stayed there for a while and then left and went through the countries of Galatia and Phrygia. He traveled from town to town in these countries, giving strength to all the followers.

²⁴A Jew named Apollos came to Ephesus. He was born in the city of Alexandria. He was an educated man who knew the Scriptures well. ²⁵He had been taught about the Lord. He was always very excited when he spoke and taught the truth about Jesus. But the only baptism that Apollos knew about was the baptism that John[n] taught. ²⁶Apollos began to speak very boldly in the synagogue, and Priscilla and Aquila heard him. So they took him to their home and helped him better understand the way of God. ²⁷Now Apollos wanted to go to the country of Southern Greece, so the believers helped him. They

wrote a letter to the followers there, asking them to accept him. These followers had believed in Jesus because of God's grace. When Apollos went there, he helped them very much. ²⁸He argued very strongly with the Jews before all the people. Apollos clearly proved that the Jews were wrong. Using the Scriptures, he proved that Jesus is the Christ.

19 While Apollos was in Corinth, Paul was visiting some places on the way to Ephesus. There he found some followers. ²Paul asked them, "Did you receive the Holy Spirit when you believed?"

They said, "We have never even heard of a Holy Spirit!"

³So he asked, "What kind of baptism did you have?"

They said, "It was the baptism that John[n] taught."

⁴Paul said, "John's baptism was a baptism of changed hearts and lives. He told people to believe in the One who would come after him. That One is Jesus."

⁵When they heard this, they were baptized in the name of the Lord Jesus.

[n]**John** John the Baptist, who preached to people about Christ's coming (Luke 3).

Prayer Starter: Help me, dear Lord, to tell others about you. You are the one who changes hearts and lives.

Memory Verse: I taught you . . .   *—Acts 20:35b*

Confusion at Ephesus

After these things, Paul made plans to go to Jerusalem. He planned to go through the countries of Macedonia and Southern Greece, and then on to Jerusalem. He said, "After I have been to Jerusalem, I must also visit Rome." ²²Paul sent Timothy and Erastus, two of his helpers, ahead to Macedonia. He himself stayed in Asia for a while.

²³But during that time, there was some serious trouble in Ephesus about the Way of Jesus. ²⁴There was a man named Demetrius, who worked with silver. He made little silver models that looked like the temple of the goddess Artemis.ⁿ The men who did this work made much money. ²⁵Demetrius had a meeting with these men and some others who did the same kind of work. He told them, "Men, you know that we make a lot of money from our business. ²⁶But look at what this man Paul is doing! He has convinced and turned away many people in Ephesus and in almost all of Asia! He says the gods that men make are not real. ²⁷There is a danger that our business will lose its good name. But there is also another danger: People will begin to think that the temple of the great goddess Artemis is not important! Her greatness will be destroyed. And Artemis is the goddess that everyone in Asia and the whole world worships."

²⁸When the men heard this, they became very angry. They shouted, "Artemis, the goddess of Ephesus, is great!" ²⁹The whole city became confused. The people grabbed Gaius and Aristarchus. (These two men were from Macedonia and were traveling with Paul.) Then all the people ran to the theater. ³⁰Paul wanted to go in and talk to the crowd, but the followers did not let him. ³¹Also, some leaders of Asia were friends of Paul. They sent him a message, begging him not to go into the theater.

ⁿ**Artemis** A Greek goddess that the people of Asia Minor worshiped.

Prayer Starter: Comfort and encourage me today, heavenly Father.

Memory Verse: I taught you to remember . . .   —*Acts 20:35b*

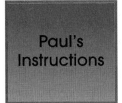

Paul's Instructions

When the trouble stopped, Paul sent for the followers to come to him. He encouraged them and then told them good-bye. Paul left and went to the country of Macedonia. [2]He said many things to strengthen the followers in the different places on his way through Macedonia. Then he went to Southern Greece. [3]He stayed there three months. He was ready to sail for Syria, but some Jews were planning something against him. So Paul decided to go back through Macedonia to Syria. [4]Some men went

with him. They were Sopater son of Pyrrhus, from the city of Berea; Aristarchus and Secundus, from the city of Thessalonica; Gaius, from Derbe; and Timothy; and Tychicus and Trophimus, two men from the country of Asia. [5]These men went first, ahead of Paul, and waited for us at Troas. [6]We sailed from Philippi after the Feast of Unleavened Bread and we met them in Troas five days later. We stayed there seven days.

[7]On the first day of the week,[n] we all met together to break bread.[n] Paul spoke to the group. Because he was planning to leave the next day, he kept on talking till midnight. [8]We were all together in a room upstairs, and there were many lamps in the room. [9]A young man named Eutychus was sitting in the window. As Paul continued talking, Eutychus was falling into a deep sleep. Finally, he went sound asleep and fell to the ground from the third floor. When they picked him up, he was dead. [10]Paul went down to Eutychus. He knelt down and put his arms around him. He said, "Don't worry. He is alive now." [11]Then Paul went upstairs again, broke bread, and ate. He spoke to them a long time, until it was early morning. Then he left. [12]They took the young man home alive and

were greatly comforted.

[13]We sailed for the city of Assos. We went first, ahead of Paul. He wanted to join us on the ship there. Paul planned it this way because he wanted to go to Assos by land. [14]When he met us at Assos, we took him aboard and went to Mitylene. [15]The next day, we sailed from Mitylene and came to a place near Chios. The next day, we sailed to Samos. A day later, we reached Miletus. [16]Paul had already decided not to stop at Ephesus. He did not want to stay too long in the country of Asia. He was hurrying to be in Jerusalem on the day of Pentecost, if that was possible.

"**first day of the week** Sunday, which for the Jews began at sunset on our Saturday. But if in this part of Asia a different system of time was used, then the meeting was on our Sunday night.

"**break bread** Probably the Lord's Supper, the special meal that Jesus told his followers to eat to remember him (Luke 22:14-20).

Prayer Starter: God, bless me when I'm at church. May I worship you and learn about you there.

Memory Verse: I taught you to remember the words of Jesus . . .

—*Acts 20:35b*

Church Leaders from Ephesus

Now from Miletus Paul sent to Ephesus and called for the elders of the church. [18]When they came to him, he said, "You know about my life from the first day I came to Asia. You know the way I lived all the time I was with you. [19]The Jews plotted against me. This troubled me very much. But you know that I always served the Lord. I never thought of myself first, and I often cried. [20]You know I preached to you, and I did not hold back anything that would help you. You know that I taught you in public and in your homes. [21]I warned both Jews and Greeks to change their lives and turn to God. And I told them all to believe in our Lord Jesus. [22]But now I must obey the Holy Spirit and go to Jerusalem. I don't know what will happen to me there. [23]I know only that in every city the Holy Spirit tells me that troubles and even jail wait for me. [24]I don't care about my own life. The most important thing is that I complete my mis-

sion. I want to finish the work that the Lord Jesus gave me—to tell people the Good News about God's grace.

[25]"And now, I know that none of you will ever see me again. All the time I was with you, I was preaching the kingdom of God. [26]So today I can tell you one thing that I am sure of: If any of you should be lost, I am not responsible. [27]This is because I have told you everything God wants you to know. [28]Be careful for yourselves and for all the people God has given you. The Holy Spirit gave you the work of caring for this flock. You must be like shepherds to the church of God.[n] This is the church that God bought with his own death. [29]I know that after I leave, some men will come like wild wolves and try to destroy the flock. [30]Also, men from your own group will rise up and twist the truth. They will lead away followers after them. [31]So be careful! Always remember this: For three years I never stopped warning each of you. I taught you night and day. I often cried over you.

[32]"Now I am putting you in the care of God and the message about his grace. That message is able to give you strength, and it will give you the blessings that God has for all his holy people. [33]When I was with you, I never wanted anyone's money or fine clothes. [34]You know that I always worked to take care of my own needs and the needs of those who were with me. [35]I showed you in all things that you should work as I did and help the weak. I taught you to remember the words of Jesus. He said, 'It is more blessed to give than to receive.' "

[36]When Paul had said this, he knelt down with all of them and prayed. [37-38]And they all cried because Paul said that they would never see him again. They put their arms around him and kissed him. Then they went with him to the ship.

[n]**of God** Some Greek copies say, "of the Lord."

Prayer Starter: Help me remember that more blessings come from giving than receiving.

Memory Verse: I taught you to remember the words of Jesus. He said, "It is more blessed . . ."
             —*Acts 20:35b*

Philip's Daughters

We all said good-bye to them and left. We sailed straight to Cos island. The next day, we reached Rhodes, and from Rhodes we went to Patara. ²There we found a ship that was going to Phoenicia. We went aboard and sailed away. ³We sailed near the island of Cyprus. We could see it to the north, but we sailed on to Syria. We stopped at Tyre because the ship needed to unload its cargo there.

⁴We found some followers in Tyre, and we stayed with them for seven days. Through the Holy Spirit they warned Paul not to go to Jerusalem. ⁵When we finished our visit, we left and continued our trip. All the followers, even the women and children, came outside the city with us. We all knelt down on the beach and prayed. ⁶Then we said good-bye and got on the ship. The followers went back home.

⁷We continued our trip from Tyre and arrived at Ptolemais. We greeted the believers there and stayed with them for a day. ⁸We left Ptolemais and went to the city of Caesarea. There we went into the home of Philip and stayed with him. Philip had the work of telling the Good News. He was one of the seven helpers.ⁿ ⁹He had four unmarried daughters who had the gift of prophesying. ¹⁰After we had been there for some time, a prophet named Agabus arrived from Judea. ¹¹He came to us and borrowed Paul's belt. Then he used the belt to tie his own hands and feet. He said, "The Holy Spirit says, 'This is how the Jews in Jerusalem will tie up the man who wears this belt. Then they will give him to the non-Jewish people.' "

¹²We all heard these words. So we and the people there begged Paul not to go to Jerusalem. ¹³But he said, "Why are you crying and making me so sad? I am ready to be tied up in Jerusalem. And I am ready to die for the Lord Jesus!"

¹⁴We could not persuade him to stay away from Jerusalem. So we stopped begging him and said, "We pray that what the Lord wants will be done."

ⁿ**helpers** The seven men chosen for a special work described in Acts 6:1-6.

Prayer Starter: Dear God, help more and more people to place their faith in Jesus Christ.

Memory Verse: I taught you to remember the words of Jesus. He said, "It is more blessed to give than to receive."

—*Acts 20:35b*

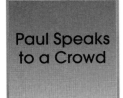

**Paul Speaks
to a Crowd**

The soldiers were about to take Paul into the army building. But he spoke to the commander, "May I say something to you?"

The commander said, "Do you speak Greek? ³⁸I thought you were the Egyptian who started some trouble against the government not long ago. He led 4,000 killers out to the desert."

³⁹Paul said, "No, I am a Jew from Tarsus in the country of Cilicia. I am a citizen of that important city. Please, let me speak to the people."

⁴⁰The commander gave permission, so Paul stood on the steps. He waved with his hand so that the people would be quiet. When there was silence, Paul spoke to them in the Jewish language.ⁿ

22Paul said, "Brothers and fathers, listen to me! I will make my defense to you." ²When the Jews heard him speaking the Jewish language,ⁿ they became very quiet. Paul said, ³"I am a Jew. I was born in Tarsus in the country of Cilicia. I grew up in this city. I was a student of Gamaliel.ⁿ He carefully taught me everything about the law of our ancestors. I was very serious about serving God, just as are all of you here today. ⁴I hurt the people who followed the Way of Jesus. Some of them were even killed. I arrested men and women and put them in jail. ⁵The high priest and the whole council of older Jewish leaders can tell you that this is true. These leaders gave me letters to the Jewish brothers in Damascus. So I was going there to arrest these people and bring them back to Jerusalem to be punished.

⁶"But something happened to me on my way to Damascus. It was about noon when I came near Damascus. Suddenly a bright light from heaven flashed all around me. ⁷I fell to the ground and heard a voice saying, 'Saul, Saul, why are you doing things against me?' ⁸I asked, 'Who are you, Lord?' The voice said, 'I am Jesus from Nazareth.' "

ⁿ**Jewish language** Aramaic, the language of the Jews in the first century.
ⁿ**Gamaliel** A very important teacher of the Pharisees, a Jewish religious group (Acts 5:34).

Prayer Starter: Lord, help me not to do anything that would hurt you or any of your followers.

Memory Verse: So men . . .   —*Acts 27:25*

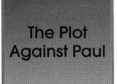

The Plot Against Paul

In the morning some of the Jews made a plan to kill Paul. They made a promise that they would not eat or drink anything until they had killed him. ¹³There were more than 40 Jews who made this plan. ¹⁴They went and talked to the leading priests and the older Jewish leaders. They said, "We have made a promise to ourselves that we will not eat or drink until we have killed Paul! ¹⁵So this is what we want you to do: Send a message to the commander to bring Paul out to you. Tell him you want to ask Paul more questions. We will be waiting to kill him while he is on the way here."

¹⁶But Paul's nephew heard about this plan. He went to the army building and told Paul about it. ¹⁷Then Paul called one of the officers and said, "Take this young man to the commander. He has a message for him."

¹⁸So the officer brought Paul's nephew to the commander. The officer said, "The prisoner, Paul, asked me to bring this young man to you. He wants to tell you something."

¹⁹The commander led the young man to a place where they could be alone. The commander asked, "What do you want to tell me?"

²⁰The young man said, "The Jews have decided to ask you to bring Paul down to their council meeting tomorrow. They want you to think that they are going to ask him more questions. ²¹But don't believe them! There are more than 40 men who are hiding and waiting to kill Paul. They have all made a promise not to eat or drink until they have killed him! Now they are waiting for you to agree."

²²The commander sent the young man away. He said to him, "Don't tell anyone that you have told me about their plan."

Prayer Starter: Protect me from the evil one, dear Lord.

Memory Verse: So men, be cheerful! . . .   *—Acts 27:25*

Agrippa and Bernice

The next day Agrippa and Bernice appeared. They dressed and acted like very important people. Agrippa and Bernice, the army leaders, and the important men of Caesarea went into the judgment room. Then Festus ordered the soldiers to bring Paul in. ²⁴Festus said, "King Agrippa and all who are gathered here with us, you see this man. All the Jewish people, here and in Jerusalem, have complained to me about him. They shout that he should not live any longer. ²⁵When I judged him, I could find nothing wrong. I found no reason to order his death. But he asked to be judged by Caesar. So I decided to send him."

26 Agrippa said to Paul, "You may now speak to defend yourself." Then Paul raised his hand and began to speak. ²He said, "King Agrippa, I will answer all the charges that the Jews make against me. I think it is a blessing that I can stand here before you today. ³I am very happy to talk to you, because you know so much about all the Jewish customs and the things that the Jews argue about. Please listen to me patiently."

Prayer Starter: May the leaders of this world bow down and worship you, O Lord.

Memory Verse: So men, be cheerful! I trust in God . . .   *—Acts 27:25*

It was decided that we would sail for Italy. [7]We sailed slowly for many days.

[13]Then a good wind began to blow from the south. The men on the ship thought, "This is the wind we wanted, and now we have it!" So they pulled up the anchor. We sailed very close to the island of Crete. [14]But then a very strong wind named the "Northeaster" came from the island. [15]This wind took the ship and carried it away. The ship could not sail against it. So we stopped trying and let the wind blow us. [16]We went below a small island named Cauda. Then we were able to bring in the lifeboat, but it was very hard to do. [17]After the men took the lifeboat in, they tied ropes around the ship to hold it together. The men were afraid that the ship would hit the sandbanks of Syrtis.[n] So they lowered the sail and let the wind carry the ship. [18]The next day the storm was blowing us so hard that the men threw out some of the cargo. [19]A day later they threw out the ship's equipment. [20]For many days we could not see the sun or the stars. The storm was very bad. We lost all hope of staying alive—we thought we would die.

[21]The men had gone without food for a long time. Then one day Paul stood up before them and said, "Men, I told you not to leave Crete. You should have listened to me. Then you would not have all this trouble and loss. [22]But now I tell you to cheer up. None of you will die! But the ship will be lost. [23]Last night an angel from God came to me. This is the God I worship. I am his. [24]God's angel said, 'Paul, do not be afraid! You must stand before Caesar. And God has given you this promise: He will save the lives of all those men sailing with you.' [25]So men, be cheerful! I trust in God. Everything will happen as his angel told me. [26]But we will crash on an island."

[27]On the fourteenth night we were floating around in the Adriatic Sea.[n] The sailors thought we were close to land. [28]They threw a rope into the water with a weight on the end of it. They found that the water was 120 feet deep. They went a little farther and threw the rope in again. It was 90 feet deep. [29]The sailors were afraid that we would hit the rocks, so they threw four anchors into the water. Then they prayed for daylight to come.

[n]**Syrtis** Shallow area in the sea near the Libyan coast.
[n]**Adriatic Sea** The sea between Greece and Italy, including the central Mediterranean.

Prayer Starter: Help me to be cheerful, Lord, for I believe you will do all you have promised.

Memory Verse: So men, be cheerful! I trust in God. Everything will happen . . .
—Acts 27:25

Shipwrecked

Some of the sailors wanted to leave the ship, and they lowered the lifeboat. These sailors wanted the other men to think that they were throwing more anchors from the front of the ship. ³¹But Paul told the officer and the other soldiers, "If these men do not stay in the ship, your lives cannot be saved!" ³²So the soldiers cut the ropes and let the lifeboat fall into the water.

³³Just before dawn Paul began persuading all the people to eat something. He said, "For the past 14 days you have been waiting and watching. You have not eaten. ³⁴Now I beg you to eat something. You need it to stay alive. None of you will lose even one hair off your heads." ³⁵After he

said this, Paul took some bread and thanked God for it before all of them. He broke off a piece and began eating. ³⁶All the men felt better. They all started eating too. ³⁷(There were 276 people on the ship.) ³⁸We ate all we wanted. Then we began making the ship lighter by throwing the grain into the sea.

³⁹When daylight came, the sailors saw land. They did not know what land it was, but they saw a bay with a beach. They wanted to sail the ship to the beach, if they could. ⁴⁰So they cut the ropes to the anchors and left the anchors in the sea. At the same time, they untied the ropes that were holding the rudders. Then they raised the front sail into the wind and sailed toward the beach. ⁴¹But the ship hit a sandbank. The front of the

ship stuck there and could not move. Then the big waves began to break the back of the ship to pieces.

⁴²The soldiers decided to kill the prisoners so that none of them could swim away and escape. ⁴³But Julius, the officer, wanted to let Paul live. He did not allow the soldiers to kill the prisoners. Instead he ordered everyone who could swim to jump into the water and swim to land. ⁴⁴The rest used wooden boards or pieces of the ship. And this is how all the people made it safely to land.

28When we were safe on land, we learned that the island was called Malta.

Prayer Starter: Thank you, Lord, for helping us when we are in danger.

Memory Verse: So men, be cheerful! I trust in God. Everything will happen as his angel told me.   —*Acts 27:25*

**Paul Bitten
by a Snake**

It was raining and very cold. But the people who lived there were very good to us. They made us a fire and welcomed all of us. ³Paul gathered a pile of sticks for the fire. He was putting them on the fire when a poisonous snake came out because of the heat and bit him on the hand. ⁴The people living on the island saw the snake hanging from Paul's hand. They said to each other, "This man must be a murderer! He did not die in the sea, but Justice" does not want him to live." ⁵But Paul shook the snake off into the fire. He was not hurt. ⁶The

people thought that Paul would swell up or fall down dead. The people waited and watched him for a long time, but nothing bad happened to him. So they changed their minds about Paul. Now they said, "He is a god!"

¹⁰⁻¹¹The people on the island gave us many honors. We stayed there three months. When we were ready to leave, they gave us the things we needed.

We got on a ship from Alexandria. The ship had stayed on the island during the winter. On the front of the ship was the sign of the twin gods." ¹²We stopped at Syracuse for three days and then left.
¹³From there we sailed to Rhegium. The next day a wind began to blow from the southwest, so we were able to leave. A day later we came to Puteoli. ¹⁴We found some believers there, and they asked us to stay with them for a week. Finally, we came to Rome.

"**Justice** The people thought there was a god named Justice who would punish bad people.
"**twin gods** Statues of Castor and Pollux, gods in old Greek tales.

Prayer Starter: Thank you for fish and birds—even for reptiles and insects.

Memory Verse: I am proud of the Good News. . . .   —*Romans 1:16*

Paul in Rome

The believers in Rome heard that we were there. They came out as far as the Market of Appius[n] and the Three Inns[n] to meet us. When Paul saw them, he was encouraged and thanked God.

[16]Then we arrived at Rome. There, Paul was allowed to live alone. But a soldier stayed with him to guard him.

[17]Three days later Paul sent for the Jewish leaders there. When they came together, he said, "Brothers, I have done nothing against our people. I have done nothing against the customs of our fathers. But I was arrested in Jerusalem and given to the Romans. [18]The Romans asked me many questions. But they could find no reason why I should be killed. They wanted to let me go free, [19]but the Jews there did not want that. So I had to ask to come to Rome to have my trial before Caesar. But I have no charge to bring against my own people. [20]That is why I wanted to see you and talk with you. I am bound with this chain because I believe in the hope of Israel."

[21]The Jews answered Paul, "We have received no letters from Judea about you. None of our Jewish brothers who have come from there brought news about you or told us anything bad about you. [22]We want to hear your

ideas. We know that people everywhere are speaking against this religious group."

²³Paul and the Jews chose a day for a meeting. On that day many more of the Jews met with Paul at the place he was staying. Paul spoke to them all day long, explaining the kingdom of God to them. He tried to persuade them to believe these things about Jesus. He used the law of Moses and the writings of the prophets to do this.

³⁰Paul stayed two full years in his own rented house. He welcomed all people who came and visited him. ³¹He preached about the kingdom of God and taught about the Lord Jesus Christ. He was very bold, and no one tried to stop him from speaking.

ⁿ**Market of Appius** A town about 27 miles from Rome.
ⁿ**Three Inns** A town about 30 miles from Rome.

Prayer Starter: Dear Lord, help me to be an encouraging friend.

Memory Verse: I am proud of the Good News. It is the power God uses . . .
—*Romans 1:16*

**Paul's Letter
to the
Romans**

From Paul, a servant of Christ Jesus. God called me to be an apostle and chose me to tell the Good News.

²God promised this Good News long ago through his prophets. That promise is written in the Holy Scriptures. ³⁻⁴The Good News is about God's Son, Jesus Christ our Lord. As a man, he was born from the family of David. But through the Spirit of holiness he was appointed to be God's Son with great power by rising from death. ⁵Through Christ, God gave me the special work of an apostle. This was to lead people of all nations to believe and obey. I do this work for Christ. ⁶And you who are in Rome are also called to belong to Jesus Christ.

⁷This letter is to all of you in Rome whom God loves and has called to be his holy people.

May God our Father and the Lord Jesus Christ show you kindness and give you peace.

⁸First I want to say that I thank my God through Jesus Christ for all of you. I thank God because people everywhere in the world are talking about your great faith. ⁹⁻¹⁰God knows that every time I pray I always mention you. God is the One I serve with my whole heart by telling the Good News about his Son. I pray that I will be allowed to come to you, and this will happen if God wants it. ¹¹I want very much to see you, to give you some spiritual gift to make you strong. ¹²I mean that I want us to help each other with the faith that we have. Your faith will help me, and my

faith will help you. [13]Brothers, I want you to know that I planned many times to come to you. But this has not been possible. I wanted to come so that I could help you grow spiritually. I wanted to help you as I have helped the other non-Jewish people.

[14]I must serve all people—Greeks and non-Greeks, the wise and the foolish. [15]That is why I want so much to preach the Good News to you in Rome.

[16]I am proud of the Good News. It is the power God uses to save everyone who believes—to save the Jews first, and also to save the non-Jews. [17]The Good News shows how God makes people right with himself. God's way of making people right with him begins and ends with faith. As the Scripture says, "The person who is made right with God by faith will live forever."[n]

5 We have been made right with God because of our faith. So we have peace with God through our Lord Jesus Christ. [2]Through our faith, Christ has brought us into that blessing of God's grace that we now enjoy. And we are happy because of the hope we have of sharing God's glory. [3]And we also have joy with our troubles because we know that these troubles produce patience. [4]And patience produces character, and character produces hope. [5]And this hope will never disappoint us, because God has poured out his love to fill our hearts. God gave us his love through the Holy Spirit, whom God has given to us.

[6]Christ died for us while we were still weak. We were living against God, but at the right time, Christ died for us. [7]Very few people will die to save the life of someone else. Although perhaps for a good man someone might possibly die. [8]But Christ died for us while we were still sinners. In this way God shows his great love for us.

[9]We have been made right with God by the blood of Christ's death. So through Christ we will surely be saved from God's anger. [10]I mean that while we were God's enemies, God made friends with us through the death of his Son. Surely, now that we are God's friends, God will save us through his Son's life. [11]And not only that, but now we are also very happy in God through our Lord Jesus Christ. Through Jesus we are now God's friends again.

[n]**"The person . . . forever."** Quotation from Habakkuk 2:4.

Prayer Starter: Make me proud of the good news about Jesus, dear God.

Memory Verse: I am proud of the Good News. It is the power God uses to save everyone who believes . . .   —*Romans 1:16*

This Is My Body

In the things I tell you now I do not praise you. Your meetings hurt you more than they help you. [18]First, I hear that when you meet together as a church you are divided. And I believe some of this. [19](It is necessary for there to be differences among you. That is the way to make it clear which of you are really doing right.) [20]When you all come together, you are not really eating the Lord's Supper." [21]This is because when you eat, each person eats without waiting for the others. Some people do not get enough to eat, while others have too much to drink. [22]You can eat and drink in your own homes! It seems that you think God's church is not important. You embarrass those who are poor. What should I tell you? Should I praise you for doing this? I do not praise you.

[23]The teaching that I gave you is the same teaching that I received from the Lord: On the night when Jesus was handed over to be killed, he took bread [24]and gave thanks for it. Then he broke the bread and said, "This is my body; it is for you. Do this to remember me." [25]In the same way, after they ate, Jesus took the cup. He said, "This cup shows the new agreement from God to his people. This new agreement begins with the blood of my death. When you drink this, do it to remember me." [26]Every time you eat this bread and drink this cup, you show others about the Lord's death until he comes.

[27]So a person should not eat the bread or drink the cup of the Lord in a way that is not worthy of it. If he does he is sinning against the body and the blood of the Lord. [28]Everyone should look into his own heart before he eats the bread and drinks the cup. [29]If someone eats the bread and drinks the cup without recognizing the body, then he is judged guilty by eating and drinking. [30]That is why many in your group are sick and weak. And many have died. [31]But if we judged ourselves in the right way, then God would not judge us. [32]But when the Lord judges us, he punishes us to show us the right way. He does this so that we will not be destroyed along with the world.

"**Lord's Supper** The meal Jesus told his followers to eat to remember him.

Prayer Starter: Help me to be well behaved in church and school, Lord. Help me to respect my teachers.

Memory Verse: I am proud of the Good News. It is the power God uses to save everyone who believes—to save the Jews first . . . —*Romans 1:16*

Paul Corrects Peter

od gave Peter the work of telling the Good News to the Jews. But God gave me the work of telling the Good News to the non-Jewish people. ⁸God gave Peter the power to work as an apostle for the Jewish people. But he also gave me the power to work as an apostle for those who are not Jews. ⁹James, Peter, and John, who seemed to be the leaders, saw that God had given me this special grace. So they accepted Barnabas and me. They said, "Paul and Barnabas, we agree that you should go to the people who are not Jews. We will go to the Jews." ¹⁰They asked us to do only one thing—to remember to help the poor. And this was something that I really wanted to do.

¹¹When Peter came to Antioch, I was against him because he was wrong. ¹²This is what happened: When Peter first came to Antioch, he ate with the non-Jewish people. But then some Jewish men were sent from James. When they arrived, Peter stopped eating with the non-Jewish people and separated himself from them. He was afraid of the Jews who

believe that all non-Jewish people must be circumcised. [13]So Peter was a hypocrite. The other Jewish believers joined with him and were hypocrites, too. Even Barnabas was influenced by what these Jewish believers did. [14]I saw what they did. They were not following the truth of the Good News. So I spoke to Peter in front of them all. I said: "Peter, you are a Jew, but you are not living like a Jew. You are living like the non-Jewish people. So why do you now try to force the non-Jewish people to live like Jews?"

[15]We were not born as non-Jewish "sinners," but we were born as Jews. [16]Yet we know that a person is not made right with God by following the law. No! It is trusting in Jesus Christ that makes a person right with God. So we, too, have put our faith in Christ Jesus, that we might be made right with God. And we are right with God because we trusted in Christ—not because we followed the law. For no one can be made right with God by following the law.

[17]We Jews came to Christ to be made right with God. So it is clear that we were sinners too. Does that mean that Christ makes us sinners? No! [18]But I would really be wrong to begin teaching again those things of the Law of Moses that I gave up. [19]I stopped living for the law. It was the law that put me to death. I died to the law so that I can now live for God. I was put to death on the cross with Christ. [20]I do not live anymore—it is Christ living in me. I still live in my body, but I live by faith in the Son of God. He loved me and gave himself to save me. [21]This gift is from God, and it is very important to me. If the law could make us right with God, then Christ did not have to die.

Prayer Starter: Give me wisdom, Lord, to know when to tell others that they are wrong.

Memory Verse: I am proud of the Good News. It is the power God uses to save everyone who believes—to save the Jews first, and also to save the non-Jews.
—*Romans 1:16*

Christ Brings Spiritual Blessings

From Paul, an apostle of Christ Jesus. I am an apostle because that is what God wanted.

To God's holy people living in Ephesus, believers in Christ Jesus.

²Grace and peace to you from God our Father and the Lord Jesus Christ.

³Praise be to the God and Father of our Lord Jesus Christ. In Christ, God has given us every spiritual blessing in heaven. ⁴In Christ, he chose us before the world was made. In his love he chose us to be his holy people—people without blame before him. ⁵And before the world was made, God decided to make us his own children through Jesus Christ. That was what he wanted and what pleased him. ⁶This brings praise to God because of his wonderful grace. God gave that grace to us

freely, in Christ, the One he loves. [7]In Christ we are set free by the blood of his death. And so we have forgiveness of sins because of God's rich grace. [8]God gave us that grace fully and freely. God, with full wisdom and understanding, [9]let us know his secret purpose. This was what God wanted, and he planned to do it through Christ. [10]His goal was to carry out his plan when the right time came. He planned that all things in heaven and on earth would be joined together in Christ as the head.

[11]In Christ we were chosen to be God's people. God had already chosen us to be his people, because that is what he wanted. And God is the One who makes everything agree with what he decides and wants. [12]We are the first people who hoped in Christ. And we were chosen so that we would bring praise to God's glory. [13]So it is with you. You heard the true teaching—the Good News about your salvation. When you heard it, you believed in Christ. And in Christ, God put his special mark on you by giving you the Holy Spirit that he had promised. [14]That Holy Spirit is the guarantee that we will get what God promised for his people. This will bring full freedom to the people who belong to God, to bring praise to God's glory.

[15-16]That is why I always remember you in my prayers and always thank God for you. I have always done this since the time I heard about your faith in the Lord Jesus and your love for all God's people. [17]I always pray to the God of our Lord Jesus Christ—to the glorious Father. I pray that he will give you a spirit that will make you wise in the knowledge of God—the knowledge that he has shown you. [18]I pray that you will have greater understanding in your heart. Then you will know the hope that God has chosen to give us. I pray that you will know that the blessings God has promised his holy people are rich and glorious. [19]And you will know that God's power is very great for us who believe. That power is the same as the great strength [20]God used to raise Christ from death and put him at his right side in heaven. [21]God made Christ more important than all rulers, authorities, powers, and kings. Christ is more important than anything in this world or in the next world. [22]God put everything under his power. And God made him the head over everything for the church. [23]The church is Christ's body. The church is filled with Christ, and Christ fills everything in every way.

Prayer Starter: I praise you, Father, for the spiritual blessings Christ brought from heaven.

Memory Verse: Do not worry about anything . . .   —*Philippians 4:6*

**The Armor
That God
Gives**

Finally, be strong in the Lord and in his great power. ¹¹Wear the full armor of God. Wear God's armor so that you can fight against the devil's evil tricks. ¹²Our fight is not against people on earth. We are fighting against the rulers and authorities and the powers of this world's darkness. We are fighting against the spiritual powers of evil in the heavenly world. ¹³That is why you need to get God's full armor. Then on the day of evil you will be able to stand strong. And when you have finished the whole fight,

you will still be standing. [14]So stand strong, with the belt of truth tied around your waist. And on your chest wear the protection of right living. [15]And on your feet wear the Good News of peace to help you stand strong. [16]And also use the shield of faith. With that you can stop all the burning arrows of the Evil One. [17]Accept God's salvation to be your helmet. And take the sword of the Spirit—that sword is the teaching of God. [18]Pray in the Spirit at all times. Pray with all kinds of prayers, and ask for everything you need. To do this you must always be ready. Never give up. Always pray for all God's people.

[19]Also pray for me. Pray that when I speak, God will give me words so that I can tell the secret truth of the Good News without fear. [20]I have the work of speaking that Good News. I am doing that now, here in prison. Pray that when I preach the Good News I will speak without fear, as I should.

[21]I am sending to you Tychicus, our brother whom we love. He is a faithful servant of the Lord's work. He will tell you everything that is happening with me. Then you will know how I am and what I am doing. [22]That is why I am sending him. I want you to know how we are. I am sending him to encourage you.

[23]Peace and love with faith to you from God the Father and the Lord Jesus Christ. [24]God's grace to all of you who love our Lord Jesus Christ with love that never ends.

Prayer Starter: Help me to stand strong for you, Lord, and to keep praying for your people.

Memory Verse: Do not worry about anything. But pray and ask God . . .
                                                                    —*Philippians 4:6*

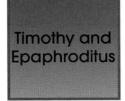

Timothy and Epaphroditus

My dear friends, you have always obeyed. You obeyed God when I was with you. It is even more important that you obey now while I am not with you. Keep on working to complete your salvation, and do it with fear and trembling. ¹³Yes, God is working in you to help you want to do what pleases him. Then he gives you the power to do it.

¹⁴Do everything without complaining or arguing. ¹⁵Then you will be innocent and without anything wrong in you. You will be God's children without fault. But you are living with crooked and mean people all around you. Among them you shine like stars in the dark world. ¹⁶You offer to them the teaching that gives life. So when Christ comes again, I can be happy because my work was not wasted. I ran in the race and won.

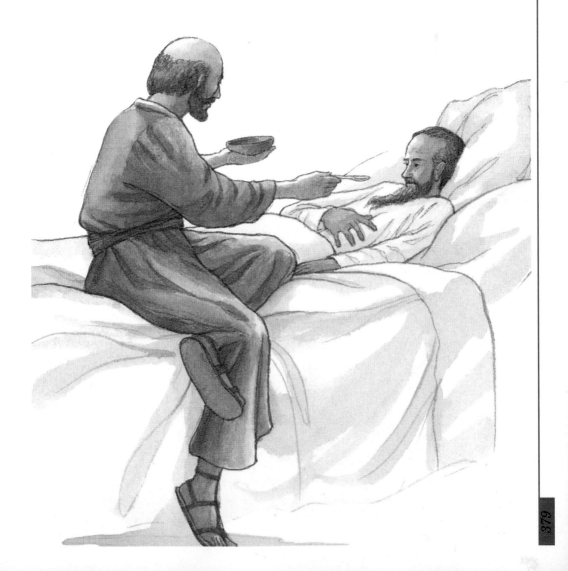

¹⁷Your faith makes you offer your lives as a sacrifice in serving God. Perhaps I will have to offer my own blood with your sacrifice. But if that happens, I will be happy and full of joy with all of you. ¹⁸You also should be happy and full of joy with me.

¹⁹I hope in the Lord Jesus to send Timothy to you soon. I will be happy to learn how you are. ²⁰I have no other person like Timothy. He truly cares for you. ²¹Other people are interested only in their own lives. They are not interested in the work of Christ Jesus. ²²You know the kind of person Timothy is. You know that he has served with me in telling the Good News, as a son serves his father. ²³I plan to send him to you quickly when I know what will happen to me. ²⁴I am sure that the Lord will help me to come to you soon.

²⁵Epaphroditus is my brother in Christ. He works and serves with me in the army of Christ. When I needed help, you sent him to me. I think now that I must send him back to you ²⁶because he wants very much to see all of you. He is worried because you heard that he was sick. ²⁷Yes, he was sick, and nearly died. But God helped him and me too, so that I would not have more sadness. ²⁸So I want very much to send him to you. When you see him, you can be happy. And I can stop worrying about you. ²⁹Welcome him in the Lord with much joy. Give honor to people like Epaphroditus. ³⁰He should be honored because he almost died for the work of Christ. He put his life in danger so that he could help me. This was help that you could not give me.

Prayer Starter: Please help those who are sick, Lord, and keep us well.

Memory Verse: Do not worry about anything. But pray and ask God for everything you need. . . .   —*Philippians 4:6*

I Continue Trying

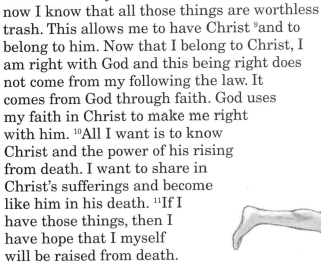

I was circumcised eight days after my birth. I am from the people of Israel and the tribe of Benjamin. I am a Hebrew, and my parents were Hebrews. The law of Moses was very important to me. That is why I became a Pharisee. ⁶I was so enthusiastic that I tried to hurt the church. No one could find fault with the way I obeyed the law of Moses. ⁷At one time all these things were important to me. But now I think those things are worth nothing because of Christ. ⁸Not only those things, but I think that all things are worth nothing compared with the greatness of knowing Christ Jesus my Lord. Because of Christ, I have lost all those things. And now I know that all those things are worthless trash. This allows me to have Christ ⁹and to belong to him. Now that I belong to Christ, I am right with God and this being right does not come from my following the law. It comes from God through faith. God uses my faith in Christ to make me right with him. ¹⁰All I want is to know Christ and the power of his rising from death. I want to share in Christ's sufferings and become like him in his death. ¹¹If I have those things, then I have hope that I myself will be raised from death.

¹²I do not mean that I am already as God wants me to be. I have not yet reached that goal. But I continue trying to reach it and to make it mine. Christ wants me to do that. That is the reason Christ made me his. ¹³Brothers, I know that I have not yet reached that goal. But there is one thing I always do: I forget the things that are past. I try as hard as I can to reach the goal that is before me. ¹⁴I keep trying to reach the goal and get the prize. That prize is mine because God called me through Christ to the life above.

Prayer Starter: Thank you, Lord, for all your promises about the future.

Memory Verse: Do not worry about anything. But pray and ask God for everything you need. And when you pray . . .   —*Philippians 4:6*

**Continue
Following
the Lord**

My dear brothers, I love you and want to see you. You bring me joy and make me proud of you. Continue following the Lord as I have told you.

²I ask Euodia and Syntyche to agree in the Lord. ³And because you serve faithfully with me, my friend, I ask you to help these women to do this. They served with me in telling people the Good News. They served together with Clement and others who worked with me. Their names are written in the book of life.ⁿ

⁴Be full of joy in the Lord always. I will say again, be full of joy.

⁵Let all men see that you are gentle and kind. The Lord is coming soon. ⁶Do not worry about anything. But pray and ask God for everything you need. And when you pray, always give thanks. ⁷And God's peace will keep your hearts and minds in Christ Jesus. The peace that God gives is so great that we cannot understand it.

⁸Brothers, continue to think about the things that are good and worthy of praise. Think about the things that are true and honorable and right and pure and beautiful and respected. ⁹And do what you learned and received from me. Do what I told you and what you saw me do. And the God who gives you peace will be with you.

ⁿ**book of life** God's book that has the names of all God's chosen people (Revelation 21:27).

Prayer Starter: Help me not to worry about anything, but to pray about everything.

Memory Verse: Do not worry about anything. But pray and ask God for everything you need. And when you pray, always give thanks.
—*Philippians 4:6*

The Lord Will Return

Brothers, we want you to know about those who have died. We do not want you to be sad as others who have no hope. [14]We believe that Jesus died and that he rose again. So, because of Jesus, God will bring together with Jesus those who have died. [15]What we tell you now is the Lord's own message. We who are living now may still be living when the Lord comes again. We who are living at that time will be with the Lord, but not before those who have already died. [16]The Lord himself will come down from heaven. There will be a loud command with the voice of the archangel[n] and with the trumpet call of God. And those who have died and were in Christ will rise first. [17]After that,

those who are still alive at that time will be gathered up with them. We will be taken up in the clouds to meet the Lord in the air. And we will be with the Lord forever. [18]So comfort each other with these words.

5 Now, brothers, we do not need to write to you about times and dates. [2]You know very well that the day the Lord comes again will be a surprise like a thief that comes in the night.

[10]Jesus died for us so that we can live together with him. It is not important if we are alive or dead when Jesus comes. [11]So comfort each other and give each other strength, just as you are doing now.

[n]**archangel** The leader among God's angels or messengers.

Prayer Starter: Lord, I can hardly wait for the Lord Jesus Christ who is coming again from heaven.

Memory Verse: You know very well . . .   *—1 Thessalonians 5:2*

Tell These Things

Tell these things to the brothers. This will show that you are a good servant of Christ Jesus. You will show that you are made strong by the words of faith and good teaching that you have been following. ⁷People tell silly stories that do not agree with God's truth. Do not follow what those stories teach. But teach yourself only to serve God. ⁸Training your body helps you in some ways, but serving God helps you in every way. Serving God brings you blessings in this life and in the future life, too. ⁹What I say is true, and you should fully accept it. ¹⁰For this is why we work and struggle: We hope in the living God. He is the Savior of all people. And in a very special way, he is the Savior of all who believe in him.

¹¹Command and teach these things. ¹²You are young, but do not let anyone treat you as if you were not important. Be an example to show the believers how they should live. Show them with your words, with the

way you live, with your love, with your faith, and with your pure life. [13]Continue to read the Scriptures to the people, strengthen them, and teach them. Do these things until I come. [14]Remember to use the gift that you have. That gift was given to you through a prophecy when the group of elders laid their hands on[n] you. [15]Continue to do those things. Give your life to doing them. Then everyone can see that your work is progressing. [16]Be careful in your life and in your teaching. Continue to live and teach rightly. Then you will save yourself and those people who listen to you.

5 Do not speak angrily to an older man, but talk to him as if he were your father. Treat younger men like brothers. [2]Treat older women like mothers, and younger women like sisters. Always treat them in a pure way.

[3]Take care of widows who are all alone.

[17]The elders who lead the church well should receive great honor. Those who work hard by speaking and teaching especially should receive great honor.

[21]Before God and Jesus Christ and the chosen angels, I command you to do these things. Be careful to do them without showing favor to anyone.

[n]**laid their hands on** A sign to show that Timothy was being given a special work of God.

Prayer Starter: Forgive me, Father, for the times I haven't treated other people nicely.

Memory Verse: You know very well that the day the Lord comes again . . .
—*1 Thessalonians 5:2*

Eunice and Lois

From Paul, an apostle of Christ Jesus by the will of God. God sent me to tell about the promise of life that is in Christ Jesus.

²To Timothy, a dear son to me. Grace, mercy, and peace to you from God the Father and Christ Jesus our Lord.

³I always remember you in my prayers, day and night. And I thank God for you in these prayers. He is the God my ancestors served. And I serve him, doing what I know is right. ⁴I remember that you cried for me. And I want very much to see you so that I can be filled with joy. ⁵I remember your true faith. That kind of faith first belonged to your grandmother Lois and to your mother Eunice. And I know that you now have that same faith. ⁶That is why I remind you to use the gift God gave you. God gave you that gift when I laid my hands on" you. Now let it grow, as a small flame grows into a fire. ⁷God did not give us a spirit that makes us afraid. He gave us a spirit of power and love and self-control.

[8]So do not be ashamed to tell people about our Lord Jesus. And do not be ashamed of me. I am in prison for the Lord. But suffer with me for the Good News. God gives us the strength to do that. [9]God saved us and made us his holy people. That was not because of anything we did ourselves but because of what he wanted and because of his grace. That grace was given to us through Christ Jesus before time began. [10]It was not shown to us until our Savior Christ Jesus came. Jesus destroyed death. And through the Good News, he showed us the way to have life that cannot be destroyed. [11]I was chosen to tell that Good News and to be an apostle and a teacher. [12]And I suffer now because I tell the Good News. But I am not ashamed. I know Jesus, the One I have believed in. And I am sure that he is able to protect what he has trusted me with until that Day.[n] [13]Follow the true teachings you heard from me. Follow them as an example of the faith and love we have in Christ Jesus. [14]Protect the truth that you were given. Protect it with the help of the Holy Spirit who lives in us.

[n]**laid . . . on** A sign to show that Paul had power from God to give Timothy a special blessing.
[n]**Day** The day Christ will come to judge all people and take his people to live with him.

Prayer Starter: Thank you, God, for all the people who love me.

Memory Verse: You know very well that the day the Lord comes again will be a surprise . . .
        —1 Thessalonians 5:2

Philemon

I remember you in my prayers. And I always thank my God for you. ⁵I hear about the love you have for all God's holy people and the faith you have in the Lord Jesus. ⁶I pray that the faith you share will make you understand every blessing that we have in Christ. ⁷My brother, you have shown love to God's people. You have made them feel happy. This has given me great joy and comfort.

⁸There is something that you should do. And because of your love in Christ, I feel free to order you to do it. ⁹But because I love you, I am asking you instead. I, Paul, am an old man now, and a prisoner for Christ Jesus. ¹⁰I am asking you a favor for my son Onesimus. He became my son while I was in prison. ¹¹In the past he was useless to you. But now he has become useful for both you and me.

¹²I am sending him back to you, and with him I am sending my own heart. ¹³I wanted to keep him with me to help me while I am in prison for the Good News. By helping me he would be serving you. ¹⁴But I did not want to do anything without asking you first. Then any favor you do for me will be because you want to do it, not because I forced you to do it.

¹⁵Onesimus was separated from you for a short time. Maybe that happened so that you could have him back forever— ¹⁶not to be a slave, but better than a slave, to be a loved brother. I love him very much. But you will love him even more. You will love him as a man and as a brother in the Lord.

¹⁷If you think of me as your friend, then accept Onesimus back. Welcome him as you would welcome me. ¹⁸If Onesimus has done anything wrong to you, charge that to me. If he owes you anything, charge that to me. ¹⁹I, Paul, am writing this with my own hand. I will pay back anything Onesimus owes. And I will say nothing about what you owe me for your own life. ²⁰So, my brother, I ask that you do this for me in the Lord. Comfort my heart in Christ.

Prayer Starter: Lord, use my love to make others happy.

Memory Verse: You know very well that the day the Lord comes again will be a surprise like a thief . . .
—*1 Thessalonians 5:2*

Faith

It was by faith that Enoch was taken to heaven. He never died. He could not be found, because God had taken him away. Before he was taken, the Scripture says that he was a man who truly pleased God. 6Without faith no one can please God. Anyone who comes to God must believe that he is real and that he rewards those who truly want to find him.

7It was by faith Noah heard God's warnings about things that he could not yet see. He obeyed God and built a large boat to save his family. By his faith, Noah showed that the world was wrong. And he became one of those who are made right with God through faith.

8It was by faith Abraham obeyed God's call to go to another place that God promised to give him. He left his own country, not knowing where he was to go. 9It was by faith that he lived in the country God promised to give him. He lived there like a visitor who did not belong. He lived in tents with Isaac and Jacob, who had received that same promise from God. 10Abraham was waiting for the city[n] that has real foundations—the city planned and built by God.

13All these great men died in faith. They did not get the things that God promised his people. But they saw them coming far in the future and were glad. They said that they were like visitors and strangers on earth. 14When people say such things, then they show that they are looking for a country that will be their own country. 15If they had been thinking about that country they had left, they could have gone back. 16But those men were waiting for a better country—a heavenly country. So God is not ashamed to be called their God. For he has prepared a city for them.

Prayer Starter: Increase my faith, Lord. Help me believe that you are real and that you reward those who seek you.

Memory Verse: You know very well that the day the Lord comes again will be a surprise like a thief that comes in the night.—*1 Thessalonians 5:2*

Religion That Pleases God

My dear brothers, always be willing to listen and slow to speak. Do not become angry easily. [20]Anger will not help you live a good life as God wants. [21]So put out of your life every evil thing and every kind of wrong you do. Don't be proud but accept God's teaching that is planted in your hearts. This teaching can save your souls.

[22]Do what God's teaching says; do not just listen and do nothing. When you only sit and listen, you are fooling yourselves. [23]A person who hears God's teaching and does nothing is like a man looking in a mirror. [24]He sees his face, then goes away and quickly forgets what he looked like. [25]But the truly happy person is the one who carefully studies God's perfect law that makes people free. He continues to study it. He listens to God's teaching and does not forget what he heard. Then he obeys what God's teaching says. When he does this, it makes him happy.

[26]A person might think he is religious. But if he says things he should not say, then he is just fooling himself. His "religion" is worth nothing. [27]Religion that God accepts is this: caring for orphans or widows who need help; and keeping yourself free from the world's evil influence. This is the kind of religion that God accepts as pure and good.

2 My dear brothers, you are believers in our glorious Lord Jesus Christ. So never think that some people are more important than others. [2]Suppose someone comes into your church meeting wearing very nice clothes and a gold ring. At the same time a poor man comes in wearing old, dirty clothes. [3]You show special attention to the one wearing nice clothes. You say, "Please, sit here in this good seat." But you say to the poor man, "Stand over there," or "Sit on the floor by my feet!" [4]What are you doing? You are making some people more important than others. With evil thoughts you are deciding which person is better.

[5]Listen, my dear brothers! God chose the poor in the world to be rich with faith. He chose them to receive the kingdom God promised to people who love him. [6]But you show no respect to the poor man. And you know that it is the rich who are always trying to control your lives. And they are the ones who take you to court. [7]They are the ones who say bad things against Jesus, who owns you.

[8]One law rules over all other laws. This royal law is found in the Scriptures: "Love your neighbor as you love yourself."[n] If you obey this law, then you are doing right. [9]But if you are treating one person as if he were more important than another, then you are sinning. That royal law proves that you are guilty of breaking God's law. [10]A person might follow all of God's law. But if he fails to obey even one command, he is guilty of breaking all the commands in that law. [11]God said, "You must not be guilty of adultery."[n] The same God also said, "You must not murder anyone."[n] So if you do not take part in adultery, but you murder someone, then you are guilty of breaking all of God's law. [12]You will be judged by the law that makes people free. You should remember this in everything you say and do. [13]Yes, you must show mercy to others, or God will not show mercy to you when he judges you. But the person who shows mercy can stand without fear when he is judged.

[14]My brothers, if someone says he has faith, but does nothing, his faith is worth nothing. Can faith like that save him? [15]A brother or sister in Christ might need clothes or might need food. [16]And you say to him, "God be with you! I hope you stay warm and get plenty to eat." You say this, but you do not give that person the things he needs. Unless you help him, your words are worth nothing. [17]It is the same with faith. If faith does nothing, then that faith is dead, because it is alone.

[n]**"Love . . . yourself."** Quotation from Leviticus 19:18.
[n]**"You . . . adultery."** Quotation from Exodus 20:14 and Deuteronomy 5:18.
[n]**"You . . . anyone."** Quotation from Exodus 20:13 and Deuteronomy 5:17.

Prayer Starter: Give me love and concern for those who don't have as much as I have.

Memory Verse: But if we confess our sins, he will forgive our sins . . .
—1 John 1:9

You Should Pray

Brothers, be patient until the Lord comes again. A farmer is patient. He waits for his valuable crop to grow from the earth. He waits patiently for it to receive the first rain and the last rain. ⁸You, too, must be patient. Do not give up hope. The Lord is coming soon. ⁹Brothers, do not complain against each other. If you do not stop complaining, you will be judged guilty. And the Judge is ready to come! ¹⁰Brothers, follow the example of the prophets who spoke for the Lord. They suffered many hard things, but they were patient. ¹¹We say they are happy because they were able to do this. You have heard about Job's patience. You know that after all his trouble, the Lord helped him. This shows that the Lord is full of mercy and is kind.

¹²My brothers, it is very important that you not use an oath when you make a promise. Don't use the name of heaven, earth, or anything else to prove what you say. When you mean yes, say only "yes." When you mean no, say only "no." Do this so that you will not be judged guilty.

[13]If one of you is having troubles, he should pray. If one of you is happy, he should sing praises. [14]If one of you is sick, he should call the church's elders. The elders should pour oil on him[n] in the name of the Lord and pray for him. [15]And the prayer that is said with faith will make the sick person well. The Lord will heal him. And if he has sinned, God will forgive him. [16]Confess your sins to each other and pray for each other. Do this so that God can heal you. When a good man prays, great things happen. [17]Elijah was a man just like us. He prayed that it would not rain. And it did not rain on the land for three and a half years! [18]Then Elijah prayed again. And the rain came down from the sky, and the land grew crops again.

[19]My brothers, one of you may wander away from the truth. And someone may help him come back. [20]Remember this: Anyone who brings a sinner back from the wrong way will save that sinner's soul from death. By doing this, that person will cause many sins to be forgiven.

[n]**pour oil on him** Oil was used like medicine, so that is probably how the believers used it.

Prayer Starter: Teach me to sing praises to you, Lord, when I am happy. And help me to pray when I am having troubles.

Memory Verse: But if we confess our sins, he will forgive our sins. We can trust God. . . .
—*1 John 1:9*

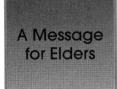

A Message for Elders

Now I have something to say to the elders in your group. I am also an elder. I myself have seen Christ's sufferings. And I will share in the glory that will be shown to us. I beg you to ²take care of God's flock, his people, that you are responsible for. Watch over it because you want to, not because you are forced to do it. That is how God wants it. Do it because you are happy to serve, not because you want money. ³Do not be like a ruler over people you are responsible for. Be good examples to them. ⁴Then when Christ, the Head Shepherd, comes, you will get a crown. This crown will be glorious, and it will never lose its beauty.

⁵In the same way, younger men should be willing to be under older men. And all of you should be very humble with each other.

"God is against the proud,
but he gives grace to the humble."

⁶So be humble under God's powerful hand. Then he will lift you up when the right time comes. ⁷Give all your worries to him, because he cares for you.

⁸Control yourselves and be careful! The devil is your enemy. And he goes around like a roaring lion looking for someone to eat. ⁹Refuse to give in to the devil. Stand strong in your faith. You know that your Christian brothers and sisters all over the world are having the same sufferings you have.

¹⁰Yes, you will suffer for a short time. But after that, God will make everything right. He will make you strong. He will support you and keep you from falling. He is the God who gives all grace. He called you to share in his glory in Christ. That glory will continue forever. ¹¹All power is his forever and ever. Amen.

Prayer Starter: Bless and encourage the pastor of my church, O Lord.

Memory Verse: But if we confess our sins, he will forgive our sins. We can trust God. He does what is right. . . .   —*1 John 1:9*

God Is Light

We write you now about something that has always existed.
We have heard.
We have seen with our own eyes.
We have watched,
and we have touched with our hands.
We write to you about the Word[n] that gives life. [2]He who gives life was shown to us. We saw him, and we can give proof about it. And now we tell you that he has life that continues forever. The one who gives this life was with God the Father. God showed him to us. [3]Now we tell you what we have seen and heard because we want you to have fellowship with us. The fellowship we share together is with God the Father and his Son, Jesus Christ. [4]We write this to you so that you can be full of joy with us.

[5]Here is the message we have heard from God and now tell to you: God is light,[n] and in him there is no darkness at all. [6]So if we say that we have fellowship with God, but we continue living in darkness, then we are liars. We do not follow the truth. [7]God is in the light. We should live in the light, too. If we live in the light, we share fellowship with each other. And when we live in the light, the blood of the death of Jesus, God's Son, is making us clean from every sin.

⁸If we say that we have no sin, we are fooling ourselves, and the truth is not in us. ⁹But if we confess our sins, he will forgive our sins. We can trust God. He does what is right. He will make us clean from all the wrongs we have done. ¹⁰If we say that we have not sinned, then we make God a liar. We do not accept God's true teaching.

ⁿ**Word** The Greek word is "logos," meaning any kind of communication. It could be translated "message." Here, it means Christ. Christ was the way God told people about himself.
ⁿ**light** This word is used to show what God is like. It means goodness or truth.

Prayer Starter: Show me when I sin, Father, so that I can ask for your forgiveness.

Memory Verse: But if we confess our sins, he will forgive our sins. We can trust God. He does what is right. He will make us clean . . . —*1 John 1:9*

Island of Patmos

I am John, and I am your brother in Christ. We are together in Jesus, and we share in these things: in suffering, in the kingdom, and in patience. I was on the island of Patmos[n] because I had preached God's message and the truth about Jesus. [10]On the Lord's day the Spirit took control of me. I heard a loud voice behind me that sounded like a trumpet. [11]The voice said, "Write what you see and send that book to the seven churches: to Ephesus, Smyrna, Pergamum, Thyatira, Sardis, Philadelphia, and Laodicea."

[12]I turned to see who was talking to me. When I turned, I saw seven golden lampstands. [13]I saw someone among the lampstands who was "like a Son of Man."[n] He was dressed in a long robe. He had a gold band around his chest. [14]His head and hair were white like wool, as white as snow. His eyes were like flames of fire. [15]His feet were like bronze that glows hot in a furnace. His voice was like the noise of flooding water. [16]He held seven stars in his right hand. A sharp two-edged sword came out of his mouth. He looked like the sun shining at its brightest time.

[17]When I saw him, I fell down at his feet like a dead man. He put his right hand on me and said, "Do not be afraid! I am the First and the Last. [18]I am the One who lives. I was dead, but look: I am alive forever and ever! And I hold the keys of death and where the dead are."

[n]**Patmos** A small island in the Aegean Sea, near the coast of Asia Minor (modern Turkey).
[n]**"like . . . Man"** "Son of Man" is a name Jesus called himself. It showed he was God's Son, but he was also a man.

Prayer Starter: Dear God, help me realize how glorious Jesus Christ really is.

Memory Verse: But if we confess our sins, he will forgive our sins. We can trust God. He does what is right. He will make us clean from all the wrongs we have done.
—*1 John 1:9*

I Stand at the Door

"Write this to the angel of the church in Laodicea:

"The Amen" is the One who is the faithful and true witness. He is the ruler of all that God has made. He says this to you: 15I know what you do. You are not hot or cold. I wish that you were hot or cold! 16But you are only warm—not hot, not cold. So I am ready to spit you out of my mouth. 17You say you are rich. You think you have become wealthy and do not need anything. But you do not know that you are really miserable, pitiful, poor, blind, and naked. 18I advise you to buy gold from me—gold made pure in fire. Then you can be truly rich. Buy from

me clothes that are white. Then you can cover your shameful nakedness. Buy from me medicine to put on your eyes. Then you can truly see.

¹⁹"I correct and punish those whom I love. So be eager to do right. Change your hearts and lives. ²⁰Here I am! I stand at the door and knock. If anyone hears my voice and opens the door, I will come in and eat with him. And he will eat with me.

²¹"He who wins the victory will sit with me on my throne. It was the same with me. I won the victory and sat down with my Father on his throne. ²²Everyone who has ears should listen to what the Spirit says to the churches."

"**Amen** Used here as a name for Jesus, it means to agree fully that something is true.

Prayer Starter: Dear God, help me to love you with all my heart, mind, and strength.

Memory Verse: Jesus is the One . . .   —*Revelation 22:20*

The Lamb

Then I saw a scroll in the right hand of the One sitting on the throne. The scroll had writing on both sides. It was kept closed with seven seals. [2]And I saw a powerful angel. He called in a loud voice, "Who is worthy to break the seals and open the scroll?" [3]But there was no one in heaven or on earth or under the earth who could open the scroll or look inside it. [4]I cried and cried because there was no one worthy to open the scroll or look inside. [5]But one of the elders said to me, "Do not cry! The Lion[n] from the tribe of Judah has won the victory. He is David's descendant. He is able to open the scroll and its seven seals."

[6]Then I saw a Lamb standing in the center of the throne with the four living things around it. The elders were also around the Lamb. The Lamb looked as if he had been killed. He had seven horns and seven eyes. These are the seven spirits of God that were sent into all the world. [7]The Lamb came and took the scroll from the right hand of the One sitting on the throne. [8]After he took the scroll, the four living things and the 24 elders bowed down before the Lamb. Each one of them had a harp. Also, they were holding golden bowls full of incense. These bowls of incense are the prayers of God's holy people. [9]And they all sang a new song to the Lamb:

> "You are worthy to take the scroll
> > and to open its seals,
> because you were killed;
> > and with the blood of your death you bought men for God
> > from every tribe, language, people, and nation.
> [10] You made them to be a kingdom of priests for our God.
> > And they will rule on the earth."

[n]**Lion** Here refers to Christ.

Prayer Starter: You, Lord, are worthy of all my love and worship.

Memory Verse: Jesus is the One who says that these things are true. . . .
         —*Revelation 22:20*

Worship in Heaven

Then I looked, and there was a great number of people. There were so many people that no one could count them. They were from every nation, tribe, people, and language of the earth. They were all standing before the throne and before the Lamb. They wore white robes and had palm branches in their hands. [10]They were shouting in a loud voice, "Salvation belongs to our God, who sits on the throne, and to the Lamb." [11]The elders[n] and the four living things were there. All the angels were standing around them and the throne. The angels bowed down on their faces before the throne and worshiped God. [12]They were saying, "Amen! Praise, glory, wisdom, thanks, honor, power, and strength belong to our God forever and ever. Amen!"

[13]Then one of the elders asked me, "Who are these people in white robes? Where did they come from?"

[14]I answered, "You know who they are, sir."

And the elder said, "These are the people who have come out of the great suffering. They have washed their robes[n] with the blood of the Lamb. Now they are clean and white. [15]And they are before the throne of God. They worship God day and night in his temple. And the One who sits on the throne will protect them. [16]Those people will never be hungry again. They will never be thirsty again. The sun will not hurt them. No heat will burn them. [17]For the Lamb at the center of the throne will be their shepherd. He will lead them to springs of water that give life. And God will wipe away every tear from their eyes."

[n]**elders** Elder means "older." Here the elders probably represent God's people.
[n]**washed their robes** This means they believed in Jesus so that their sins could be forgiven by Christ's blood.

Prayer Starter: Amen! Praise, glory, wisdom, thanks, and strength belong to our God forever and ever! Amen!

Memory Verse: Jesus is the One who says that these things are true. Now he says . . .
                                                                            —*Revelation 22:20*

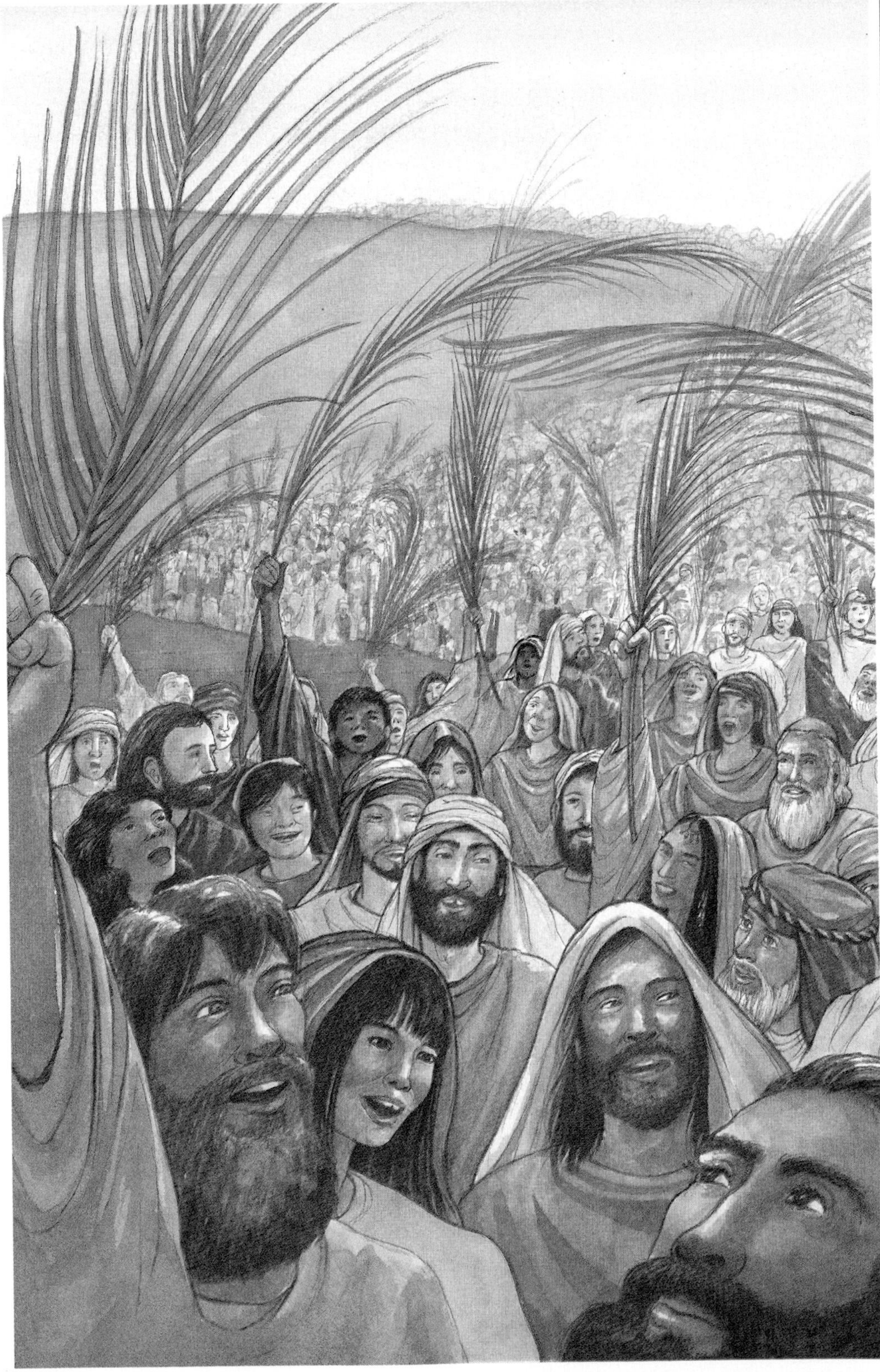

King
of Kings

Then the angel said to me, "Write this: Those who are invited to the wedding meal of the Lamb are happy!" Then the angel said, "These are the true words of God."

¹⁰Then I bowed down at the angel's feet to worship him. But he said to me, "Do not worship me! I am a servant like you and your brothers who have the truth of Jesus. Worship God! Because the truth about Jesus is the spirit that gives all prophecy."

¹¹Then I saw heaven open. There before me was a white horse. The rider on the horse is called Faithful and True. He is right when he judges and makes war. ¹²His eyes are like burning fire, and on his head are many crowns. He has a name written on him, but he is the only one who knows the name. No other person knows the name. ¹³He is dressed in a robe dipped in blood. His name is the Word of God. ¹⁴The armies of heaven were following him on white horses. They were dressed in fine linen, white and clean. ¹⁵A sharp sword comes out of the rider's mouth. He will use this sword to defeat the nations. He will rule them with a scepter of iron. He will crush out the wine in the winepress of the terrible anger of God All-Powerful. ¹⁶On his robe and on his leg was written this name: "KING OF KINGS AND LORD OF LORDS."

¹⁷Then I saw an angel standing in the sun. The angel called with a loud voice to all the birds flying in the sky, "Come together for the great feast of God."

¹⁹Then I saw the beast and the kings of the earth. Their armies were gathered together to make war against the rider on the horse and his army. ²⁰But the beast was captured and with him the false prophet.

Prayer Starter: You, O Lord God, are King of kings and Lord of lords.

Memory Verse: Jesus is the One who says that these things are true. Now he says, "Yes, I am coming soon." . . .
—*Revelation 22:20*

Please Come Soon

Then I saw a new heaven and a new earth. The first heaven and the first earth had disappeared. Now there was no sea. ²And I saw the holy city coming down out of heaven from God. This holy city is the new Jerusalem." It was prepared like a bride dressed for her husband. ³I heard a loud voice from the throne. The voice said, "Now God's home is with men. He will live with them, and they will be his people. God himself will be with them and will be their God. ⁴He will wipe away every tear from their eyes. There will be no more death, sadness, crying, or pain. All the old ways are gone."

¹⁰The angel carried me away by the Spirit to a very large and high mountain. He showed me the holy city, Jerusalem. It was coming down out of heaven from God. ¹¹It was shining with the glory of God. It was shining bright like a very expensive jewel, like a jasper. It was clear as crystal.

22 "Listen! I am coming soon! I will bring rewards with me. I will repay each one for what he has done. ¹³I am the Alpha and the Omega," the First and the Last, the Beginning and the End.

¹⁶"I, Jesus, have sent my angel to tell you these things for the churches. I am the descendant from the family of David. I am the bright morning star."

¹⁷The Spirit and the bride say, "Come!" Everyone who hears this should also say, "Come!" If anyone is thirsty, let him come; whoever wishes it may have the water of life as a free gift.

²⁰Jesus is the One who says that these things are true. Now he says, "Yes, I am coming soon."

Amen. Come, Lord Jesus!

²¹The grace of the Lord Jesus be with all. Amen.

"**new Jerusalem** The spiritual city where God's people live with him.
"**Alpha and the Omega** The first and last letters in the Greek alphabet. This means "the beginning and the end."

Prayer Starter: Lord Jesus, please come soon!

Memory Verse: Jesus is the One who says that these things are true. Now he says, "Yes, I am coming soon." Amen. Come, Lord Jesus!

—*Revelation 22:20*

Subject List